MONEY SENSE is an excellent resource for the many women in our society who bear the burden of financial management without the necessary financial training. Judith has a good mix of truth and humor, making this an easy book to read.

Larry Burkett
Christian Financial Concepts

money sense

WHAT EVERY WOMAN MUST KNOW TO BE FINANCIALLY CONFIDENT

Judith Briles

MOODY PRESS

CHICAGO

For Linda, a visionary

Also by Judith Briles

— ◆ — ◆ — ◆ — ◆ — ◆ — ◆ — ◆ — ◆ — ◆ — ◆ — ◆ — ◆ — ◆ — ◆ — ◆ — ◆ — ◆ —

Gender Traps
The Briles Report on Women in Healthcare
The Confidence Factor
The Dollars and Sense Divorce
Woman to Woman
The Workplace
When God Says NO
Judith Briles' Money Guide for Christian Women
Faith and Savvy Too!
Money Phases
The Woman's Guide to Financial Savvy

Contents

—•—•—•—•—•—•—•—•—•—•—•—•—•—•—•—•—

Life Phase 5: 50–65

Life Phase 6: 65 and Over

Acknowledgments

—•—•—•—•—•—•—•—•—•—•—•—•—•—•—•—•—•—•—

Every book has its genesis. For me, the real awareness of money stirred when, in 1969, I went to work as a secretary in a stock brokerage firm in Los Angeles. Al Pierce was the primary broker I worked for. Each day I was given a new lesson in the money market—and I was hooked.

I became a stockbroker in 1972, and began teaching classes for women in 1974. Out of those classes, my first book was birthed, *The Woman's Guide to Financial Savvy*, in 1981.

Since that time, I have written several other money books; *Money Sense* is the latest, and, in my opinion, the best primer I have written on the topic of money, and, specifically, on money matters for and about women. In the past twenty-five years I've accumulated data from a myriad of sources: television, radio, magazines, books, interviews with women just like you—all too numerous to even mention. My business and financial library is extensive, and it grows each year with the works of financial masters in the field.

Money Sense is in your hands because of the vision of Moody's managing editor, Linda Holland. Her charge to me was to do something different for our Christian woman reader—and we did, with the assistance of master editors, Cheryl Dunlop and Anne Scherich. They were able to reduce a seven-pound baby to the volume you are holding. Without their guidance and help it would have been impossible.

Finally, the completion of the manuscript never would have been possible without my husband, John Maling.

Every woman should have a purse of her own.

—Judith Briles

Foundations

Chapter 1

—◆—◆—◆—◆—◆—◆—◆—◆—◆—◆—◆—◆—◆—

Money Sense Matters

*Y*ears ago my son came home sobbing with deep teeth marks on his arm. The attacker, it turned out, was my neighbor's three-year-old son. When I approached the defendant, inquired as to the motive behind such an act, and suggested that he would be unwise to repeat it, he stuck his tongue out at me, turned on his heel, and walked away. Certain that his mother would be anxious to know of her son's dangerous, antisocial behavior, I told her what had happened. She smiled knowingly, shrugged her shoulders, and said, "It's just a phase." Years later, when my nine- and eleven-year-olds engaged in a breadstick swordfight in our town's finest Italian restaurant, I smiled at the waiter and said, "It's just a phase."

Those magic words explained, if not excused, a variety of behaviors, from my teenager's inability to get up before noon on holidays to the latest fad diet. But those "phases" don't last forever. They mysteriously disappear at about the time a person turns eighteen. When my I flunked my driver's license renewal test at the age of twenty-five, the surly man behind the counter didn't smile and say, "It's just a phase." When I overdrew my checking account because I forgot to enter several checks, my banker didn't say, "It's just a phase."

It just wasn't fair! We *all* need phases. They were good for us as children. They provided us with comfy little identity slots. When we left one slot, by change either in age or behavior, we were immediately filed into another. Phases provided a real sense of security—and security is necessary at any age.

That is why this book is organized around the phases of a woman's life. Financial strategies appropriate for a woman of twenty-five are not appropriate for a woman of fifty-five—and vice-versa. Physical, psychological, and emotional circumstances influence us in different ways at different times in our lives. Recognizing current and future phases is essential in determining how best to react to current conditions and plan for future circumstances.

We need to talk about life phases to make sense of financial strategies; we need to talk about finances because of inflation. The value of money declines as the years unfold. If inflation averages a 4 percent increase each year, your money will lose almost half of its value in less than eighteen years. If inflation runs at 12 percent per year, a thousand dollar stored under your pillow will only buy $880 worth of goods and services at the end of twelve months.

Similarly, it is foolish to believe that the Social Security system will be able to supply the funds you need when you are in your sixties, seventies, and eighties. The Social Security system has substantial problems that will certainly affect everyone who is now under fifty years of age and possibly even people who are already receiving retirement benefits from Social Security.

If you choose not to take steps to fight the effects of inflation, you will have less next year. If you choose not to plan for the financial needs you will have during your retirement years, you are likely to suffer for it in the end. If you do nothing about what you presently have, earn, and invest, and what you hope to have tomorrow the odds are that you are in fact, doing something: losing it.

WHERE DO WE STAND?

Money sense matters to women because greater numbers of women are managing more money than ever before. Consider the following figures for the nineties:

- The IRS reveals that 35 percent of all estates in excess of
  $5 million are currently controlled by women.

- According to the Bureau of Labor Statistics, more than 60 percent of women work outside the home.

- The Oppenheimer Management Corporation surveyed households and learned that women pay 56 percent of all family bills.

- The National Foundation for Women Business Owners states that more than 5.4 million businesses in the United States are owned by women.

- The U.S. House of Representatives' Committee on Small Business reports that by the year 2000, 50 percent of all businesses·in this country will be female-owned.

Yet the 1992 Oppenheimer nationwide survey concerning women and their financial acumen revealed the following:

- Only 9 percent of women describe themselves as "very confident" when making an investment decision.

- Women between the ages of thirty-five and fifty-four are the least knowledgeable; 71 percent said that they did not know how to invest.

- Of this age group, 37 percent reported they had never made an investment decision. An identical number said they spend no time on their savings and investments.

Subsequent Oppenheimer Management Corporation surveys taken since then revealed the following:

- Although women are widely responsible for day-to-day management of household finances, only 12 percent make investment decisions on their own.

- Eighty-nine percent had no idea of the level of the Dow Jones Industrial Average—or even what it is.

- Sixty-two percent said that they didn't understand how a mutual fund works.

- Sixty-nine percent said they didn't know that stocks have historically outperformed bonds, CDs, savings accounts, and money market instruments.

- Fifty-two percent said they feel financially unprepared for retirement.

- Yet fully 82 percent of these women believe that they will be solely responsible for their own financial well-being at some point in their lives.

Women are absolutely right. They must be responsible. According to the United States Bureau of the Census:

- Forty-eight percent of women aged sixty-five and older are or will be widowed.

- Fifty percent of women who married within the last twenty years will divorce.

- Ten percent will remain single.

The message these statistics bring is sobering: At some point in their lives, an overwhelming majority of American women will have to bear responsibility for their own financial security.

A woman may be an expert in any field from science to the arts, but we still don't know what to do with our salaries, our savings, our investments. Instead of learning about investment programs and money management, we have depended on parents, husbands, or friends to take care of our money matters. We forget that other people make mistakes too.

Worse, they sometime die or become disabled or are lost through divorce. We are satisfied with the safety and ease of savings accounts, letting a professional, our friendly banker, be our guide. We forget that bankers have vested interests of their own, that inflation often runs higher than bank interest rates, or that bankers, too, make mistakes.

WHAT TO DO?

The most practical way of dealing with money is to devise a plan for increasing your income, net worth, and/or investable moneys each year. And how do you do that?

1. Learn what the life phases and their financial requirements are. Identify your own life phase and financial profile.

2. Learn about money management, the terms used in finances, and the types of investments and financial strategies available, all in the context of your own life phase.

3. Put what you know to work in your daily life.

The wise woman starts saving and planning today—no matter her age or her life phase. She takes active steps to avoid the perils of poor advice, miscalculated investments, and simple neglect. She puts into practice the advice given in Proverbs 19:20, "Listen to advice and accept instruction, and in the end you will be wise."

With *Money Sense*, you will become confident, capable, and in control of your and your family's money matters—a must for today, and for the years to come.

Let's begin . . .

Chapter 2

— ◆ — ◆ — ◆ — ◆ — ◆ — ◆ — ◆ — ◆ — ◆ — ◆ — ◆ — ◆ — ◆ — ◆ —

The Six Life Phases

LIFE PHASE 1: 18–25

The first life phase is a time of making choices and decisions without having a lot of experience to back them up. You are a builder setting foundations without really knowing the dimensions of the building. You make decisions that provide you with the information you should have had before making the decision in the first place. To set the best foundation in this life phase for later financial security, you will need to discipline yourself to save money and keep from spending a lot on personal pleasures (great clothes, meals out, vacations, and general "fun" things). After all, some day you'll be in Life Phase 6 and will wish you had been more careful earlier.

Life Phase 1 is the time to establish a relationship with a bank and other financial contacts, to borrow money for the first time, and to begin to establish your credit history.

In Life Phase 1 you take the first steps in financial planning. You need to compute your net worth and cash flow, establish a liquidity fund and a retirement account, set up a system of record keeping for tax and other purposes, purchase insurance, tithe to your church, and (yes) make a will. You also need to develop background knowledge of finances and financial terms and understand the risk elements in investments. Money markets, Treasuries, certificates of deposit, and EE bonds will be on your mind.

LIFE PHASE 2: 25–35

Life Phase 2 is a time of decision making. By now you are likely to have completed your formal education and will probably have made some career decisions. You are also perfecting various skills and possibly experiencing healthy increases in salary that underscore your need for a financial strategy. You are becoming aware of tax obligations. You are extremely protective of your dependents, if you have them.

By this time you will probably have formulated a set of values that includes the importance of money and just how much of it is enough for you. Women in this phase are able to take risks. They can make substantial mistakes in career choices and/or investments and still fully recover and even turn those mistakes to their advantage. This also may be a likelier time to purchase a home as a personal residence.

Tax advantages, liquidity, life insurance, banking relations, stocks, mutual funds, deferred compensation, the purchase of a home, and having kids and obtaining the funds for their college education are on your mind during this life phase.

LIFE PHASE 3: 35–40

By the time you reach Life Phase 3 you are likely to have achieved a sense of substance, be fairly stable, and have an overall understanding of where you are going. In addition, you are likely to be "tuned in" to your overall tax situation. You may even develop a sense of urgency to rectify it. During this period you are still able to take risks. As with the twenty-five- to thirty-five-year-old age group, if you place your funds in an unsuccessful venture, it will probably not seriously dampen your overall investment and monetary confidence.

This is a period in your financial career when you are most likely to start your own business, join an investment club, explore possible stock options, and invest in rental property. Tax shelters and adjustments to your will are on your mind.

LIFE PHASE 4: 40–50

Life Phase 4 is a phase of reduced risk taking and a time to assume a nonaggressive investment posture, especially as you reach the far end of the phase. This is usually not the time to go into venture capital deals unless you are fairly secure financially.

This is often a critical time, especially in the family area. Your adolescent children may be sowing their oats. You are beginning to face the fact that you are not immortal. It is also an age of abrupt reversals. In the previous life phase you probably had a sense of stability and substance and knowing exactly who you were and where you were going. In Life Phase 4, however, you are more likely to experience unexpected changes. If there is a dissolution in a marital relationship, it often occurs now and can have a dramatic impact on your financial security.

Lines of credit, Social Security, gifts and taxes, cash accumulation, tax obligations, short-term markets, change of residence, and transfer of tax-deferred moneys are on your mind.

LIFE PHASE 5: 50–65

During Life Phase 5 you find that there is less time to reap long-term rewards from investments, and you may look forward to retiring. (You probably have felt you wanted to retire at some time during each one of the previous phases—I wanted to do so at least half a dozen times between thirty-five and forty.) You are now in a period of asset building, and you are more conservative. You begin to eliminate unrewarding activities and endeavors.

At this point you have acquired a great deal of knowledge and experience and can often use it to your best advantage. I often find that women in this phase tend to be more philosophical about life and choose to share their experiences openly with the younger generation—who, of course, are generally unwilling to listen (but that's "just a phase"). In this phase, as well as the next, it is possible that you may become a widow. The economic impact of the death of a spouse can be disastrous, especially if you have made no plans for it.

Investment opportunities in undervalued corporations, annual reports, a possible change of residence, annuities, home equity, reverse mortgages, estate planning, trusts, living wills, and your parents and their money are on your mind.

LIFE PHASE 6: 65 AND OVER

Life Phase 6 is generally thought of as the retirement phase. It should be a period of reward and comfort. It is no longer necessary or wise to make long-term investments, and your primary focus should be on liquidity (the ability to turn investments back into cash quickly if you choose) and using current funds as income to meet ongoing needs. This is often a time for having fun, and possibly even nurturing members of the younger generation through their own phases.

Some old and some new friends are on your mind: liquidity, money market funds, short-term certificates of deposit, Treasury obligations, zero coupon bonds, municipal bonds, short-term bonds, utility stocks, sale of primary residence, Social Security, and gifts.

Common Themes in All the Life Phases

Each life phase has a different challenge. Sometimes you will make financial mistakes. Sometimes you will lose money, energy, and sleep. But I firmly believe that out of every negative situation you will reap at least some positive result.

You will note that the life phases overlap. That's because they are not intended to be hard and fast divisions. They are intended only as loose guidelines—a way of identifying to some extent where you are in order to determine where you are going and how best to get there.

You will also notice that some aspects of money sense apply to all the life phases. All those topics are at least begun in the first chapters of the book; some are recurring themes throughout the book.

1. You will always need to be on top of daily money management. That means you need to manage your checking and savings accounts, credit cards, cash flow, net worth,

and record keeping for tax and other purposes.

2. You will always need to know how to establish and maintain a good credit rating.

3. You will always need to know about income and investments: kinds of income, kinds of investments, what liquidity is and why it's important, and the tax implications of your investments. The basics are covered in the first chapters of this book, but elements are also dealt with elsewhere in the book.

4. You will always need to know what types of financial consultants are necessary for intelligent money management and how to choose those consultants.

5. You will always need to know the principles behind the wise purchase of insurance and which types of insurance are available to you and best for you at a given phase in your life.

6. You will always need to know the steps in buying real estate, either for personal use or as an investment, and the tax implications of real estate transactions.

7. You will always need to know what constitutes good retirement planning and how your retirement planning needs to shift with each life phase.

8. You will always need to know about wills and estate planning: what a will is, the difference between a will and a living trust, what probate is, what the executor of a will must do, and how and why to make a living will.

Because Life Phases 1 and 2 set the foundation for your financial program, they are a "must read" for any woman who is just beginning the money maze—whether she is eighteen or fifty-two. Those first two phases are the key components in building your money foundation.

Life Phase 1: 18–25

All the abundance you desire is here. You just have to tune into it.

—Judith Briles

Chapter 3

━ ◆ ━ ◆ ━ ◆ ━ ◆ ━ ◆ ━ ◆ ━ ◆ ━ ◆ ━ ◆ ━ ◆ ━ ◆ ━

Getting Started

INCOME, NET WORTH, AND CASH FLOW

*B*etween the ages of eighteen and twenty-five you are likely to be gathering data, completing or upgrading your education, and/or entering the job market. You are probably more carefree than women who are older, and you are as much of a risk-taker as you are ever likely to be.

This is an exciting period of awakening to what money is and what it can do. You will make financial mistakes, but as you approach the end of this phase, you will have learned from those mistakes and begun to understand how money can work for you. Your main task during this life phase is to lay the foundation of your finances.

You will need to know how to:

- Efficiently manage income, net worth, and cash flow (covered in this chapter)

- Find places to park your cash (chapter 4)

- Use credit and credit cards responsibly (chapter 5)

- Understand tax policies and know how to use them to your benefit (chapter 6)

- Purchase insurance (chapter 7)

- Plan for retirement (chapter 9)

- Tithe to your church (covered in this chapter)

- Hire financial experts (chapter 10)

The last task—hiring expert advisers—is probably the most important task in this life phase. Probably the task next in importance is establishing a solid credit rating by doing what Americans do best—borrowing. But before you can do either of these you need to have developed the habit of saving, and you need to figure your net worth.

DETERMINING YOUR NET WORTH

The first step in developing a financial profile is to determine your *net worth*. You do this by adding up your assets, subtracting your debits and liabilities, and looking at the final figure.

Single women will have an easier time in determining their net worth because all assets are theirs exclusively. Married women have an additional initial decision to make: whether to determine net worth as a family or as an individual. A married woman needs to determine which assets—and liabilities—are hers alone, which assets are her spouse's, and which assets are joint.

How assets are listed and legally held, how insurance policies are set up, how savings accounts are listed, in whose name the cars are owned, what mortgages or loans have your name on them, and which credit cards are in his name or your name or joint names will make a difference in assessing your true financial condition.

However, for the sake of simplicity, most net worth statements can be calculated for the family; nearly all assets acquired and income earned during a marriage are considered jointly owned. (The exceptions will be discussed later.) Unless you hold significant separate assets, it is not only acceptable, but realistic to calculate net worth as a family.

What Is Separate Property?

Separate property includes assets you acquired prior to marriage or assets that were given to you or that you inherited during your marriage. These assets should be kept separate from assets commonly held by you and your husband. If your Aunt Martha gave you three hundred shares of Apple Computer stock and you sell that stock in order to purchase others, the new stocks are still your separate property because they were bought with money raised from the sale of that stock.

Because states differ in how they regard assets obtained during a marriage, a married woman, or a woman contemplating marriage, should find out exactly how her state treats assets, income, and separate property. This is especially important in the community property states (Arizona, California, Idaho, Louisiana, Texas, Nevada, New Mexico, Washington, and Wisconsin).

Your Personal Assessment

You can calculate your net worth by using the form on pages 32–34. I have added columns for your calculations for the next two years, so that you can see how your situation changes over the years. If some of the terms in the chart are unfamiliar, skip to the glossary at the back of this book, where definitions of a number of financial terms appear.

FUTON CHAIR/COUCH.
FUTON BED/MATTRESS,
BED/FRAME
DAD/MOMS ART.
FUTON CHAIR
NORDI TRACK
TELEPHONE — CORDLESS,
4-DAD CHAIRS
CLOTHES,
LINENS/BLANKETS.
DESK/FILE CABINETS
COMPUTER, SOFTWARE
PAINTINGS
PHOTOGRAPHS
BOOKS,
(2) DESK CHAIRS
POTS & PANS-SILVERWARE
BATHROOM TOILETRIES)

$ JB tip

Even if you have a negative net worth now, you are the single biggest asset you have. Your creativity and hard work will allow you to create a positive net worth.

BICYCLE
GARDEN TOOLS
VACUUM.
VASES - POTTERY
FRAME RACK
1- BUREAU.
1- NIGHT STAND
4- LAMPS.
SPARE BED/COT
ROLLER BLADES
ICE SKATES
QUILTS.
CATS
DRAFTING TABLE
CHINA - PORCELAIN.
OLD STEREO - SPEAKERS
CD's.
BREAD MAKER
TOASTER OVEN
MICROWAVE BLENDER

CALCULATE YOUR NET WORTH

• ASSETS	TODAY 10/15/95	Dec. 31, 1996	Dec. 31, 1997
List exactly what you have in:			
Certificates of Deposit			
Checking Accounts			
Collectible Debts Owed to You			
Credit Unions			
Deposits with Utilities			
Deferred Compensation, 401(k)			
IRA or SEP			
Keogh			
Money Market Funds			
Savings Accounts			
Tax Refunds			
U.S. Treasury Bills, Notes, Bonds			
Present cash value of your:			
Annuities			
Life Insurance			
Corporate Retirement Funds (Pensions, Profit Sharing)			
Stock Options			
U.S. Savings Bonds			
Present market value of your:			
Bonds and Notes			
Business (if owned by you or spouse)			
Commodities			
Home(s)			
Mortgages You Hold on Others' Property			

Mutual Funds — _____ _____
Notes Due You — _____ _____
Other Real Estate — _____ _____
Stocks — _____ _____

What you would get if you sold your:

Boat, Motorcycle, Plane, Trailer,
    Skis, Bicycle(s) *BICYCLE*   50. _____ _____
Car(s) *TOYOTA*   8000 _____ _____
Horses, Dogs, Other Animals — _____ _____
Patents or Publication Rights — _____ _____
Sports or Photo Equipment   600 _____ _____
    NORDITRACK, COMPUTER

Appraisal or estimate of what you would get if you sold your:

Collections (stamps, coins, etc.) _____ _____ _____
Home Furnishings (including
    appliances) *RAINBOW, BREADMAKER* 600 _____ _____
Household Valuables (paintings,
    silver, etc.)   300 _____ _____
Jewelry and Furs   400 _____ _____
Any Other Soluble Property or
    Collectible Moneys _____ _____ _____

TOTAL ASSETS _____ _____ _____

• LIABILITIES

Now list all:

Child and Special Support You Owe   — _____ _____
Bank, Insurance Policy, and Other
    Loans _____ _____ _____
      CAR
      CAR INSURANCE
      HOUSE INSURANCE
      HEALTH INSUR.
      MORTGAGE

Credit Card Charges and Cash
   Advances *CITI BANK, SEARS,*   _____   _____   _____
Fixed Commitments
   (college tuition, etc.)   _____   _____   _____
Mortgages You Owe (total amount)   _____   _____   _____
Payments Due on Purchases *NORDTRACK* _____   _____   _____
Student Loans   _____   _____   _____
Taxes Due That Have Not Been
   Withheld   _____   _____   _____
Any Other Money You Owe   _____   _____   _____

TOTAL LIABILITIES   _____   _____   _____

TOTAL NET WORTH
(assets minus liabilities)   _____   _____   _____

EVALUATING YOUR CASH FLOW

Calculating cash flow is something like making up a budget in reverse. Instead of planning where your dollars should go, you chart exactly where they went. A cash flow chart enables you to prepare for those months when you have bigger than usual expenditures—and hence need more cash on hand. Seeing where your money goes is more than half the job of seeing where it *should* go.

Proverbs 24:3–4 says it succinctly: "Any enterprise is built by wise planning, becomes strong through common sense, and profits wonderfully by keeping abreast of the facts" (TLB).

DEVELOPING A PLAN

• INCOMING:	Budgeted	Actual
Alimony/Child Support	_____	_____
Bonuses	_____	_____
Capital Gains (the increase in value of an asset over the purchase price at the time you sell it)	_____	_____
Commissions	_____	_____
Dividends	_____	_____
Gifts	_____	_____
Interest	_____	_____
Other Income	_____	_____
Rental Property	_____	_____
Retirement, Pensions	_____	_____
Salary	_____	_____
TOTAL CASH IN	_____	_____

• OUTGOING:	Budgeted	Actual
Child Care	_____	_____
Clothing	_____	_____
Contributions	_____	_____
Credit Card Payments	_____	_____
Deferred Compensation(401(k), IRA)	_____	_____
Education (books, tuition, seminars)	_____	_____
Entertainment (eating out, movies, cable TV)	_____	_____
Gasoline	_____	_____
Gifts	_____	_____
Groceries	_____	_____
Home Furnishings	_____	_____
Household Supplies	_____	_____
Housing (mortgage or rent)	_____	_____

Installment Payments	_____	_____
Insurance:		
Life	_____	_____
Auto	_____	_____
Medical	_____	_____
Dental	_____	_____
Home	_____	_____
Other	_____	_____
Medical Expenses	_____	_____
Savings	_____	_____
Subscriptions	_____	_____
Taxes:		
Federal (withheld)	_____	_____
Federal (quarterly)	_____	_____
State (withheld)	_____	_____
State (quarterly)	_____	_____
FICA (Social Security)	_____	_____
Property	_____	_____
State Disability Insurance	_____	_____
General Sales	_____	_____
County or City	_____	_____
Transportation	_____	_____
Car Payments	_____	_____
Gas	_____	_____
Repair/Maintenance	_____	_____
Utilities:		
Gas or Oil	_____	_____
Electricity	_____	_____
Garbage	_____	_____
Telephone	_____	_____
Vacation	_____	_____
Other	_____	_____
TOTAL CASH OUT	_____	_____

- **NET CASH FLOW**   _____   _____
  (The difference between the cash you put in and the cash you take out)

Now You See It, Now You Don't

When I worked with clients, the topic of cash flow . . . a lack of it . . . almost always surfaced. Money ran out before the end of the month . . . and no one knew where it went!

I do, and I bet you do too. Modern technology has two faces: A time-saving benefit can make life become too simple and too convenient. Welcome to the world of ATMs—Automatic Teller Machines.

If money is unaccounted for or is used for impulse items, the ATM card is often a player in the event. Granted, those machines at banks, grocery stores, even malls are convenient and so easy to use. That's the problem. You decide you need $20 (usually the minimum amount that can be withdrawn).

By the time you've walked over to the machine, you've begun to wonder whether $20 will be enough. You rationalize that the "Quick Forty" or "Fast Fifty" might better suit your needs over the weekend. Fair enough, you may need extra cash and this will save you from coming back. You may not need the $50. But it would be nice to have it . . . just in case.

In case of what? My experience has been that (1) many forget to enter the withdrawal in their checkbooks (it must be treated as an immediate debit, an invisible check), and (2) most take more than what they actually need . . . and spend it. Once cash goes into a pocket, wallet or purse, it just disappears. You can't remember where it was spent; it just was spent.

$ JB *tip*

If your money runs out before the end of the month—Stop using your ATM card NOW!

I wish I could say it went to cash heaven! Alas, it didn't. How about movies, sodas, lunch out, a snazzy doodah—whatever? Most Christians have been told about the perils of credit cards, to pay for things in cash. I definitely agree that cash is the preferred method, but most financial and consumer debt counselors will tell you that ATM cash usually goes for incidentals, rarely necessities.

If you are having trouble tracking what you spend your income on, *immediately* stop using this card. Put it in your freezer and forget it. Only thaw it out for real emergencies! From now on, write checks—even for $1.50 if the merchant will take it. Why? Because you now have a written track record of what you spent; and most financial institutions are now charging a "use" fee every time you withdraw from the ATM, a fee that is more than the cost per check from your checking account.

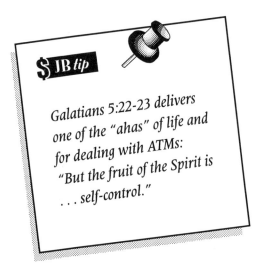

$ JB *tip*

Galatians 5:22-23 delivers one of the "ahas" of life and for dealing with ATMs: "But the fruit of the Spirit is . . . self-control."

"What," you ask, "give up my cash card? I need it because I can only get to the bank during non-business hours." Nonsense! Many banks open at 7 A.M. today and most have Saturday hours. If you buy groceries, most stores have a cash overage policy when you write a check—although taking advantage of that benefit can also be risky.

Cash dwindling to nothing is a problem for many. If you are trying to get a handle on where your cash goes, pick up a few receipt envelopes from any stationery store. Any time you spend money, write the date, item, and amount on the front of the envelope, put the receipt in the envelope, and tally the total spent at the end of the month. You will be surprised at where your money goes . . . and it's not to cash heaven! I have done this for years to identify cash spent for business-related purposes. All I do at tax time is add up each month's envelope total.

The bottom line is this: ATM cards are real culprits when it comes to money problems. Unless you really track where cash goes, are not prone to impulse spending and shopping, and don't spend more than you make, trash the card.

THE VALUE OF MONEY GOES UP . . .
AND GOES DOWN.
WHO CARES? YOU SHOULD.

If it costs you more to live next year, your income and investments need to increase to keep up. You can get a quick reading on what you'll need to protect yourself against inflation by using the compounding table below. This table can also be used to calculate how much your present net worth will grow if you can increase it at a specified annual rate and to find out how your savings and investments will increase at various annual rates.

FIFTEEN-YEAR COMPOUNDING TABLE

Years from Now	Compounding Factor If Annual Rate of Inflation Is:										
	5%	6%	7%	8%	9%	10%	11%	12%	13%	14%	15%
1	1.05	1.06	1.07	1.08	1.09	1.10	1.11	1.12	1.13	1.14	1.15
2	1.10	1.12	1.14	1.17	1.19	1.21	1.23	1.25	1.27	1.29	1.32
3	1.16	1.19	1.23	1.26	1.30	1.33	1.36	1.40	1.44	1.48	1.52
4	1.22	1.26	1.31	1.36	1.42	1.46	1.52	1.57	1.63	1.68	1.74
5	1.28	1.34	1.40	1.47	1.54	1.61	1.68	1.76	1.84	1.92	2.01
6	1.34	1.42	1.50	1.59	1.68	1.77	1.87	1.97	2.08	2.19	2.31

7	1.41	1.50	1.61	1.71	1.83	1.95	2.07	2.21	2.35	2.50	2.66
8	1.48	1.59	1.72	1.85	1.99	2.14	2.30	2.47	2.65	2.85	3.05
9	1.55	1.69	1.84	2.00	2.17	2.36	2.55	2.77	3.00	3.25	3.51
10	1.63	1.79	1.97	2.16	2.37	2.59	2.83	3.10	3.39	3.70	4.04
15	2.08	2.40	2.76	3.17	3.64	4.18	4.78	5.47	6.25	7.13	8.13
20	2.65	3.21	3.87	4.66	5.60	6.73	8.06	9.64	11.52	3.71	6.36
25	3.39	4.29	5.43	6.85	8.62	10.83	13.58	17.00	21.23	26.46	32.91
30	4.32	5.74	7.61	10.06	13.27	17.45	22.89	29.95	39.11	50.90	66.21

Example: *What you must make fifteen years from now to maintain your present standard of living if inflation is 5 percent annually and your annual income is now $25,000.*

After-tax income times appropriate compounding figure equals income needed: $25,000: $25,000 x 2.08 = $52,000.

Example: *What your net worth would be in fifteen years if you started out with $10,000 and increased it by 6 percent a year.*

Current net worth times appropriate compounding figure equals new net worth: $10,000 x 2.4 = $24,000.

Net worth at 15 percent: $10,000 x 8.13 = $81,300.

Example: *How your savings and investments would increase if you could invest $5,000 today at a 6 percent yield compared to what you would get if you earned a 10 percent return annually on the same $5,000.*

$5,000 x 1.34 = $6,700
$5,000 x 1.61 = $8,050

The generally accepted method of tracking inflation and deflation is the Consumer Price Index (CPI), an annual listing of common consumer items along with their prices, but it is not always the most accurate means of determining how inflation affects you. It consists of items many of us do not buy very often and tends to reflect the overall buying and not the buying habits of specific of groups of individuals (the twenty-six-year-old professional woman with a $30,000-a-year job, a husband, and one child, or the fifty-five-year-old widow with minimum income). Looking at your personal expenses through the years is a more accurate indicator.

ALL INCOME IS NOT EQUAL

One of the best things you can do for yourself as a money manager is to remember that income includes a lot more than the paycheck you get at work. There are four basic types of income, plus a fifth, "phantom income."

1. *Straight reportable and taxable.* These are the dollars you receive from various jobs you hold; from dividends or interest; from notes or bonds, capital gains, and distributions from partnerships; from pensions; and from various retirement accounts.

2. *Tax-exempt.* Municipal bond income is tax-exempt. It is different from the salary you receive as an employee or the income you receive if you are self-employed, which is, generally speaking, reported on a gross (that is, pre-tax) basis.

3. *Tax-deferred.* Tax-deferred income may be generated from a 401(k), an IRA, a SEP, a Keogh, an annuity, or other tax-deferred options. Funds are allowed to accumulate, and taxes are deferred to a later date when such funds are withdrawn.

4. *Tax-sheltered.* This form of income is often generated by investments that have special accounting provisions attached. Most often this involves declaring the depreciation of an asset (property, equipment, or some other good) on your income tax form by reducing its estimated value due to wear and usage. For example, when you own and rent out a house you can deduct from your taxable income a monetary amount representing this loss of value over time. There are strict formulas for the computation of depreciation.

5. *Phantom income.* Phantom income is usually a surprise. In the case of real estate, when rental or investment property is sold, and depreciation has been declared during the time it was owned, the IRS says you must "recapture," or "reclaim" (declare as income), the depreciation you deducted on your taxes during the time you owned the property.

When you work through the math, there are instances where this accounting feature will result in your making money on a real estate sale even though you sold the property for less than you paid for it after all expenses are adjusted.

DEPRECIATION: THE HOME SELLERS' PHANTOM

Regular Purchase Price $60,000
Sale Price $65,000
Sale Expense $ 5,000

Gross Return $ 0

Reclaim 10 Years Depreciation $16,360
($45,000 / 27 1/2 = $1,636;
$1,636 x 10 = $16,360)*

* Only the building can be depreciated, not the total purchase price of $60,000; 75 percent of $60,000 = $45,000.

THE SIX FACES OF RISK

As you save and invest through each life phase, you will encounter some form of risk on each path you take.

Market Risk

Market risk is the risk you take each time you invest your money. Stocks, bonds, mutual funds, and anything else you can put your money into can do three things: increase in value, decrease in value, or stay put. Market risk is when your investment lies there like a wet noodle or shrinks like a raisin. Either way, you lose money.

Business Risk

This risk is tied into the economy and usually reflects it. Business risk affects investments that do well when the economy is strong and limp along when the economy is weak.

Environmental Risk

Environmental risk tap dances around Mother Nature. When California was plagued by disasters a few years ago, real estate and stock in insurance companies carried greater risk. Between the earthquakes and the fires, the land didn't look so terrific. Millions of dollars in insurance claims impacted the earnings of the insurers, in turn affecting those who had invested in insurance companies.

Political Risk

Political risk includes change. Taxes, policies, Social Security, and health care pop into mind as I write this. When Congress is in session, your money may be at risk.

Inflation Risk

Inflation risk means that unless your investments earn more than the prevailing inflation rate—as well as any taxes that might be due on the earnings—you are losing money.

Interest Rate Risk

This risk affects any investment that is interest sensitive—fixed income, utilities, annuities, and bonds—usually investments that are identified as conservative. If you buy long-term bonds (bonds that mature in more than ten years) when rates are low, and rates increase over the years—you lose. The value of your bonds will decline because the bonds purchased with a higher return factor will be more attractive.

As you consider a possible investment, check it against the six faces of risk. Ask yourself how changes in any of the elements of risk might alter your investment. That way, you will have your eyes open.

IT PAYS TO KEEP GOOD RECORDS

Besides knowing your net worth and monthly income and expenses, paying bills on time, and limiting credit purchases, sane money management also includes record keeping. You may think it boring, but it is critical.

Keeping accurate records can save you money—not to mention irritation—when it comes time to prepare your tax documents, track investment performance, or manage your daily finances. Organizing records that may be scattered among desk drawers, filing cabinets, and shop boxes may seem a daunting task, but it's more than worthwhile.

What should you keep?

Tax Preparation

If an accountant prepares your tax return, your cost is likely to be lower if you can provide orderly and complete information. Accurate records can also remind you of deductible items you might otherwise overlook.

The IRS has three years after the due date of a tax return to challenge your filing. That means you should save files—including receipts, canceled checks, and other backup material—for at least that long. After that time, checks and receipts backing up most itemized deductions can be discarded.

In many cases, however, old records will continue to have a bearing on future returns. For example, if you use a computer in your work and are depreciating it, you need to keep your documentation for three years after the final tax return on which you claimed the write-off for the computer.

To play it safe, you should hold onto supporting documentation for at least six years—the amount of time the IRS has to audit your return if you under-report your income by at least 25 percent. No time limit applies in cases of fraud or failure to file.

Retirement Account Documentation

Keep transaction confirmations and summary statements for employer-sponsored retirement plans indefinitely. The same goes for salary-deferral programs. These accounts are all tax-deferred, which means one day taxes will be due.

If you fund an IRA, keep all supporting documentation, whether you're eligible for current tax deductions or not. Keep Form 8606 for any year in which you report non-tax-deductible contributions until you withdraw all the money in your IRA. You should also keep the forms you receive from your IRA trustees or custodians: Form 5498 reports contributions and Forms 1099R or W-2P report distributions.

One way to simplify this record-keeping task is to consolidate all your IRA accounts into one. This reduces the number of transaction and summary statements you need to track. Many IRA trustees or custodians allow you to diversify your IRA investment within one account, so you don't need to lose investment options by paring down your accounts.

Investments

Monthly brokerage account and mutual fund statements can usually be discarded once you receive your year-end summary, which lists all transactions for the year. But save every trade confirmation statement—both purchase and sale—for at least six years after you sell the investments.

You'll need confirmation documents to establish your investment cost basis, the figure from which you'll calculate the amount of your capital gain or loss when you do sell. Without such proof, you may end up paying more in taxes than you should.

It's especially important for investors who participate in mutual fund and stock dividend reinvestment plans to keep statements that will establish cost basis. You pay taxes on dividends in the year you receive them, even if you reinvest the dividends in more shares. When you sell you can add the cost of reinvesting shares to your original investment cost, which will reduce the size of taxable gains or increase the size of deductible losses.

If you have been purchasing the same security over a period of time and want to sell all or a portion of your holding, well-kept records allow you to identify which shares you are selling. If you don't identify the shares, the IRS normally considers the first shares sold to be the shares you first acquired. This could result in an increase in your reportable capital gains.

The IRS, in fact, allows sellers of mutual fund shares to figure their taxable gains or losses in a number of ways. The calculations may be complicated, but you can seek help from your accountant or tax adviser in determining which method is most beneficial for you. If you have neglected to save the documents you need or have misplaced them, many brokerage firms will provide you with copies, often for a fee.

Homeowner's Records

Homeowners also need to prove the cost basis of their home when it comes time to sell. The starting point is to keep property deeds and all purchase and sale documents.

Improvements that have prolonged your home's useful life or added value to it become part of your cost basis and can reduce the taxable gains you must report to the IRS. Keep records of everything you spend on these home-improvement projects, whether minor or major.

Tax laws allow you to defer taxes on the gain from a home sale by rolling over the profits into another home of equal or greater value within twenty-four months of your sale. If you do this, keep all records regarding your old home and begin to keep records on your new home. Documents for each house can be used to provide proof of your cost basis when you finally do report gains.

The Case for Forever

You may not like setting aside the space necessary to keep all of your financial documents indefinitely, but the idea has merit. Aged documents can come in handy.

For example, the Social Security Administration keeps track of your annual earnings in order to estimate your eventual benefits. Down the road, however, if you want to challenge their records, you'll need tax records of your own to prove your version of your earnings record.

Devise a filing system that will help you put your hands on documents when you need them. Store your records in a fire-resistant box, or keep hard-to-replace items in a safe deposit box. Once you get organized, maintaining good records is a lot easier than you might think—and a good investment of your time.

I was a shoeboxer for years. Now, my records go into specific files (mutual funds, loans, taxes, etc.) which I store in a labeled box in the basement. In the eighties, I experienced four IRS audits. Because I could support my deductions with backup records, no additional taxes were owed.

If I hadn't had the appropriate records, I would not have "known the state of my flocks or herds," as Proverbs 27:23 counsels. Every woman must watch her interests—personal and business—closely.

Tithing, of Course!

When a new puppy was welcomed into our home, I became the "walker." Each day I'm home, I take Tsasha on an hour walk. Within a short time, she expected, even demanded, our time together. Without realizing it, I had allotted a portion of each day to her. After just a few weeks, a habit was formed. A tithe.

Do you shuffle tithing to your "back closet"—something to be dealt with on a rainy day? Must do, unfortunately. Throughout the Old and New Testaments, giving, sharing, even tithing, are presented as opportunities.

To tithe is to trust. It is to acknowledge that God will provide, that God will protect. When you, tithe, or give to God, you create an investment in your own spirituality, your community, your family, and your faith.

◆ MS. MISC. ◆

During this life phase, and more particularly the next life phase (discussion starting with chapter 10), you may elect to purchase stocks and mutual funds. You can purchase both of these with minimal dollars. Look for stocks in the high-growth areas. Purchase only "no-load" mutual funds. For more information on mutual funds, read Austin Pryor's booklet *Mutual Funds* (Moody, 1994).

Participate in an IRA, a SEP, a Keogh account, or a 401(k) plan, if available. All offer tax-shelter advantages and tax deferral on the income or gain that accumulates.

Become aware of the tax deductions and/or credits that are available to you so that you may take advantage of them. It's worth it to buy at least an hour of a CPA's time.

During this life phase, or more likely, during the next life phase, you may purchase your first home. It takes a while to build the assets necessary to acquire the house of your dreams. But there are several home-owning opportunities even with the current interest rates and high housing costs. Keep your eyes open. In chapter 12 I will discuss the purchase of a home in detail.

Quiz

Your Aunt Harriet dies and leaves you $75,000. You have three children under ten years of age. What is the first thing to do with the money?

(a) Give it to your husband because money scares you.

(b) Buy 36,000 jars of peanut butter.

(c) Put it in a high-yielding, liquid account like a money market fund.

Answer: The money market fund is a good temporary place to put money while deciding how it should be invested. Do not jump into anything. Take the next six months to explore your options and then make investments.

◆ PHASING UP ◆

During Life Phase 1, most women feel that they can do anything. It's almost a holdover from the teen years when people feel invincible—nothing bad will come their way—in fact, they will live forever. Women are at their best physically during this phase. For many, pursuing a blooming social life, education, career, and marriage top their priority lists.

Most women imagine that someday the man of their dreams will arrive at their doorstep—accompanied by his mythical white horse. And many women have been raised to believe that regardless of how successful they become, there will still one day be a man to take care of finances.

But in the real world, most men and women are on equal footing—neither knows much about money. The difference is that women usually admit it.

God has given each of us gifts. One of those gifts is a brain. Use it. If you are married, communication is key—determine how each of you feels about risk and identify what each of you defines as risk. Most likely, one of you is stronger in the numbers department.

When it comes to couples and money, breakdowns are frequent. Set goals—short- and long-term. If you are better at budgeting and paying bills, do it. If your spouse is better at spotting trends or probing the strengths and weaknesses of potential investments, let him do that. Whatever your strengths are, build on them. Whatever your weaknesses, learn more about them so you can turn them into strengths.

During this phase, most of your money will go for rent, food, fun, and clothes—lots of them. If there is anything left at the end of the month, it usually evaporates. Do yourself a favor: Tithe to yourself. Whatever you make a month, take 10 percent off the top and put it in a savings account. Skip some of the great clothes and a little of the fun—this newly acquired habit will be one of the most critical things you do in your financial life.

Your Phase Focus:

$ Begin to live independently.

$ Identify short-term (vacation), intermediate-term (car) and long-term (home) goals.

$ Establish good credit (see chapters 5).

$ Keep credit card debt to a minimum (see chapter 5).

$ Tithe to yourself; save 10 percent of your income each month.

$ Tithe to your church.

$ Set up a liquidity fund—something you can access within days (see chapter 4).

$ Determine which insurance you need: life, health, disability, renters, or homeowners. Use discount services and make sure you have adequate coverage.

$ Begin to prepare for retirement (see chapter 9).

$ If you have funded your liquidity fund, begin to explore invest-ment possibilities.

◆   **RETIREMENT BONUS**   ◆

If you had started your IRA at the age of eighteen and contributed $2,000 per year, averaging 12 percent per year, at the end of this life phase its accumulated value would be $22,459.40.

Chapter 4
Parking Your Cash

*I*deally, the time to talk about bankers and the other financial counselors you need to place on your financial team is before you assess your net worth and cash flow, but in real life it is probably better to have some idea of where you stand financially before you seek out financial counselors and find places to park your money.

This chapter will focus on the first adviser you need, your banker, and the way you treat that basic financial commodity, cash.

A GOOD BANKER

Banking is an expanding field, and the choice of a bank (or banks) is an important and integral part of your plan. Your banker should not be a junior member of a management team but someone who has spent several years with the particular institution you deal with—preferably not someone who has been transferred from branch to branch every six months while gaining experience. You need someone who knows you, will grow with you, and will be willing to work with you in the bad times as well as the good.

Get to Know Your Banker

In a rapidly changing economy, it might make sense to have more than one banker. For example, in a tight dollars market (also known as a tight money market), which is usually paired with increasing or high interest rates, it is more expensive to borrow, and you may need to set up an account with a bank new to you to get a better market rate.

Bankers are often very flexible and willing to answer questions and offer assistance over the phone. This, of course, will be the case only after you have established a relationship with them and after they know you as an individual. Make an appointment to say hello to your bankers, explain your financial goals, and present your situation and let them know you look forward to a long-term relationship. You will be remembered.

Test Your Banker's IQ

Banks use a zillion ways (or at least it seems like it) to calculate the amount of interest they pay on an account. Everything from "current rates," "annual rates," "simple interest," "daily average rate"—you name it—are bantered around by financial institutions. The advertised high rate could be a dud when the small print is read.

Your banker should be able to answer, in English that you understand, the following questions:

1. What does the bank pay interest on? The answer should be the balance accumulated in your savings account every day, normally known as *day of deposit to day of withdrawal*. Some institutions pay on your *average balance* over the month, which generally yields less. Be wary when interest is paid on only the lowest balance each month—credit unions often do this. If you had $3,000 in the account twenty-nine days, then drew out $2,500 on the thirtieth, you'd earn interest only on the remaining $500. Also, if your bank pays interest only on your *investable balance*, it could mean that only 80 to 90 percent of your deposit earns interest. That lowers your yield.

2. How often does interest compound? "Compounding" means that the bank adds the interest you earn to your

account, and then pays interest on the combined interest and principal. The more often your interest is compounded, the more money you make. Daily, or continuous, compounding yields the most, followed by monthly, quarterly, then semiannual, then annual compounding.

With "simple" interest there is no compounding at all. What difference does it make? Lots. At 8 percent interest, compounding daily, your savings are worth 9 percent more after six years than if you had earned only simple interest. Compounding is the Eighth Wonder of the World!

COMPOUND INTEREST: THE EIGHTH WONDER OF THE WORLD
—◆—◆—◆—◆—◆—◆—◆—◆—◆—◆—◆—◆—◆—◆—◆—◆—◆—

Compounding Method	A $10,000 Deposit at 8 Percent		
	One Year	Three Years	Six Years
Daily	$10,833	$12,712	$16,160
Monthly	10,830	12,702	16,135
Quarterly	10,824	12,682	16,084
Semiannually	10,816	12,653	16,010
Annually	10,800	12,597	15,869
Simple Interest	10,800	12,400	14,800

---

3. How often will interest be credited? Most banks that compound interest daily do not actually give you the money until the end of the month or the end of the quarter. If this is how your banker responds, ask what happens to the interest if you close your account before the end of the quarter. Usually, you will lose it, even though the bank claims that it's paying you right to the day of withdrawal. If the banker says interest will be credited to the day of withdrawal, get it in writing!

4. What is the *annual percentage yield* on your savings? This yield brings all kinds of mathematical nuances into play —not only interest rate and frequency of compounding, but also such technical details as how many days the bank counts as a year. (Some banks use 366 days, some use 365, some use 360.) As a rule, the higher the annual percentage yield, the better your return.

5. What is the *periodic payment rate*? That's the rate the bank applies when figuring how much interest you have earned. Knowing it, you can check the bank's calculations to see if it paid you properly. Mistakes are not uncommon. A good bank will give you its periodic payment rate and show you how to use it.

6. Here's the bottom-line question for all purposes: If you put $1,000 (or $100, whatever you have) into this account today, how much money—in dollars and cents—will it earn in one year? This is the only true way of comparing one savings account with another. Some bankers don't like to answer the question, because it takes a little time and is revealing. But their attitude in telling you is critical. If the banker is clear with his response and helpful in other areas, this may be more important than earning an extra $5 in interest.

A LIQUIDITY FUND

You need a liquidity fund: ready cash or accessible money. Safe money. Investments that have a guaranteed principal, where there is no likelihood of a change in value. *This should be money you can get access to within seven days, with no strings attached.* This instant access will give you protection against the unexpected: the forgotten bill, the tax supplement, a medical emergency, or property damage from a storm or fire.

Six months of after-tax income is your goal. You should have enough on hand to meet your mortgage or rent payment; auto loan payments and auto expenses (such as gas and maintenance); utilities (including phone, gas, and electric); credit card payments; auto, home, and personal health or life insurance premiums, and daily living expenses, such as groceries.

Liquidity is also valuable in the recession that almost always follows inflation. If you have liquidity then, you can participate in the bargains that are available in investments and personal purchases.

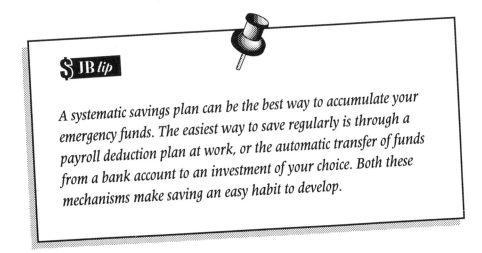

$ JB tip

A systematic savings plan can be the best way to accumulate your emergency funds. The easiest way to save regularly is through a payroll deduction plan at work, or the automatic transfer of funds from a bank account to an investment of your choice. Both these mechanisms make saving an easy habit to develop.

Passbook Savings Account

The most obvious, and probably most familiar, place to park your cash is the bank. The parable of the talents, as retold by Luke, takes on special significance here, for it introduced the concept that at the very least cash money can always be put in the bank:

> But the third man brought back only the money he had
> started with. "I've kept it safe," he said, "because I was afraid
> (you would demand my profits), for you are a hard man to
> deal with, taking what isn't yours and even confiscating the
> crops that others plant." "You vile and wicked slave," the
> king roared. "Hard, am I? That's exactly how I'll be toward
> you! If you knew so much about me and how tough I am,

then why didn't you deposit the money in the bank so that I could at least get some interest on it?" (Luke 19:20–23 TLB)

A passbook savings account can be obtained from any financial institution, with interest earning approximately 3–4 percent (sometimes lower and sometimes higher—your responsibility is to monitor the rates your financial institution is giving you).

A passbook account allows you to deposit and withdraw funds on a daily basis. The interest rates will not vary and you can call your bank or savings and loan and ask them to transfer funds from your passbook savings account into your checking account if the need arises.

Money Market Funds

An excellent alternative to bank savings is a money market fund, a mutual fund that purchases money instruments only. Interest rates for these funds will vary, and there are minimum dollar requirements for most. Those of you who are just beginning to save should open a savings account first. Then, as you build up your account, transfer most of your savings to such instruments as money market funds, leaving only what you may need for an emergency in your savings account.

A money market fund is simply a mutual fund. It is a portfolio of money market instruments—treasury bills, bonds, notes, commercial paper, banker's acceptances, certificate of deposits. They are not guaranteed by any federal agency and do not carry Federal Deposit Insurance Corporation (FDIC) insurance. With the pooling of funds from people like you and me, amounting to many millions of dollars on a daily basis, they are able to participate in very large investments.

Due to the volume of money market instruments they purchase, they often get a higher interest rate—a rate that you and I don't enjoy with our smaller funds. Having access to a money market fund makes good financial sense. Money market funds outside of banks and savings and loans usually pay a higher interest rate.

You can obtain a prospectus or offering memorandum from the funds by contacting them directly. If you scout the newspapers you will find several advertisements for local and national funds. Most of them indicate "800" numbers which you can call to request a prospectus and ask questions. Stock brokerages also offer money market funds to their customers. Mutual fund companies offer money funds to their fund customers. If someone wants to step out of the market for awhile, the change to cash is only a phone call away.

William Donoghue and Thomas Tilling's book *The Complete Money Market Guide* can be of assistance in describing the various categories of funds. In the appendix, a partial listing includes the address, minimum requirements, and phone number of each fund. Any cash should be earning more money for you. Period.

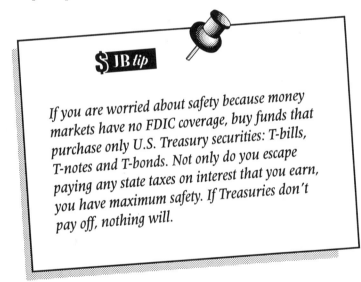

$ JB tip

If you are worried about safety because money markets have no FDIC coverage, buy funds that purchase only U.S. Treasury securities: T-bills, T-notes and T-bonds. Not only do you escape paying any state taxes on interest that you earn, you have maximum safety. If Treasuries don't pay off, nothing will.

Bank Certificates of Deposit

Another option for your liquidity fund is to keep some of your money in individual bank certificates of deposit (CDs) or time deposits. Since certificates of deposits have distinct maturity dates, preserve your liquidity by purchasing several CDs with differing maturity dates, splitting your money between CDs maturing in three, six, and nine months. That way you'll have some money available at regular intervals.

Certificates of deposit are usually purchased in $500 units. To participate, you simply place your funds on deposit and sign up for the various programs your particular financial institution offers. The time frame could be as little as thirty days or as long as eight years. Depending on how much you have on deposit at any given bank, your CDs might be backed by the FDIC. The FDIC limits coverage to $100,000 per separately titled account.

If you're considering placing money above the insured limit in any banking institution, contact Veribanc (800-44-BANKS) and ask for their bank safety rating on that institution. The cost is $10.

Certificates of deposit guarantee you a higher interest rate than that paid by a normal passbook savings account. They also offer you immediate liquidity—but at a price. Banks are obligated to charge a penalty should you withdraw your funds before a certificate matures. These penalties are substantial—the loss of up to six months' interest while the remaining interest reverts to what a standard passbook would have paid during the same period. In other words, if you wish to receive the advertised high interest rate, your money isn't really liquid at all.

If you've already bought certificates and find you need immediate cash, calculate the amount of money you will lose from the penalty if you withdraw and compare it to the cost of a loan for the remainder of the period during which your cash is committed. It's quite possible it would make more sense to take out a loan to satisfy your cash needs and let the certificate come to maturity. The higher interest you will earn from the matured certificate may more than cover the interest charged on the loan. (Most banks will lend up to 90 percent of the face value of a deposit certificate.)

The bottom line? Before tying up any funds, ask how much money you will get at the end of the proposed period. Then compare.

If you are thinking of buying a CD, it's important to shop around. Rates on CDs of any maturity can vary by as much as 2 percentage points from bank to bank, city to city, and state to state. Local competition usually guarantees that interest rates on CDs are fairly competitive.

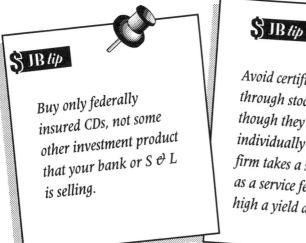

> **$ JB *tip***
>
> Buy only federally insured CDs, not some other investment product that your bank or S & L is selling.

> **$ JB *tip***
>
> Avoid certificates of deposit offered through stock brokerage firms, even though they promise that your CD is individually insured. The brokerage firm takes a small bite out of your yield as a service fee, so you are not getting as high a yield as you deserve on your CD.

Central Asset Accounts

Central asset accounts are brokerage accounts that work in conjunction with money market funds to invest in investment grade short-term corporate, government, or municipal bonds. Money that is not otherwise invested and interest and dividends earned on the securities held in your account are automatically swept into the fund or funds of your choice on a regular basis. This way, your money is virtually always working for you. You can access funds in your account by writing checks, using a debit or credit card, or through cash machines.

TREASURY BILLS

If you accumulate more substantial sums, you can purchase Treasury bills (T-bills). A T-bill is a United States Government obligation that is guaranteed by the government and can be purchased from a Federal Reserve Bank, through a stock-brokerage firm, or through a savings and loan or a commercial bank. To participate in this market you must have $10,000 on deposit with the particular entity with which you are dealing before you instruct them to buy the T-bill; T-bills are issued for a minimum of $10,000 with increments of $5,000.

T-bills come with a three-month, six-month, or one-year maturity. Proceeds from Treasury bills are used to finance the day-to-day operations of the U.S. Government and are one of the primary monitors of what is happening in the interest market.

$ JB tip

T-bills are considered short term. When you buy one, definitely plan on holding it until maturity. If you have to liquidate, it may be expensive in relation to the actual interest you earn.

Treasury bills are sold at auction each week. When you buy a T-bill, you receive the entire amount of the interest within a few days of the auction. Since individuals purchase T-bills through the Treasury Direct system, your interest is deposited directly into your bank account or money market account as you specify. When you purchase T-bills, you'll need to supply your bank or money market account number and the bank routing number of the institution that will be receiving the interest for your account. Your bank or mutual fund company will give you the routing number when you request it.

Since interest on the T-bill is paid to you immediately and not at the maturity of the bill, your true yield or return on T-bills will be higher than the stated auction "discount" rate because you actually have less than the full $10,000 tied up in your investment. Your true yield is also announced at the time of the auction. In fact, your ultimate yield could be even higher since the interest you earn can sit in your bank or money market fund and earn additional interest.

> **$ JB tip**
>
> *T-bills allow you to defer taxable income. Although you receive your interest within a few days from purchase, you don't declare it until the T-bill matures. If you purchased a one-year T-bill in June, 1995, the interest does not get reported until 1996's return (which you file in 1997!).*

Several weeks before your T-bills mature, you'll receive a letter from the Federal Reserve asking whether you'd like the proceeds deposited in your local bank account, or whether you want to "roll over" the T-bill when it matures and accept the average rate at the next week's auction. Or at the time you purchase the T-bills you can request automatic rollover at maturity.

If you do not elect to roll over your T-bills, at maturity the full proceeds (i.e., your original investment) will be automatically credited to your bank account.

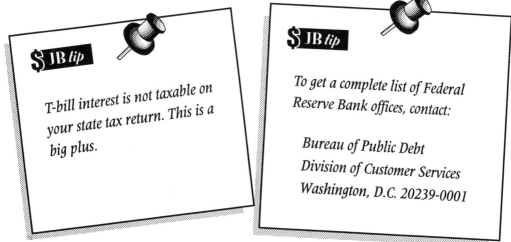

> **$ JB tip**
>
> *T-bill interest is not taxable on your state tax return. This is a big plus.*

> **$ JB tip**
>
> *To get a complete list of Federal Reserve Bank offices, contact:*
>
> *Bureau of Public Debt*
> *Division of Customer Services*
> *Washington, D.C. 20239-0001*

U.S. SAVINGS BONDS

Series EE U.S. savings bonds are safe, although they do require you to forget your money for five years to earn the promised interest. U.S. savings bonds offer market rates of interest, tax deferral, and ease of purchase in small dollar amounts. They can also be used to get a special tax break on money saved for college. In fact, although savings bonds were once marketed as a strictly "patriotic" investment, they have some dramatic advantages over other safe money strategies.

U.S. savings bonds can be purchased through banks and other financial institutions, or through regular payroll deductions at most major companies. Savings bonds are purchased at a discount from face value. For example, a $50 face value bond has a purchase price of $25.

As long as you hold the bond, interest will continue to build up. The bond will continue to accrue interest at whatever the floating rate is up to thirty years from the purchase date. The highest rate paid since the EE bond was established was in 1982–83: 11.09 percent. Since 1982, they have averaged 7.66 percent.

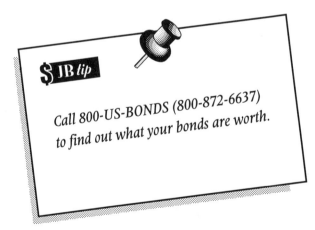

$ JB *tip*

Call 800-US-BONDS (800-872-6637) to find out what your bonds are worth.

You never pay any state income tax on savings bond interest, and you don't pay any federal income tax on the interest you earn until you cash the bonds in at some time in the future.

Beginning in 1990, savings bonds purchased in the parents' names and cashed in to pay for college tuition may be completely tax-free in certain income brackets. Check with your accountant since tax laws, and tax brackets, keep changing.

There are limits to how much you can invest in savings bonds each year. An individual may purchase only $30,000 face value ($15,000 purchase price) of savings bonds in a calendar year. If you purchase bonds in joint names with different people, you can bypass—or at least stretch—this rule.

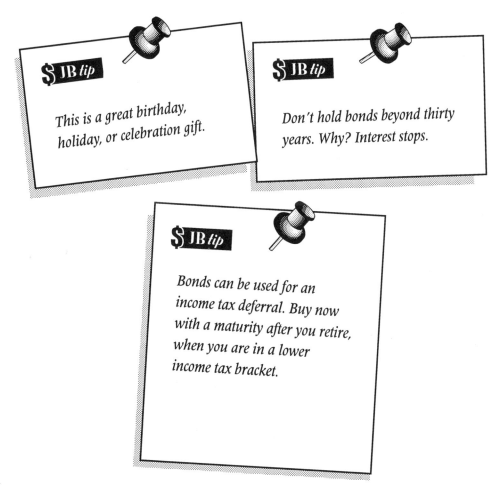

$ JB tip

This is a great birthday, holiday, or celebration gift.

$ JB tip

Don't hold bonds beyond thirty years. Why? Interest stops.

$ JB tip

Bonds can be used for an income tax deferral. Buy now with a maturity after you retire, when you are in a lower income tax bracket.

—◆—◆—◆—◆—◆—◆—◆—◆—◆—◆—◆—◆—◆—◆—◆—

Chapter 5

Credit Cards: Friend and Foe

*A*mericans owe a lot of money. In 1994, Americans owed more than $700 billion in consumer debt.

- More than $250 billion is owed on credit cards.

- More than $250 billion is owed on auto loans.

- Mortgage debt exceeds $3 trillion.

- Corporations have $3.6 trillion debt reported on their books.

- State and local governments owe in excess of $900 billion.

- The national debt exceeds $4 trillion.

Looking at these numbers, no wonder many of you don't worry about a few thousand dollars you owe! But you should. Credit can be expensive.

No verse in the Bible forbids us to borrow money. On the other hand, no one verse tells us to borrow either. The Bible does say that when you borrow money you put yourself under obligation to the lender (see Proverbs 22:7). It cautions us in the extremes of just about anything people can do. Credit and borrowing are no exception.

USING CREDIT THE RIGHT WAY

Having credit available to you is similar to having savings in a bank. If you have taken the trouble to establish a good credit rating by buying on credit and paying off on time, have focused on building a proper relationship with the bank manager over the years, and have demonstrated that you are a good, responsible citizen with stable employment or ability to repay, the bank will be delighted to lend you $5,000 on an unsecured basis. Having the ability to borrow $5,000 has the same effect as actually having $5,000 in the bank. It's there in case you need it.

The same reasoning applies to credit cards. Credit cards represent the ability to obtain cash, goods, or services. In the early eighties, another woman and I owned a business. Part of our business was buying old buildings and restoring them. My business partner took on another partner—drugs. Several hundred thousand dollars were missing from a construction loan that my signature was on. The bank demanded that I pay it. Eventually, I did.

Over the next few years my family lost our home, cars, and all investments; even jewelry was sold. Everything material built up over a ten-year period—gone. More than one million dollars in value!

The stress was unbelievable. My health was a mess, my marriage in jeopardy—even the dog lost her hair! If I had not had a credit card, many times my family would not have eaten.

Eventually, the bank got back all its money. (And it never even said, "Thank you.") Because I had credit set up, when disaster hit, my family was able to meet the bare essential needs. Pressure was taken off me for a few months until I could get cash flow going again.

Only a Few Cards Are Really Needed

Today, because many stores and vendors accept credit cards other than their own, you don't need to carry lots of cards. A Visa and MasterCard make sense, as well as one of the business cards, such as American Express or Diners Club. If you travel, a business card is vital, especially for your airline tickets, hotel, and car rental costs. You cannot rent a car without a credit card, even if your intent is to pay cash.

Cards Are Useful in Tracking Expenses

Credit cards can be used to keep track of many different types of payments. Put expenses that are tax deductible or business related on one card and personal expenses on another card. A word of caution here: Beware of the danger of running too many charges that cannot be paid when the bill comes. In order to avoid any finance charges, your credit card statements must be paid in full before the due date.

Low Interest May Not Be in Yours

If you decide to get a lower credit card interest rate by applying for a new card, get your magnifying glass out. The rates may be too good to be true. One bank might offer a low 11.9 percent rate (sounds good if you pay 21 percent). But after you transfer the old balance to it, any new purchases trigger a change—the interest rate on the entire balance will be increased to 15.9 percent.

You *must* read all the fine print and conditions. Before you jump ship, call your present bank representative or the toll-free number on your bill and remind the person you speak with that your mailbox is brimming with rival offers—*and ask for a lower rate*. This technique has worked to get annual fees waived and interest points lowered. *You can't get it if you don't ask for it.*

A nonprofit consumer education group, Bankcard Holders of America, publishes a monthly list of low-rate cards for $4. You can contact them at 800-327-7300 or 703-481-1110. Many of the lowest rate cards are from regional or smaller banks that do not send out mass solicitations—they can't afford to because their profit margins are much smaller than the banks that bombard you with mail box hype. In July of 1994, *Money* magazine reported the best credit card deals (see table). Each month, *Money* updates its list.

THE BEST CREDIT CARD DEALS

Institution (state) Telephone	Rate	Annual Fee
National Average	17.66%	

FOR PEOPLE WHO CARRY BALANCES

Institution (state) Telephone	Rate	Annual Fee
Federal Savings (AR) 800-374-5600	7.92%	$33
Arkansas Federal 800-477-3348	8.00%	$35
First Union (NC) 800-377-3404	9.15%	$39
AFBA Industrial (CO) 800-776-2265	9.25%	$35

FOR PEOPLE WHO PAY IN FULL

Institution (state) Telephone	Rate	Annual Fee
Amalgamated Bank (IL) 800-723-0303	12.25%	$0
USAA Federal Savings (TX) 800-922-9092	12.50%	$0
Oak Brook Bank (IL) 800-536-3000	12.65%	$0
Transflorida Bank 305-434-5111	12.90%	$0

Source: "Money Monitor," *Money*, July 1994.

Your research should find the following information about credit cards and rates:

- Does the rate sound too good to be true? It probably is. Find out how long that rate is guaranteed. Six months is the norm.

- Is the percentage rate based on the prime rate? Depending on the economic climate, the interest rate could increase (or decrease) significantly.

- What is the grace period in which you pay no interest, if you pay off your balance in full? Ideally, twenty-five days.

- The interest rate on purchases may be low, but the cash advance rate could be significantly different. Many credit cards provide checks; do they count as a cash advance?

- Is there an annual fee? How much is it?

- What are the amenities? Are they worth the percentage rate?

- Read the fine print. It's all there. Banks are required by law to disclose the above information, and more.

SECURE CARDS

If you don't have a credit history or have had problems in the past, a secure credit card may be for you. Deposit funds into a savings type of account, earning interest, and your financial institution issues credit equal to your deposit.

Warning: Go straight to your bank or savings and loan for this card. Do not use a card shipping service or other type of middleman. Nationally, you can contact Citibank at 800-743-1332, Key Federal Savings Bank at

800-228-2230, or American Pacific Bank at 800-879-8745. Bankcard Holders of America can offer you a complete list.

DEBIT CARDS

Debit cards are different from secure cards in that when your charge slip is processed, the amount of the purchase is deducted directly from your checking account. If there is not enough money in your account, the transaction won't go through. The big plus here is that you have the convenience of a credit card and the discipline of a *finite* spending limit.

FOLLOW THE RULES OF THE ROAD

Before credit gets out of control, identify and follow the following guidelines for credit card use.

Limit How Many Cards You Apply For

Don't apply for more than one or two credits cards at a time. Each inquiry about your credit is included in your credit report. If too many credit grantors inquire at once, they may become suspicious of your intention.

Don't Charge Disposable Items

Make it a personal rule not to charge "disposable" items such as gasoline and food on your credit card. These items are long gone by the time you receive your credit card bill. Unless you need the records for a business deduction, pay cash for food, restaurant meals, and gasoline.

Apply to Card Issuers Directly

Avoid companies that promise to get you a low-interest-rate credit card for a fee. Contact the card issuer directly, using the lists available from Bankcard Holders of America at 800-327-7300. Do not pay a fee unless the card is actually issued to you, at which time the fee will be added to your account balance.

Avoid Cards with Costly Billing Practices

In spite of advertised lower rates, consider the following cards taboo:

- Cards that charge interest from date of purchase with no grace period.

- Cards that charge interest immediately on a cash advance, plus charge a fee for each cash advance.

- Cards that charge late fees and over-the-limit fees.

Keep an Updated List of All Your Cards

Make a list of all the credit cards (and other cards such as insurance and driver's license) you keep in your wallet. Note each account number, and next to it place the toll-free phone number you have been given to call in case of loss or theft. (You'll find that number on your monthly bill.)

Know Your Liability If Cards Are Lost or Stolen

If you report the loss of your credit cards *before* they are used, you have no liability for *any* charges. If you report the loss of your credit cards, and they have been used, you are liable for the first $50 charged on each card. Many creditors waive their right to charge you for the first $50. If a lost or stolen card is used for a mail order purchase and is not presented directly to the merchant, you are not liable for any of the purchase.

There are registration services that offer to limit your entire liability on lost or stolen cards. This service isn't free, but it is convenient. If your card is lost or stolen, you make one call—to the registration service. In turn, the service will contact all your creditors. Check your homeowner or rental insurance policy to see if it covers the $50 deductible on each credit card.

Know Your Credit Card Rights

All merchants sign their own agreements with card issuers such as Visa,

MasterCard, and American Express. These are your rights:

- Merchants cannot ask for your phone number, address, or driver's license in order to accept your card.

- Merchants should not ask for your credit card number in order to accept a check, nor should you allow your credit card number to be written on the back of your check. Also, merchants are not allowed to charge the cost of a bounced check to your credit card, even if they have your card number.

- Visa and MasterCard prohibit merchants from requiring a minimum dollar amount purchase in order to use your card. American Express has the same policy in most states.

Avoid Credit Card Fraud

Use your credit card carefully.

- Do not make mail order purchases or give out your credit card number to individuals or companies that solicit you over the phone.

- Use credit cards for mail orders only with well-known companies, and only when you initiate the purchase.

- Do not write your credit card number on your personal check.

- Take possession of all carbons used in credit card transactions.

Deal with Credit Card Disputes Properly

Many people mistakenly believe that using a credit card to make a purchase automatically protects them in case of a dispute. Although some premium cards do offer buyer protection plans that guarantee products that are lost, stolen, or defective, using a standard card does not absolve the shopper of the need to use discretion in purchasing.

You cannot stop payment after a purchase by notifying your credit card issuer to decline payment once you have signed the charge slip. Instead, you must wait until the disputed charge appears on your bill. Then you have sixty days to notify your card issuer—in writing—that you dispute the charge.

Your card company will then notify the merchant's processing bank, which in turn will contact the merchant. If the merchant declines the charge-back and insists the charge stays on the bill, *you must pay.* Then your only remedy is to take the merchant to court.

A strong warning: If you are in a dispute with a merchant, you must continue to make payments on your charge or credit card account. If you don't, the damage to your credit report will be worse than any gains you feel you get by harassing the merchant.

CREDIT REPORTS

If you have ever borrowed money, received a credit card, purchased a home, or applied for life insurance, the odds are that one or more of the three major credit bureaus has a file on you. Although the bureaus do have overlap files on many people, the information in each company's file may be different. To thoroughly check on your credit, contact all three credit bureaus and read each report. If you haven't received a copy of your credit report in the past year, get one at once. Make it an annual ritual to do this. You can contact the credit bureaus at the following addresses:

Equifax Information Service
Customer Correspondence
P.O. Box 740193
Atlanta, GA 30374
800-685-1111
Cost: $8.00

TRW
P.O. Box 749-029
Dallas, TX 75374
800-392-1122
Annual Copy, free; second copy, $7.50

TransUnion
P.O. Box 8070
North Olmsted, OH 44070
800-922-5490
Cost, $8.00

In contacting each bureau, you must supply your name, address, and Social Security Number, and you must sign your request.

What Is in a Credit Report?

Most reports will include the following:

- What charge accounts and bankcards you have and how long you've had them.

- The date of your last payment.

- The largest amount that you've ever owed to that particular creditor, or the top limit that you're allowed to charge.

- The current amount owed (usually within one month of report).

- Whether your payments are current.

- The amount that's past due, if any.

- How many times you have been past due, and for how many days (over thirty, over sixty, etc.).

- The type of loan or account, and its terms.

- Any special problems with your account—for example, that goods were repossessed or that a collection agency had to be called in.

- Any court actions, such as liens, judgments awarded to creditors, bankruptcies, and foreclosures.

- Your legal relationship to the account—are you jointly responsible? Individually responsible? A cosigner?

- Past accounts, paid in full but now closed.

- Whether you've put a statement on the record in a dispute with a lender.

Credit Reports Don't Tell All

Your credit record will identify your employer but will not include information about your salary or wages, bank accounts, kids, or assets. Some credit bureaus will report if you are married.

If you apply for a large insurance policy or mortgage, some lenders or insurance underwriters request an "investigation" report, which could contain the above information as well as information gathered from business associates and neighbors about your personal living habits. In 1992, Equifax signed an agreement with the FTC limiting investigative reporting questions.

BEFORE YOU APPLY FOR CREDIT

Once one of my daughters was rejected for a car loan. The reasoning? The creditor thought she couldn't possibly make payments based on her earnings and existing amounts owed on other obligations; he thought she hadn't reported all her outstanding debts. Sheryl was puzzled and angry. She had reported everything.

Eventually the mystery was solved. Sheryl requested a copy of her report, and she found her older sister's accounts reported as hers, as well as one of mine. Of course she couldn't handle three people's obligations! It took a few months to unravel the mess. The end result? She got her loan.

By obtaining a copy of your report prior to applying for credit, you have the opportunity to correct errors. And errors do happen—often. In 1993, Consumer's Union asked its employees to request copies of their reports. Out of 161 credit reports, 48 percent had inaccuracies, some minor, others major.

If you have been rejected on a credit application, you will usually have thirty days to get a free copy of your report (the length of time will vary, depending on the reporting agencies' policies in your area). Return a copy of your denial letter to the reporting agency with a request for a copy of your report. The address of the reporting agency will be on the denial letter.

Make the corrections that are appropriate or make a statement as to what caused you to be late on a payment. It will be entered on your report. You can even direct the agency to send corrected reports to merchants who have made inquiries. Their names will appear on your report as an "inquiry."

If you think a reporting error was made by a company you do business with, contact that company directly, asking that a written statement correcting the error be sent to the credit bureau. Many businesses send credit information to more than one credit bureau. Be sure to ask them to contact each credit bureau to which they previously made reports.

If you feel that a credit bureau has not responded promptly (give them thirty days) and fairly, contact the Federal Trade Commission (FTC) with your complaint:

Federal Trade Commission
Attn: Credit Bureau Complaints
Pennsylvania Avenue and 6th St. N.W.
Washington, D.C. 20580

MAINTAINING GOOD CREDIT

Negative information stays on your credit report for seven years, except for bankruptcy, which will hang on for a decade. This includes closed accounts. You should do everything possible to avoid ruining your credit record. That means facing up to credit and debt problems as soon as they occur. Communicate immediately if you will be late in your payments.

In the nineties, creditors understand the difference between credit problems caused by excessive spending and those caused by unexpected situations, such as illness or job loss. Creditors are usually willing to work with you—if you face up to the situation early and fully.

If you feel the situation will be temporary, you can try to talk to your creditors about arranging an extended payment plan or an interest-only payment plan. If creditors are not responsive, or if you have too many creditors, it's time to seek help.

Here's what lenders *don't* like to see:

- You already have a lot of credit cards, with large credit lines that have been used.

- You have been chased for payment by a collection agency.

- You were sued for money owed.

- There's a lien on your property.

- A creditor closed one of your accounts.

- You have been applying for a lot of credit lately. (Most assume that you're in trouble.)

CREDIT COUNSELING ASSISTANCE

Here are four legitimate places to seek credit counseling assistance:

The National Foundation for Consumer Credit
8611 Second Avenue
Silver Spring, MD 20910
800-388-2227

Family Service America, Inc.
11700 West Lake Park Drive
Milwaukee, WI 53224
800-221-2681

Christian Financial Concepts
601 Broad St. S.E.
Gainesville, GA 30501
404-534-1000

Consumer Credit Counseling Service
800-388-2227
(This 800# will refer you directly to the CCCS office closest to your city.)

Each of these agencies will put you in touch with a local office or representative that will provide consumer credit counseling. These organizations will work with you in two ways. They'll contact, or assist you in contacting, your creditors and help work out a repayment plan if possible. And they'll help you understand how to deal with a spending problem if you have one, so you can avoid future credit woes.

HOW TO TELL YOU'RE IN TROUBLE

Here are twenty telltale signs that you are stretched to the max and need help:
    1. You can afford to pay only the minimum on your
        credit cards every month.

2. You have to charge purchases that you used to pay in cash.

3. You took a debt-consolidation loan, and now you're running up fresh debts.

4. You can't save, period.

5. You look forward to the junk mail, hoping that a new bank will offer you a credit card.

6. You're taking cash advances from one card in order to make payments on another.

7. You can't pay your basic bills on time.

8. You're being called by creditors.

9. You get turned down for credit.

10. You don't even want some of the things you buy.

11. Without overtime or another job, you'd lose your house or your car.

12. You're taking cash advances for daily expenses like food and rent.

13. You borrow money from others at work, until the end of the week. You borrow money from your relatives.

14. You don't open an envelope that you think contains a bill.

15. When you buy on credit, you always choose the longest time period to repay.

16. You never pay off your credit cards completely.

17. You delay paying by fiddling your creditors—putting the bill for the phone company in the envelope addressed to the utilities company and vice versa. Or, you "forget" to sign your checks.

18. You bounce checks or overdraft your account.

19. You get scared about money in the middle of the night.

20. You don't dare tell your spouse (or, sometimes, yourself) that there isn't enough money!

Credit card issuers have developed sophisticated systems for identifying borrowers who are likely to default. They call it "behavior scoring." Here are six of the warning signals that creditors look for:

1. You pay only the bare minimum every month and never more than the minimum.

2. You make partial payments.

3. You started falling behind on your payments soon after opening the account.

4. You have taken the maximum cash advance.

5. Your account balance always grows: You can't ever seem to pay it off.

6. You have periodic bouts of late payment.

Does this sound like you? If so, your number-one job is to get out of debt. It's the only way you will get rich. Believe it or not, the Bible has several passages dealing with this subject. For example, the twenty-fifth chapter of Matthew teaches about the management and distribution of surplus. With surpluses, you can give freely to others.

ZAPPING CONSUMER DEBT

If you are serious about kicking the habit, there is one simple solution: Don't borrow any more! Debt doesn't have to be forever. If you pay the minimum amount the bank requires, it may seem like debt lasts forever. The longer you have it, the more interest you pay.

Necessity is often the mother of invention. Bankcard Holders of America has a Debt Zapper program that shows consumers the quickest way to pay back what they owe, at the lowest cost. For information contact BHA at 560 Herndon Parkway, Suite 120, Herndon, VA 22070, or call 800-327-7300.

American Express has also gotten into the act. They have created a brochure comparing plastic card costs with cash. For example, if your card carries a 19.8 percent rate and you buy a new TV for $500 and spread the payoff over a twenty-four-month period, you actually pay $637. The add-on interest increases your real cost by 27 percent! To get a free copy of *How to Use Credit Cards Wisely*, send a self-addressed envelope to American Express, Dept. N.W., Office of Public Responsibility, 200 Vessey St., New York, NY 10285.

$ JB *tip*

Warning: Avoid credit-repair "clinics" and "specialists" who promise to solve your credit report problems. Don't give them a dime of your money.

GETTING CREDIT IN YOUR OWN NAME

Many married women carry credit cards with their married name imprinted on the card (for example, Mrs. Robert Evans, instead of *Susan* Evans) but find out only later that the credit card itself was issued to their spouse. In this case, regular monthly payments are credited to the spouse whose financial information was used to establish the credit account. Make sure the credit bureau lists you as "jointly responsible" for the credit, not as an "authorized signer" on the card. It is vital to establish credit in your own name while you are married so that you won't be left without credit if your spouse should suddenly die or file for divorce.

Credit bureaus do not have joint credit reports; if you have credit in joint names, transactions on that account are reported separately under individual names. Joint accounts opened since 1977 are generally reported separately to the credit bureau by any creditor you have a transaction with.

If a credit grantor has not been reporting payment history separately, you should request a change in writing. Then check back a few months later to see if the change was made. You do not have to have a job or income to have credit in your own name. You do have to have your payment history reported separately to the credit bureau on joint accounts so that credit bureaus know you exist.

If you are legally separated or divorced, immediately close all joint accounts. If you are widowed, and your accounts are held in JTWROS (joint tenants with the right of survivorship) or community property, close them and set up a new account in your name. If they are held as joint tenants in common, your spouse's will will dictate how his money is to be distributed. Seek legal counsel before withdrawing funds or closing an account. Open new ones in your own name, then check with the credit bureaus in a few months to make sure your old account is reported closed.

Chapter 6

—•—◆—•—◆—•—◆—•—◆—•—◆—•—◆—•—◆—•—◆—•—◆—•—

Taxes: Lightening the Burden

*W*hen it comes to taxes, the one thing you can be assured of is they will change—up, down, even sideways. The ever-changing tax environment demands that you take the responsibility to keep up with areas that will have a direct impact on you and your family. *The tax information presented in this chapter is subject to change. I strongly advise that, before you begin an action plan, you check with your financial consultant, accountant, or tax lawyer to verify what is current and whether a suggested strategy or deduction is still allowable.*

One place to start is with your itemized deductions. An appalling majority of my clients would come to me failing to have claimed all deductions due them. If you're serious about a financial plan, you need to become familiar with what can be deducted and how to substantiate the deductions. Because this area changes so much, I will not focus on any specifics. Rather, I encourage you to seek outside professional help. Even the IRS has pamphlets on deductions that are reader friendly.

Most people could pay far less income tax than they do and still remain in the good graces of the Internal Revenue Service. Much of your early effort in executing a financial strategy will be aimed at whittling down, by legal means, the amount of your taxable income. Tax planners and lawmakers have decided that certain tax exemptions and incentives will stimulate the economy, benefit the family, and serve the capitalistic system.

The areas I will address are your tax brackets—yes, indeed, they change too—and your withholding declarations if you work for pay (all women work—some get a paycheck, some don't). Read on.

RECORD KEEPING IS VITAL

If you are going to use the tax laws to your advantage, you must keep accurate records of your financial transactions. If you are meticulous about tracking every dollar you spend, and if you spend time on record keeping and detailing expenses, when tax time comes around, you will only need to total the bottom lines. However, there is no one correct way to do this.

I'm a stockpiler. I accumulate all tax-related data during the year (receipts, bank records, canceled checks, stock and interest information, etc.) in one place—a folder or drawer designated for that purpose—and then spend two days each year dividing, organizing, and totaling. My accountant then pushes all the totals to their appropriate spots. Whatever method you use, be consistent about it. If you question a receipt or expense, keep or record it anyway. An accountant can advise you, but only if the information is there to work with.

A useful tool for record keeping is a detailed, accurate desk journal or calendar. It's a central place to record business, including your travel—destination mileage, and purpose for the trip; business-related meals and expenses, including who you met and why; child care and medical expenses; cash donations and other related areas. To be successful in the area of record keeping for the tax game, especially if an audit comes your way, think documentation, documentation, documentation.

I have had only one audit with the IRS in the nineties. It/They (I'm never sure what to call them!) wanted to check all my travel-related expenses. My accountant and I thought that was a hoot—half of my time is on the road. Three items were taken to the audit: the year-end statement with my business credit card that showed air, hotel, car rentals, and food expenses all broken out by category and date; a few samples of programs at which I spoke that showed my name, sponsor, date, and topic; and a calendar.

Now, this calendar wasn't one where you turned a page for each date. It measured 2 1/2 by 3 1/2 feet with the entire year on one sheet. On it were a variety of dots—green, red, blue, and yellow, on each of which was written a city and state. The IRS agent was told that each dot represented an engagement (red was vacation, green was a paid speech, etc.) and all he had to do was match the date dot with a program with a travel expense. Within an hour, the audit was cleared!

TAX RATE TABLES BEGINNING IN 1993

The law contains five regular tax brackets: 15 percent, 28 percent, 31 percent, 36 percent, and 39.6 percent. The following tax rate schedule illustrates these rates.

1993 FEDERAL INCOME TAX RATE SCHEDULE
— ♦ — ♦ — ♦ — ♦ — ♦ — ♦ — ♦ — ♦ — ♦ — ♦ — ♦ — ♦ — ♦ — ♦ — ♦ —

	Taxable Income	Tax	Rate on Excess (in percentages)
Married Filing Jointly*	$ 0	$ 0	15
	36,900	5,535	28
	89,150	20,165	31
	140,000	35,929	36
	250,000	75,529	39.6
Single	$ 0	$ 0	15
	22,100	3,315	28
	53,500	12,107	31
	115,000	31,172	36
	250,000	79,772	39.6
Head of Household	$ 0	$ 0	15
	29,600	4,440	28
	76,400	17,544	31
	27,500	33,385	36
	250,000	77,485	39.6
Married Filing Separately	$ 0	$ 0	15
	18,450	2,768	28
	44,575	10,083	31
	70,000	17,964	36
	125,000	37,764	39.6

* The joint return rates can be used by a qualifying surviving spouse.

Any strategy you use or consider using will tie into your tax rate at some time or another. If you buy a house with a mortgage, it reduces your taxable income; if you have a loss or gain on any investment, it adjusts your taxable income.

Therefore, you are going to need to get out your calculator, pencil, and paper, and determine whether your income will increase, as in a gain, or be reduced. Any changes in overall tax liability should be reflected by an adjustment on your W-4 if you and/or your spouse are employed.

Remember, Uncle Sam does not pay interest on tax refunds, and you may risk a penalty if you underwithhold on taxes.

WHAT IS A STANDARD DEDUCTION?

Tax preparers and individuals who complete tax returns that include itemized deductions are quite familiar with the term *Standard Deduction*.

In order to do an itemized return (almost anyone who has a home mortgage in excess of $10,000 does an itemized return), you need to have total (or gross) deductions in excess of the Standard Deduction benchmark.

For example, if you are single, pay state taxes, contribute to your church and other causes, etc., you should have total deductions in excess of $3,700 before you itemize. If you paid $1,200 in state taxes and tithed $1,200, the combined $2,400 qualified deductions don't exceed the $3,700 mark for itemizing. Therefore, you would most likely file a short form.

But if you buy a home that carries a mortgage, the picture changes. The interest from the mortgage plus real estate taxes would be added to your state taxes, contributions, etc. Anything over the $3,700 would be deducted from your taxable income to determine your overall obligation.

YOUR STANDARD DEDUCTION

Filing Status 1994

— ◆ — ◆ — ◆ — ◆ — ◆ — ◆ — ◆ — ◆ — ◆ — ◆ — ◆ — ◆ — ◆ — ◆ — ◆ —

Married filing jointly	$6,200
Surviving spouse	6,200
Single	3,700
Head of household	5,450
Married filing separately	3,100

THE W-4 AND YOU

Legitimate deductions offer just one area for tax savings; knowledgeable use of the W-4 withholding form is another. The problem is that few people bother to read it. In fact, most merely count themselves and dependents, if they have any, as their only withholding allowance.

If you get a refund at the end of each year, you are losing a lot of money. You are providing a twelve-month interest-free loan to the government with moneys you could be using. It is simply not necessary to have huge amounts withheld from your paycheck if you have the proper deductions to back up a lesser withholding figure.

The odds are that if you receive a check in excess of $500, the withholding sum is too great. It's time to complete a new W-4.

Today's W-4 consists of two pages. It can be completed within minutes if you know what your deductions will be—home mortgage interest, the allowable percentage of personal interest, charitable contributions, state and local taxes (no sales tax), medical expenses in excess of 7.5 percent of your adjusted income, and miscellaneous deductions (most miscellaneous deductions are now deductible only in excess of 2 percent of your income). If you don't know the exact numbers (nobody will until after the year has ended), keep in mind that this is an estimate—when in doubt use last year's tax return as a guide, and ask your accountant.

Calculate twice a year what your overall tax liability will be. If you withhold at least 90 percent of what your obligation is, you will incur no penalties. People the IRS identify as "tax protestors" or others who deliberately understate their withholdings will be hit with a $500 penalty.

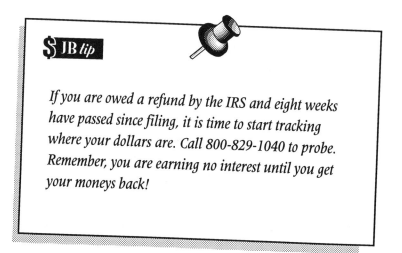

$ JB *tip*

If you are owed a refund by the IRS and eight weeks have passed since filing, it is time to start tracking where your dollars are. Call 800-829-1040 to probe. Remember, you are earning no interest until you get your moneys back!

Chapter 7
—•—•—•—•—•—•—•—•—•—•—•—•—•—•—•—
Insurance: Who, What, and How

*I*nsurance can be confusing. This chapter will give a brief overview of insurance: the kinds available, the purposes for each, and some ideas to help you sort through how much you need.

LIFE INSURANCE

The only people for whom your life insurance will be useful are those you leave behind when you die. Life insurance is not for you—it's for them. Do not buy any if you have no one financially dependent upon you, or buy only the insurance necessary to cover funeral expenses for yourself if you believe these would be a burden for your family.

There are three reasons for buying life insurance:

1. To replace income if you die prematurely and family members depend on that income.

2. To provide money to buy out a business partner, repay business loans, or hire a successor in case of an owner's death.

3. To provide immediate, liquid money to pay estate taxes, burial costs, and debts.

As you begin to probe the maze that is insurance land—and believe me, it is a maze—keep two rules in mind:

- *Keep it simple.* It is easy to go brain numb when considering insurance. If you really don't understand the concept of what an agent is proposing, pass.

- *Frugality wins.* Buy the lowest cost insurance you can. Stretching your dollar to get the most for the least is your guide.

Life insurance is death protection—protection for those you love and care for. Other types of insurance that go beyond pure death protection, with savings and investments attached to the policy as part of the deal, carry a hefty price tag. More later on that.

WHO NEEDS LIFE INSURANCE?

Not everyone needs life insurance. Below are several life phase scenarios. See where you fit:

1. *You're young, single, with no dependents.* Stop—you don't need it. Instead, purchase disability coverage, add to your investments, and seed your retirement account.

Agents usually make the pitch that it's less costly to buy insurance now. Here are the facts: The difference between buying a term policy at age thirty versus age forty is about $27 per year. That's not a big deal.

The call? Skip insurance and invest the amount you would have paid in premiums in a no-load mutual fund.

2. *You're older, single with no dependents.* You don't need life insurance. If you have some, does it have any cash value? What interest rate does it earn? Most likely, you can earn more in your bank and you can use the money.

The call?  Cancel life insurance and use any accumulated cash to invest, put in savings, and live on.

3. *You're single with dependents.* Dependents come in all ages: babies to elderly parents. Insurance alert! What happens if you die—tomorrow? Who will provide care for your dependents and supplement your parents' income? A policy makes sense.

If you have children from a prior marriage, things can get complicated when it comes to money. A life insurance policy could be placed in a trust that would designate disbursements—your lawyer, agent, or financial planner will help here (after you tell him what you want).

If relatives will become guardians, do your kids and them a huge favor by having insurance proceeds to fund education needs and daily expenses.

The call? If you are under fifty years of age and a nonsmoker, you can get a term insurance policy for less than $200 a year—that's $16 per month!

4. *You're a DINK—a double-income couple with no kids.* You might not need insurance. Each spouse could be self-supporting if the other dies.

The call? Buy coverage only if you need both incomes to cover obligations (don't forget the mortgage). Or, if you each have an estate valued at over $600,000, you may need cash to pay taxes.

5. *You're an OINK—a one-income couple with no kids.* The working spouse may need insurance to protect/preserve the lifestyle of the spouse at home.

The call? If the spouse at home has independent moneys, pass on life insurance.

6. *You're married, with young children.* You need insurance, lots of it. Those kids have to be raised and educated, and it's not cheap.

The call? You need up to seven times your earnings to take care of your brood. Check out low-cost term insurance. But you probably need the coverage only until they're on their own. Then this portion of your insurance can be canceled.

7. *You are married and don't work for pay.* If you don't have children, pass on insurance for yourself, but your spouse should be covered. If you have small children, would your husband need to pay for housekeeping and child-care services? You may need a policy.

The call? If your marriage assets haven't accumulated large cash and/or investments, your spouse may not have the extra income to cover child-related expense. Remember, if you are under fifty, a term policy costs less than $200 per year for $100,000 in coverage. Get it.

8. *You're retired.* You need insurance only if your spouse couldn't live on the Social Security, pension, and savings you'll leave behind.

The call? If your spouse dies, cancel the insurance. Keep it only if you have plenty of money to live on and want to leave a big check for your church, a charity, or your kids.

9. *You're a kid.* Pass unless you are a movie star or you have a genetic disorder that will make insurance coverage unattainable when you become an adult.

The call? 💡 Put your money in a no-load mutual fund.

If you have a policy your great grandmother bought for you when you were a child, cash it in. The bank will pay a higher savings interest than the insurance company will.

10. *You own a business.* Either you or the company needs a policy on your life. If you are the sole owner, your heirs may need to cover the debts you signed personally for, or to pay estate taxes. A co-owner may want to be able to buy his or her partner's share of the business if the partner dies or becomes disabled. Talk to your lawyer about a buy/sell agreement funded by life and disability insurance. This is know as "key man" insurance.

The call? 💡 Don't assume that your partner(s) will take care of your spouse and kids when you are gone. Your family may own a percentage of the business, but if the company doesn't make any cash distributions it's difficult to eat paper.

11. *You're rich.* You may need money to pay estate taxes. If your investments are illiquid (real estate and privately owned companies fit here) you need money—ready cash.

The call? 💡 If you're in this category, ideally you should have set up an irrevocable trust to keep the insurance proceeds out of your estate.

TYPES OF LIFE INSURANCE

Life insurance is sold in two types and a zillion hybrids. *Term* and *whole life* are the most common, and there are variations of each. *Universal life*, which combines term and whole life (kind of), was introduced several years ago as well.

In determining your life-insurance needs, there are several areas to consider. For example, you may have accumulated debts that should be paid off if your spouse dies, as well as initial administrative, funeral, and estate costs. If you have children, you should take a close look at your current annual living expenses. This, of course, should be adjusted for other current sources of income.

Whatever the proceeds are, the beneficiary will more than likely put them to work in order to achieve some economic growth. Unless the proceeds from a policy are extremely small, it is improbable that the beneficiary or the surviving spouse will immediately spend them all. But beware—many widows are approached to "invest" their insurance proceeds in a whole gamut of "opportunities." A better word would be scams. Mistakes are made, often to another's benefit (i.e., commissions), during times of emotional stress.

My experience has shown that women who become widowed will more than likely enter the workforce within a few years. Even though this may be the case in your particular situation, it is important for you to consider—especially in the purchase of life insurance—that you or your spouse may die tomorrow and the survivor may not be financially stable immediately. If that happens, how long will your dependents need financial assistance? I personally feel that you should always consider the worst possibility, even though everyone may be on his or her feet and off and running within a few years.

Term Insurance

Term insurance answers most needs when it comes to replacing lost income. It is pure insurance. It offers a set amount of money to the beneficiary of the policy if the insured dies, and it costs substantially less than whole life. The primary difference in the two types of insurance is that whole life has a savings account tied to it, whereas term insurance does not.

The key parts of term insurance are the following:

- You pay premiums every year (monthly, quarterly, or annually). Insurance stays in force until you stop paying. There is no cash build up—savings.

- With ordinary term, your premium increases slightly each year. You can buy a level term, which keeps the premium fixed for several years.

- Costs are determined by age, whether you smoke, and your gender (women usually pay less, although some insurance companies use unisex rates).

- Companies vary in what they charge—the same policy and amount can cost twice as much at another company.

- It should be renewable—which means you don't have to requalify with a physical every year.

Whole Life Insurance

Whole life insurance has a savings account attached to it. The longer you are in it, the more savings you will have. In order to achieve this, whole life's premiums are much greater than term's. When whole life is proposed it is always accompanied by illustrations—the "What-ifs." Projections for growth in the savings side are *always* inflated—they are *never guaranteed!*

It is easy to be misled on interest rates. Insurance companies routinely announce high interest rates to keep policy holders at bay, then they increase their operating expenses and charges for mortality (the death benefit). These expenses are deducted from your cash value before any interest is paid.

The result: You do get a higher interest rate, but it is paid on a smaller amount of cash. You therefore earn less than the promised rate.

Universal Life Insurance

Universal life insurance offers some flexibility. You can get a guaranteed policy amount for when you die; you can accumulate tax-deferred cash; you can pay extra premiums early on so that extra cash will build up (theoretically) to pay future premiums. Here's the catch: If the interest rates projected in your illustration are not achieved (after all, rates do vary) you may have a problem—your cash won't build up to pay the premiums down the road.

Canceling a universal life policy can be quite expensive. In fact, you can lose 100 percent of the money you put up on the savings side.

In the table on the next page, beneath the columns headed "25 years" and "35 years" are two percentage numbers: 75 percent and 60 percent. Those are your replacement goals, and they refer to the actual percentage of current earnings that you would like to have available to your spouse if you die or available to you if he dies. In using the table, multiply this factor by your current gross earnings. The result will tell you approximately how much life insurance you need.

If earnings and/or age of spouse fall between the indicated figures, you can determine your multiple by averaging the difference between the age span and the earnings. The replacement percentages refer to the percentage of income that is represented by your spouse. If, however, you make more than your spouse, he should carry the amount of coverage on you that the loss of your earnings would represent.

For example, let's assume that you make $30,000 a year and your spouse makes $22,500 a year. Let's also assume that your spouse is thirty-five. If you were to die tomorrow and your objective was to leave him with replacement dollars for your lost earnings, you would multiply 8 times $30,000 and arrive at $240,000. That would be the recommended amount of insurance coverage for you to carry on yourself.

MULTIPLES-OF-SALARY TABLE

Your Present Gross Earnings	25 Years		Present Age of Spouse 35 Years		45 Years		55 Years	
	75%	60%	75%	60%	75%	60%	75%	60%
$ 7,500	4.0	3.0	5.5	4.0	7.5	5.5	6.5	4.5
$ 9,000	4.0	3.0	5.5	4.0	7.5	5.5	6.5	4.5
$15,000	4.5	3.0	6.5	4.5	8.0	6.0	7.0	5.5
$23,500	6.5	4.5	8.0	5.5	8.5	6.5	7.5	5.5
$30,000	7.5	5.0	8.0	6.0	8.5	6.5	7.0	5.5
$40,000	7.5	5.0	8.0	6.0	8.0	6.0	7.0	5.5
$65,000	7.5	5.5	7.5	6.0	7.5	6.0	6.5	5.0

PAY THE PIPER

How much should you pay for life insurance? The amount you pay each year is called a premium. After you decide how much life insurance you need in your particular situation, the amount of your annual premium is based on four calculations.

1. Your age

2. Your current state of health

3. How much money the insurance company can earn by investing your premium dollars until your death

4. The insurance company's expenses for paying the agent commissions and mailing you bills

How Much Cheaper Is Term Insurance?

Picking only from lower-cost companies, the table below shows dramatically how much more coverage you get for your money with term insurance. The premiums quoted are for a $100,000 policy for a nonsmoker.

The term premiums rise every year; those for cash-value policies can stay level for life. The chart lists premiums you would pay for a particular type of insurance if you started paying for it at a particular age. But in terms of what's affordable at any given age, term insurance wins hands down.

YEARLY PREMIUMS FOR A $100,000 POLICY
–◆—◆—◆—◆—◆—◆—◆—◆—◆—◆—◆—◆—◆—◆—◆—◆—

Age	Term Insurance	Universal-Life Insurance	Whole-Life Insurance
30	$136	$ 590	$ 875
35	140	746	1,095
40	163	950	1,391
45	205	1,217	1,776
50	320	1,583	2,311
55	440	2,078	3,038
60	610	2,741	4,717
65	980	3,665	5,376

Source: National Insurance Consumer Organization

HOW TO FIND CHEAP INSURANCE

There are two ways to find the companies that lower your insurance costs.

1. *Check out the National Insurance Consumer Organization (NICO).* Write NICO at:

   121 N. Payne St.
   Alexandria, VA 22314

2. *Locate a computerized price-quote service.* All you need is your age, gender, and health status and the computer starts to crunch info. It's a good idea to recheck every three to five years—who knows what "deals" will be out there.

- *Insurance Information* (800-472-5800). For $50,
  Insurance Information sends you names and phone
  numbers of the five insurers that offer the lowest term
  rates for someone with your stats. Your $50 will be
  refunded if you don't find a policy more than $50 cheaper
  than the one you presently have.

  Insurance Information does not sell you insurance.

Other price quote services are offered by insurance agents. There is no obligation to buy, and no salesperson will call you to sell you a policy. In other words, you are in charge.

- *TermQuote*—Dayton, Ohio (800-444-8376)

- *SelectQuote*—San Francisco, California (800-343-1985)

- *InsuranceQuote*—Chandler, Arizona (800-972-1104)

Price quotes are accompanied by brief descriptions (not with great details) of the policies. Make sure you ask for *annual renewable term* quotes. Many will give you instead a *reentry* or *revertible* term, which means you will have to requalify in a few years (as in health).

Another attractive resource is the discount insurance buying service or fee adviser. Two that are worth your attention are:

- *R. K. Wilson Associates* (800-879-5433). Rick Nelson is
  located in Lake Priest, Illinois, and uses low-load policies
  to save consumers from 40 to 70 percent on anything that
  creates a commission.

- *Direct Insurance Services* (DIS) (619-587-2000). Mark
  White's firm is located in San Diego, California. His objective and policies parallel R. K. Wilson.

One other resource is *The Individual Investor's Guide to Low-Load Insur-*

ance Products by Glenn Daily. You can order it by calling International Publishing at 800-488-4149. Cost is $22.95 plus $2 shipping.

WHO'S THE FAIREST IN THE LAND?

Most insurance companies quote their A. M. Best rating when queries are made about safety. When Executive Life failed in 1991, A. M. Best was still rating the company "A+"! Go ahead and fake a yawn if you get the Best rating. What you want is the Weiss Research rating.

Weiss Research is the newest rating kid on the block—and the most conservative. Before Executive Life went belly up, Weiss's rating had been reduced to "D."

To date, libraries don't carry Weiss. You can contact Weiss directly at 800-289-9222. Your cost will be $15.

Agents won't tell you if the insurance company they are illustrating/promoting is unsafe. Nor will they tell you that any investment projections are unrealistic. You may get a low quote for future premiums, which may depend on the company making a 15 to 20 percent profit on its investment portfolio. Forget it. And it is a rare agent who will tell you that you can get a better deal someplace else.

◆ SUMMING UP ◆

In 1905, a commission led by then New York State Senator William Armstrong reported on the insurance industry:

> The business is riddled with self-dealing, unsound investments, unsuitable policies, high pressure selling and unbridled sales expenses. Consumers take large losses when they drop expensive coverage that they shouldn't have bought and can't afford.

It is not much different today. Major insurance companies—Metropolitan Life, Equitable Life Insurance Society, and Crown Life—were hit with massive lawsuits in the nineties for misrepresentation and scams, even selling phony retirement policies to nurses. Big moneys were paid in settlements.

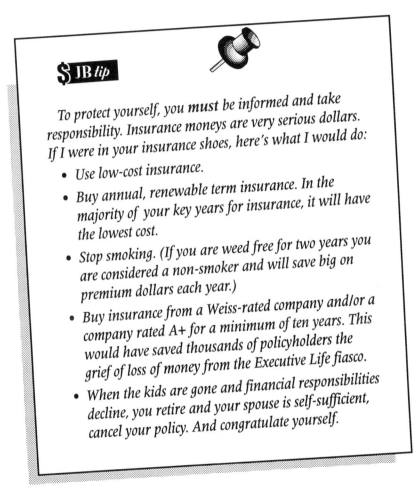

$ JB tip

To protect yourself, you **must** be informed and take responsibility. Insurance moneys are very serious dollars. If I were in your insurance shoes, here's what I would do:

- Use low-cost insurance.
- Buy annual, renewable term insurance. In the majority of your key years for insurance, it will have the lowest cost.
- Stop smoking. (If you are weed free for two years you are considered a non-smoker and will save big on premium dollars each year.)
- Buy insurance from a Weiss-rated company and/or a company rated A+ for a minimum of ten years. This would have saved thousands of policyholders the grief of loss of money from the Executive Life fiasco.
- When the kids are gone and financial responsibilities decline, you retire and your spouse is self-sufficient, cancel your policy. And congratulate yourself.

DISABILITY INSURANCE

One area many women don't think about is disability insurance. No matter what your occupation is, if you get sick or require major surgery that will keep you out of the office earning stream for more than a few weeks, disability insurance becomes essential.

Insurance companies use three different definitions of "disabled" in their policies. The first is "totally incapacitated and confined to bed." The second is "unable to work at any occupation." This does not necessarily mean that you are bedridden. The third is "unable to work at a specific occupation." As of this writing, there is no disability insurance available for a woman employed inside the home as a homemaker. Yet.

As a rule, the sooner benefits commence, the more expensive the policy. I recommend you explore disability policies that begin ninety days after you have been incapacitated. Also, the more extended the coverage, such as ten years, the more expensive the policy.

How Much Disability Do You Need?

Now, how much do you really need? If you purchase disability insurance directly and pay for the premiums with your after-tax dollars, any benefit you receive will be nontaxable. On the other hand, if you receive disability insurance and your employer pays for the premium, then any proceeds you receive during the convalescence period will be taxable. If you are dealing with nontaxable dollars, then you will probably need 50 percent to 70 percent of your current annual income after taxes. If you make $25,000 a year, 60 percent of your income after taxes will be approximately $13,000. Seventy percent will be approximately $15,000.

The next step in your calculations is to determine how much income you will receive from any savings or investments on a monthly and annual basis. How much income, if you are entitled to any, could you receive from Social Security disability benefits? How much income, if you are entitled to it, could you receive in a work-related injury from Workmen's Compensation? How much income would you receive from any employer providing disability benefits?

After you have totaled the amounts that you would receive from other sources, deduct that total from your estimated annual needs. This will give you the total amount of coverage you will need to carry. If, after checking all your sources, you determine you will receive $3,500 annually, deduct that amount from the $13,000 that was your minimum requirement, divide the remainder ($9,500) by 12, and you can determine that you will need additional coverage of $792 per month.

Your next step is to get a quote from an insurance broker who deals in long-term disability programs. Because rates vary from company to company, it is a good idea to get quotes from at least three. An insurance broker who represents several different companies will best be able to assist you. (See the discussion of discounted insurance quotes on pages 118–19.)

Demand Certain Guarantees

As in any contract, the language can make it or break it. For a disability policy, the language makes a significant difference in the type of coverage that you will receive. The policy that you purchase should have a *non-cancelable* clause. This means that as long as you keep paying the premiums, the insurance company cannot cancel it.

Secondly, it should have a *guaranteed annual premium* which means they cannot increase the premium that has already been declared within the policy. As a rule, the younger you are when you purchase your disability insurance, the less the policy will be.

Finally, you want to have a *waiver of premiums clause* which will guarantee that if you become disabled, you no longer have to pay the premiums to keep the policy in force.

The best disability policies also include a *residual benefit disability* payment. This means that the policy will pay the difference between the income that you are able to earn after you are disabled and the original amount of your guaranteed monthly payment. Sometimes residual benefits are automatically included in a new policy, and at other times, you have to purchase them as a special rider. A residual benefit comes into play if you are disabled and cannot return to your original occupation but are able to work at another function. If your new income is $2,000 per month versus your disability payment of $2,500 per month, the insurance company will continue to pay you the $500 per month difference.

$ JB *tip*

When you select residual benefits, make sure that you do not have to be totally disabled before you can claim them.

$ JB *tip*

Make sure that the wording of your policy states that it pays for any disability caused by illness as well as accident.

USAA, a life insurance company out of San Antonio, Texas, 800-531-8000, is one of the few disability underwriters that will sell direct to the consumer without working through an insurance agent. In addition to getting the other quotes from agents/brokers within your area, contact them for a direct quote.

Keep Up With Inflation and Income

If your income or inflation rises, it is safe to assume your expenses will also. Many policies have a small amount of inflation protection (a small percentage increase) within the guaranteed benefits. Make sure you understand exactly what that percent is. If your income rises, you may have to increase additional disability policies, or your policy may include a clause that allows you to increase your coverage without taking additional physical examinations or needing to prove your insurability.

Health Insurance

For the nineties healthcare and chaos go hand in hand.

Whatever the case, there is a lot of confusion, and that confusion will probably continue for the next several years while hospitals and health-care organizations downsize, right-size, and resize. Whether you buy insurance through your employer or on your own, the insurer will either allow you to choose your own doctors and plan of treatment, or it won't. If it doesn't allow you to select your own doctors, you must use physicians from its approved list and request permission for surgeries and other forms of care. If you don't follow its rules, it is improbable you will be reimbursed, at least in full.

If you work for a big company, most likely you have healthcare coverage. This type group coverage will probably give you the most for the dollars spent. A medical policy through a large employer usually includes a deductible ranging from $150 to $300 per person in the family before the insurance policy pays. It also carries a ceiling, such as $2,000 of moneys you expend before it begins to cover 100 percent on procedures.

Most insurance companies will do almost anything to keep you out of the hospital. If you require surgery, they prefer to get you to a day surgery or a clinic where you are in and out in a few hours. Many pay for these procedures 100 percent. If you insist on going into the hospital, probably the insurer won't pay the whole bill.

If you are married and you both have insurance coverage, you may choose to opt out of one of the plans, or to maintain your participation and *co-insure*. This means that where one company will be the primary insurer if a demand is made on a claim, the other company will come in and pay up to 100 percent of whatever the procedure is.

If you work for a smaller company, your coverage could be reduced, you may have to pay for it 100 percent, or there may not be any coverage offered at all. It's not unusual for employees to be required to complete a health questionnaire to participate in a smaller company's plan. Most health insurance rates have increased over the past few years. Those of smaller companies have increased at a greater percentage rate.

Extending Limits

Many insurance policies have life-time limits such as $250,000. If yours does today, you are underinsured. Ten years ago, you'd have to really push it to accumulate $250,000 in medical bills. Not so now. With organ transplants, bypasses, even back surgery, your bills could range from $50,000 to $150,000 without batting an eye. Some insurers sell a high-limit "major medical" policy that covers devastating illnesses with much higher limits. They carry deductibles of $25,000 or so. Because of the high deductible, this insurance doesn't cost much, but it can bring a great deal of peace of mind. The $25,000 is not a problem, because your regular policy would take care of that before the higher limit policy kicks in.

Changing Employers

If you leave an employer who has health insurance, you may be able to convert your policy into an individual coverage. Depending upon the circumstances of your leaving, your coverage can last up to eighteen months, and if you are totally disabled, up to twenty-nine months. There will be an increase in your premium.

Because of the public's awareness and concern over healthcare insurance, we will probably eventually get to a place where coverage will be carried from employer to employer, and that the eighteen- to twenty-nine-month window will become obsolete.

Buy health insurance when you are healthy, not when you are sick. If you wait until then, you'll pay substantially more for your policy, if you can get one at all.

Although group insurance through your employer is usually the least expensive way to go, make sure you know all the exclusions, if any. Other drawbacks include: Policies can be canceled out from under you (the employer may decide no longer to offer coverage); policies can increase markedly (state regulators don't review rate increases in advance as they do for individual policies); and group policies often have low maximum benefits.

$ JB tip

Be suspicious of any pitches for group policies that arrive through the mail. Initially, they sound terrific. But exclusions lie buried between the lines.

Ways to Have Insurance and Reduce Costs

- *Buy group insurance.*

- *Buy unisex rates if possible.* Women generally pay more for coverage than men.

- *Delete maternity.* If you are not going to have children or are out of child-bearing range, deleting maternity can save you $30 to $75 a month. Before doing so, verify whether regular gynecological coverage outside of giving birth is included.

- *Join a Health Maintenance Organization (HMO).* The granddaddy of HMO's is Kaiser Permanente. They usually cost less than traditional insurers when you use their offices, internal staff, and hospital.

- *Use a Preferred-Provider Organization (PPO).* With a PPO you usually pay less for your coverage (i.e., you only pay

$10 per doctor visit.) The catch is that you are restricted to the doctors and hospitals who've joined the plan and any specialists they refer you to.

- *Get a " managed care" or "utilization review" policy.* Utilization review means you are subject to rules of the insurance company such as mandatory secondary opinions on any hospital admissions before undergoing non-emergency surgery and limits on hospital stays. If you are willing to go along with their rules, you usually pay a lower premium. If you violate them, the insurer will limit how much will be paid.

- *Increase your deductible.* By increasing to a higher amount, such as $500 or $1,000, you could reduce your insurance premium by as much as 25 percent.

- *Purchase a "waiver of premium."* If an injury or accident keeps you out of work, a waiver of premium kicks in and enables you to quit paying health insurance premiums while retaining your policy. The waiver will pay the policy until you are able to go back to work.

- *Get a policy that is "guaranteed renewable."* This prevents the insurer from canceling your individual policy or raising your premiums because your health is poor. Don't purchase any individual policy without it.

- *Pay by the month.* Paying your premiums monthly is a few dollars higher that by quarter or annually. But if you don't have a couple of thousand dollars for an annual premium, you should be able to work out a few hundred dollars a month. Payment plans are almost always set up to work through your checking account as an automatic deduction and sent to the insurance company.

Bad Insurance

- *TV advertised insurance.* Almost anything that is "hocked" by celebrities. These policies often have long waiting periods before they cover any illness. They should be banned.

- *Accident insurance.* Pays medical bills that result from an accident, not an illness. Only 4.5 percent of deaths are accidental. You need a policy that covers both sickness and accident, which most major medical policies do.

- *One disease or catastrophe insurance.* Credit and cancer insurances come to mind. The odds are against your getting the disease you insure against. With a general policy, you shouldn't need cancer insurance.

- *Mail order policies.* Take a pass on anything that arrives in your mailbox unsolicited. It is equivalent to the TV advertised insurance.

- *Student policies.* If you have a child in a private school, college, or university, they are most likely covered within your own policy.

Buying health insurance demands that you get involved in what you are purchasing. It also means that you need to pay attention to what you can do to help reduce your cost: Stop smoking, drink less, eat right, exercise—all things that you can control.

Automobile Insurance

Most Americans drive, and the potential liability from owning and driving a car is almost unlimited. In addition to the financial cost from an accident—to your car, the other party's car, and any physical harm—there's always the threat of a lawsuit—unless you live in a no-fault state. This is where pain and suffering come in, and amounts that juries can award for pain and suffering can be stratospheric. The only people who can do without automotive insurance are those who have nothing to lose—which is not you. Automotive insurance is priced by:

- Your driving record (if you have several moving violations, you'll pay more)

- Auto theft rates in your area

- Whether you live in an urban or suburban area

- If you have made numerous claims on other policies

- If you use your car for business

- If you drive more than the annual standard (approximately 10,000 miles per year)

- If you drive a car type that is frequently stolen

- If you drive an expensive car (i.e., Mercedes or Jaguar)

- Your age and gender

There are two key factors to an auto insurance policy: the coverage and the cost. You need to understand what coverage is required by your state and what you'll have to pay to get it. There are eight basic coverages in any policy:

1. *Bodily Injury and Liability.* This insurance will pay another for medical costs and loss of earnings if you are involved in an accident. Most states require a minimum of $25,000 per person and $50,000 per accident in bodily injury insurance. If you don't live in a no-fault state, it is wise to increase the $25,000/$50,000 limits.

2. *Personal Damage Liability.* Insurance moneys paid to repair the other party's car or property that is damaged.

The minimum required here is usually $10,000. As above, if you don't live in a no-fault state, it's wise to increase the minimum limit.

3. *Uninsured Motorist.* This coverage pays off if you and/or the passenger in your car are injured by a driver who has no insurance, or if you are the victim of a hit-and-run accident.

4. *Underinsured Motorist.* If you are in an accident and the other driver's coverage is used up or not in place, this portion of your policy will kick in and cover you for expenses that the other party would have normally covered.

5. *Medical Payments.* Regardless of who is at fault, this pays hospital, medical, and funeral bills for you and members of your family. If you have extensive coverage for medical, hospital, and funeral bills under other policies, you may want to exclude this portion and save a few dollars.

6. *Personal Injury Protection (PIP).* PIP is commonly offered in states with no-fault auto insurance. It also pays medical, hospital, and funeral expenses and adds payments for lost wages and other services such as housekeeping if an accident renders you temporarily disabled. If your healthcare insurance covers you extensively, and you have disability for lost wages, you may want to take a pass on this section.

7. *Collision Coverage.* This pays for damage to your car in an accident or a replacement for a vehicle if it is covered. One of the best ways to save money in this area is to increase your deductible, which is usually set from $100 to $500.

8. *Comprehensive.* If you have financed a car when you purchased it, you will be required to carry comprehensive

coverage. It covers theft and any damage to the car, from things like vandalism, riots, fires, trees, hail, etc. Comprehensive coverage also can cover a rental car if yours is damaged or stolen, usually for up to thirty days.

Two other coverages that you might consider are towing and car rental.

Reducing Costs

Everyone wants to pay the least and get the most coverage. Here are some tips:

- *When purchasing auto insurance, comparison shop.* If you have been in the military, you can call for quotes at United Services Automobile Association (USAA) at 800-531-8000.

  In addition, *Consumer Reports* does a study of automotive insurers and their ratings for customer satisfaction as well as general pricing policy. You can obtain past copies at your local library.

  Additional references: USAA, San Antonio, Texas, 800-531-8080 and GEICO, Washington, DC, 800-842-3000.

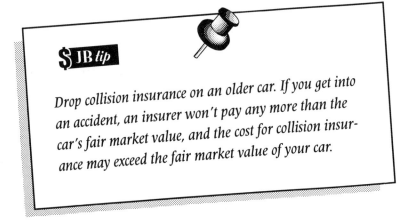

$ JB tip

Drop collision insurance on an older car. If you get into an accident, an insurer won't pay any more than the car's fair market value, and the cost for collision insurance may exceed the fair market value of your car.

- Make sure that you get all discounts available to you. Combining your auto and homeowners or renters policy or insuring more than one car under a policy can save you substantially.

- *Don't get tickets.* If you are a good driver, you will receive anywhere from 10 to 15 percent discount on your premium.

- *Own a car with airbags and antilock brakes.* Some insurers allow discounts for automobiles which have either airbags or antilock brakes.

- Use *student discounts.* If you have a male under 25 in your home, you are going to pay more. If you have a teenager at home, it is cheaper to insure him or her on your family policy rather than to list the teen as a primary driver on a car. If your teens have taken any driver training courses, and/or has good grades, they can get additional discounts.

$ JB *tip*

You can save hundreds of dollars by living in a suburb or the country versus the big city.

- *Senior drivers.* Some companies offer discounts for mature drivers with good driving records. Also contact the American Association of Retired Persons (AARP), 1909 K St. NW, Washington DC, 20049 for further information.

- *Install anti-theft and alarms.* If your car has any alarms or any anti-theft devices, notify your insurance agent to see if you will qualify for a discount.

- *Avoid TV pitches.* As with health insurance, beware of celebrities and late-night TV ads that promise insurance "no matter what your driving record is." If you have a poor driving record that has caused insurance companies to deny you coverage, your state may have a "high risk pool." In most states, any insurer who does business within the state is obligated to insure some of these drivers. Check with your state commissioner at your state capital to identify alternatives if this is your situation. No one should ever drive without automobile insurance coverage.

Ask if your state has an auto-insurance buyers guide. This guide shows what auto insurance companies charge. Call the Insurance Commissioner's office at your state capital.

Homeowner's and Renter's Insurance

Think back to hurricanes Hugo and Andrew. Millions of dollars—megamillions—were lost and most people didn't have insurance. Many of the displaced people were renters, not homeowners. It was estimated that 75 percent of the renters lost all their belongings to wind and rain from these natural disasters, and most weren't covered by insurance.

$ JB tip

If you don't own a video camera, borrow or rent one and video all of your home, including opening the closet doors and getting your clothes "on camera." Nothing supports your claim like a picture when it comes to insurance.

If you have a mortgage on your home, the lender will require property insurance. Unless you have oodles of money, everyone needs a home-owner or renter insurance policy. "Perils" are all the things that can go wrong. They include fire, lightning, smoke damage, hail, storms, explosions, riots, damage by automobiles, damage by aircraft, theft, loss of property that has been removed from a house, vandalism, and glass breakage. But that may not be enough.

If you live in a part of the country that has winter freezes, consider coverage that will include roof collapse from ice or snow, pipes freezing, or, for that matter, pipes or hot water pipes or heaters that explode. If there was a flood or major rain damage, and your closets were hit from the roof leaks, would all your clothes, rugs, and furniture be covered?

Whatever you do, make sure that you have enough coverage, and make sure that you get coverage that is for *replacement value*, not *depreciated value*. If you own items such as jewelry or art, you may be required to carry a floater or schedule items on your policy. Most policies will limit jewelry and art work in the $1,000 to $1,500 range. If your valuables exceed that amount, call your insurance agent.

How to Cut Your Cost

1. Raise your *deductible* amount. Every insurance policy has a deductible, whether it is $100, $200, etc. Consider increasing your deductible to $500, even $1,000. This could save you anywhere from 10 to 25 percent on your total annual premium.

2. If you purchase your homeowners or renters policy from the same company as your automobile insurance, it is very likely that you will get a discount.

3. If you have burglar or smoke alarms in your house, many companies will reduce your premiums.

4. If you have been with a company for several years and have never made a claim, you may be entitled to lower rates. Ask.

5. If you are retired, notify your insurance company, because many offer lower rates. They assume you will be home more often, and therefore will suffer less damage/fewer claims from "perils" or theft.

6. If your household is all non-smokers, many insurance companies offer reduced rates. Ask.

$JB Tip: Shop around for homeowners insurance. Not all companies charge the same amount for the same coverage.

7. If you can pay your homeowners coverage annually, versus semi-annually or quarterly, you can usually save as much as 5 percent.

Insurance companies usually accept your word that you've had a loss when you claim you had two TV sets and a super-duper CD system. But, if there is total destruction or loss, it is essential to be able to prove your claim.

This is where the camera or video camera comes into play. Take a walking tour of your house with a video and describe the furnishing, decorations, clothing, floor coverings, everything as you move along. If you don't have a video camera or access to one, take a regular camera and take rolls and rolls of film. Store these in a safe deposit box or in a location outside your home.

If your home is destroyed by fire or another disaster, you have proof of its contents. By having current visual proof of your assets, you will have minimal problems in getting the moneys due you in your policy. As a reminder, be sure that *all insurance coverage is noted at replacement cost*. That means you get your lost item new or, as it would cost today versus what it cost three years ago when you purchased it.

Insurance must be purchased with a money sense awareness. If it isn't, you will overpay, buy the wrong type at the wrong time, and not know until years have passed. Not good. Having the right insurance coverage for your particular needs is imperative in building your financial security.

For more information on life insurance, check the latest NICO guide: *Taking the Bite Out of Insurance* available at bookstores or by contacting NICO, 121 N. Payne St., Alexandria, VA 22314. Or for a thorough look at types of insurance, read *Buying Insurance* by Wilson J. Humber (Moody, 1994).

Chapter 8

$-\bullet-\bullet-\bullet-\bullet-\bullet-\bullet-\bullet-\bullet-\bullet-\bullet-\bullet-\bullet-\bullet-\bullet-$

Automobiles
Borrow, Lease, or Pay Cash?

The most important thing you can do in buying any car is *be prepared*. Unfortunately, when it comes to buying cars, most people, especially women, get taken for a ride. There are three critical numbers to note before you enter any car dealership.

- How much the dealer paid for the car (invoice price)

- How much you should pay for the options you want

- How much the car will be worth in four years

The moment you drive your new car off the dealer's lot, it loses 20 percent of the purchase value. By knowing what the dealer actually paid for the car and negotiating your purchase price closer to that amount, that 20 percent depreciation is reduced substantially.

Annually, *Consumer Reports* comes out with reports on the automotive industry. If you are not a subscriber, you can review copies at your local library.

Another service that is invaluable, also offered by *Consumer Reports*, is its Auto Price Service. For $11 (additional cars are less if you are getting prices on multiple cars), *Consumer Reports* gives you the base invoice price for any car—they cover more than 1,000—as well as the factory-installed options you want. By having this information at your fingertips, you'll know exactly what the dealer has paid. *Consumer Reports* can be reached at 312-347-5810.

In addition, you should become familiar with the "Blue Book." Official-ly within the trade, it is known as the *National Automotive Dealers Association Guide*. Your bank always has copies, and so does the reference area of any library. To guesstimate what your newly-purchased car will be worth in four years, deduct 40 percent of the value of the car you are consider-ing, and make sure you include all the options you want to purchase with it. In addition, if you have a car to trade in, the Blue Book will tell you its value range.

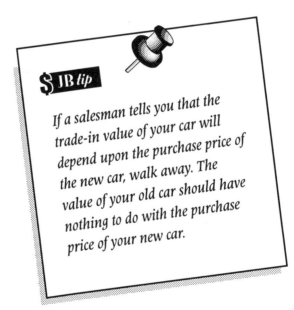

$ JB tip

If a salesman tells you that the trade-in value of your car will depend upon the purchase price of the new car, walk away. The value of your old car should have nothing to do with the purchase price of your new car.

Good Guy-Bad Guy

Salesmen are artists in their sales techniques. You should be aware that many car salesmen use a "good-guy, bad-guy routine." The bad guy is often the sales manager. The salesman pretends to be your advocate, and wants to help you out but the mean manager won't quite work the deal you want. Hang in there, and don't believe this common ploy. Whatever you do, tell the salesman that you want definite answers and you want the agreed-upon price in writing. One of the savviest things you can do if you don't have the cash to pay for your car outright, is to have your financing arranged ahead of time. But don't tell the salesman you have your own financing. Nail down the price—in writing—then tell him. This saves you hundreds—sometimes thousands in financial charges. Dealer financing is usually costly compared to your bank's.

If you finance your car, and it is not used for business purposes, any interest you pay is non-deductible. One way to alter that is to borrow from the home equity in your home. If you can get a low rate, your new mortgage rate should be low, and your interest will be 100 percent deductible.

$ JB tip

Skip the warranty. Most new cars today have excellent warranties. You don't need to spend another $200 to $300 paying for something you already have.

Other items that salesmen routinely attempt to seduce you into purchasing are rustproofing, undercoating, and glazing. Unless you live in an area of the world that has substantial damage from saltwater—sea air— pass. Most car manufacturers do an excellent job in these areas in the first place. Why pay for it again?

If you watch TV, listen to the radio, read the newspaper, or drive by automotive dealerships with big sales signs in bright, neon colors, don't believe them. Most automotive sales start with markups that the salesman then marks down to the regular price. Also, forget about any bonuses such as dinners for two or weekends for two at a resort. You are purchasing a car and you want the best deal possible.

$ JB *tip*

An excellent book for negotiating for a car is Don't Get Taken Every Time *(Penguin Books) by Remar Sutton. This is must reading.*

Should You Lease Instead of Buy?

If you want a new car, you don't have dollars for the down payment, and the automotive dealerships are not offering any special minimum or "no-down" deals, leasing becomes a strong possibility. When you lease, you put minimal dollars down, if any, and you usually pay a lower monthly payment. The drawback is that you don't own the car at the end of the lease—the dealer does.

At the end of a lease, the car has a residual value—what it is worth. The higher the value, the lower your monthly payment will be. The lower the value, the higher your payment. If your intent is to purchase the car at the end of the lease, don't go with the low monthly payment. You want your car to have a high value—especially if you will seek a loan to pay for it.

There are two kinds of leases: a *closed-end* lease and an *open-end* lease. You want the closed-end, which means you can walk away from the lease at the end of the period regardless of what the value is and not owe a dime.

With an open-end lease, you end up with an ongoing deal. If the car turns out to be worth less than the dealer originally anticipated, you make up the difference in order to close out or terminate the lease. You may have to come up with more money.

The average person drives 10,000 miles a year. Most leases factor in an allowance of 15,000 miles a year. This means that if you stay under the 15,000 miles, you won't be dinged for any extra charges. Most leases also have a clause referring to normal and acceptable wear and tear. Scratches—even small dents—could be considered normal wear and tear. Having the fender missing is not.

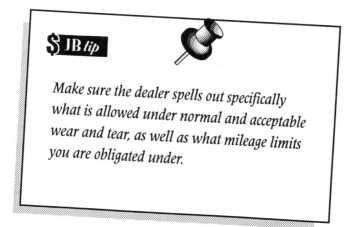

$ JB tip

Make sure the dealer spells out specifically what is allowed under normal and acceptable wear and tear, as well as what mileage limits you are obligated under.

If leasing sounds like a good option, make sure that you comparison shop. Check out several dealerships to see what they offer. Understand exactly what the terms of the lease are so that you don't overpay or get hit with an unexpected financial whammy at the time the lease terminates. And finally, don't lease a car for a time longer than you want to own it. If you expect to use it for two years, don't lease it for four even though your monthly payments may be lower.

Buying a Used Car

Used cars can be a great deal. Remember how fast new cars depreciate. When individuals advertise through the newspapers, you often can get a better financial deal.

Buying through a dealer can be more expensive, but it is usually safest because of warranties, as well as the dealer's reputation. And the car will be discounted already.

When you buy through the dealer you are protected by the federal "lemon laws"; not so with a private sale. If you have a dud, dealers will eventually have to fix the problem. With a private party, it's your problem.

Warning: do not buy a car that has been in an accident. If you buy it from a dealer, look for the words, "laundered," "rebuilt," or "salvaged." They mean that the car has had an accident and has been put back together with parts from other cars.

As with buying with new cars, *Consumer Reports* is also prepared to help you out in the used car market. The *Consumer Reports' Used Car Buying Guide*, can be ordered by calling 800-272-0722. The cost will be under $10 and worth every penny.

When it comes to used cars, specific factors that affect the price are the condition of the car as well as the total mileage. If you know that you are going to be driving a lot of miles, go for low mileage. Usually you can get better deals with family vehicles such as stationwagons and vans rather than the "sporty" cars.

Make sure that you comparison shop. Newspapers are filled with advertisements for car sales from private parties as well as dealerships. Finally, don't commit to the asking price of the vehicle; negotiate a little, and only raise your price one percent or so at a time. By referring to the *Consumer Reports' Buying Guide*, you'll know what your buying range is. Money sense also tells you to have an independent mechanic check out the car before any money passes hands.

Chapter 9

─◆─◆─◆─◆─◆─◆─◆─◆─◆─◆─◆─◆─◆─

Retirement Planning
Begins Today

*T*he best way to make sure you and your family enjoy a comfortable living at retirement is to take charge. *You can't count on Social Security and a company pension to provide all the income you need.* The only way to have a comfortable financial future is to start planning today. Not tomorrow or next month.

As I write this, my brothers and I are dealing with a problem that thousands of women and men face each day. This morning I received a call from my father. His Social Security check will be reduced $121 dollars a month. This is after a $400 reduction when my mother died a year ago.

My father is eighty-three. For the past twenty years, my brothers and I have supplemented my parents' income. When my mother died, each month we sent money to offset my father's shortfall. My parents never saved or made investments. The assumed Social Security was going to be there. Both of my parents were intelligent, but they weren't thinking clearly about retirement. It's not that they planned to have us support them the last two decades and the rest of their lives; it happened because they did NO planning.

THE RULE OF 72 IS GOLD

Dishonest money dwindles away, but he who gathers money little by little makes it grow (Proverbs 13:11).

The Rule of 72 is a formula for calculating the time it will take for your money to double when invested at any rate of compound interest. It will also explain how long it will take for the spending power of your money to be cut in half by inflation.

Take any number and divide it into 72. The resulting answer is the number of years it will take your money to double. Let's say you can earn a 6 percent interest rate; divide 72 by 6, and the resulting answer—12—is the number of years it will take your money to double. If you're earning 8 percent, it will take only nine years to double your money.

If inflation is running at 5 percent, and you divide 72 by 5, the resulting answer—14.5—is the number of years it will take for inflation to cut your buying power in half.

Watching Your Money Grow

The difference between investing taxable and tax-deferred adds up over time. Say you're earning 8 percent on your money. If you placed $2,000 each year in a taxable account, you'd have $27,568 at the end of ten years. In a tax-deferred account you'd have $31,042. In fifteen years, the difference would be $48,343 taxable versus $58,283 tax-deferred— and by thirty years, the difference would be $160,326 versus $243,532!

If you placed $2,000 a year in your IRA for just five years, from age sixteen through age twenty, and then never put in another dime, you could retire at age sixty-five with more than one million dollars (assuming an average 10 percent return). If you had $1,000 and placed it in an investment that earned 10 percent for fifteen years, never adding anything more to it, your money would quadruple.

For more information on planning for your future, consult *Saving the Best for Last* by Wilson J. Humber (Moody, 1994) or *IRAs and Annuities* by Austin Pryor (Moody, 1994).

HOW A SINGLE $1,000 INVESTMENT WILL GROW

— • — • — • — • — • — • — • — • — • — • — • — • — • — • — • — • —

Percent	5 Years	8 Years	10 Years	12 Years	15 Years
3	$1,159	$1,267	$1,344	$1,426	$1,558
4	1,217	1,369	1,480	1,601	1,801
5	1,276	1,478	1,629	1,796	2,079
6	1,338	1,594	1,791	2,012	2,397
8	1,469	1,851	2,159	2,518	3,172
10	1,611	2,144	2,594	3,138	4,177
15	2,011	3,059	4,046	5,350	8,137

If you added $1,000 each year for the fifteen years, still earning 10 percent, your $15,000 would be worth more than $30,000!

HOW A $1,000 INVESTMENT EVERY YEAR WILL GROW

— • — • — • — • — • — • — • — • — • — • — • — • — • — • — • —

Percent	5 Years	8 Years	10 Years	12 Years	15 Years
3	$5,310	$8,890	$11,460	$14,190	$18,600
4	5,420	9,210	12,010	15,030	20,020
5	5,530	9,550	12,580	15,920	21,580
6	5,640	9,900	13,180	16,870	23,280
8	5,870	10,640	14,490	18,980	27,150
10	6,110	11,440	15,940	21,380	31,770
15	6,740	13,730	20,300	29,000	47,580

* Percent annual net rate of return (compounded)

Does thinking about $1,000 (at least now) seem overwhelming? Then, let's try $25. If you squirrel away $25 per month for the next thirty years and earn 8 percent on the accumulating moneys, your grand total would be valued at $37,507. The actual moneys you put in totaled $9,000—the increase is your growth.

What if you upped the ante—saving $125 each month instead of the $25? The total amount put in would be $45,000. The value, assuming an 8 percent growth, would be $187,535.

No matter at what age you start putting dollars into savings and investments using compounding and tax deferrals, it will increase in value. The sooner you start, the better.

DON'T COUNT ON SOCIAL SECURITY

Statistics show that approximately 40 percent of the incomes of most retirees will come from company-sponsored pension plans and Social Security. The percentage may be even lower if the Social Security program continues on its present course. The U.S. government has borrowed money from the Social Security Trust Fund, and that money may or may not be paid back. Furthermore, there just aren't enough people working now to support the generations yet to retire. There are already more Americans over age sixty-five than ever in history, and the trend isn't stopping anytime soon.

Strive to be self-reliant and self-sufficient. When your time comes to pull down Social Security, think of it *only as supplemental*, not a primary source of money. By beginning your retirement investing today, you will be a savvy visionary. Social Security, and its withdrawing participants, must go through a radical restructuring after the turn of the century.

The more you plan and invest, the less likely you will be affected.

Whoever sows sparingly will also reap sparingly, and
whoever sows generously will also reap generously.
(2 Corinthians 9:6)

IRAS, SEPS, AND KEOGHS

The best tax shelters that have ever been created for millions of Americans are the IRA, SEP, and Keogh. Congress continually changes the rules regarding these retirement plans, but even if the deductibility is nil, they offer tax-deferred buildup. A giant plus.

So, what are the rules at this writing?

1. You can deduct up to $2,000, depending on your income level, if you are not a participant in a company retirement plan. If you are married, your spouse can't be in a plan at his company. Participation is defined as being "eligible" for a defined-benefit plan, even if you are not vested (which means that you can pull out dollars now). If your company has a defined-contribution plan, you don't participate until dollars actually are placed in the plan on your behalf.

2. You can place up to $2,000 that is fully deductible if your adjusted gross income is $25,000 or less if you are single, $40,000 if you are married. Any deductiblity disappears if you are single and your adjusted gross income exceeds $35,000, or, if you are married $50,000.

If you are self-employed, you not only can begin a Keogh or a SEP (Simplified Employee Pensions) account, but you can also contribute $2,000 to an IRA.

For example, assume you have gross revenues of $50,000 and, after all expenses, a net income of $25,000. Fifteen percent of $25,000 is $3,750. Therefore you could place $4,500 into a Keogh account and an additional $2,000 into an IRA account. These figures, of course, will not take into consideration individual losses or excess itemized deductions that you would normally take on your tax return.

If you are married and your spouse does not work, you can add an additional $250. If you had $25,000 in taxable income and it was reduced by a $4,500 contribution to a SEP or Keogh account and a $2,250 contribution to an IRA account, you would have a remaining taxable income of $18,250 and a federal obligation of $2,850. If you had not placed the funds into these various retirement accounts, your federal taxes alone would be an additional $1,013. This represents a 26 percent tax savings on the actual dollars invested, as well as an ability to control where the funds are placed.

If you earned enough money to make the maximum contribution of $30,000 per annum for a Keogh, as well as the contribution toward an IRA, you could claim a total deduction of $32,250. The IRS at some point in time could challenge this, but under today's law it is certainly permissible. Once you begin these accounts, however, be aware that you can neither use these funds as collateral nor borrow from them.

If you are employed (either by self or another) and your employer does not have any pension plans set up, you can set up a SEP IRA. It is primarily funded by the employer up to a maximum of 15 percent of compensation or $30,000, whichever is less. In addition, you can add the regular IRA of $2,000 to the kitty. You have immediate ownership rights (100 percent), and, if you change jobs, you can either take it with you or roll it over into a regular IRA.

If you are self-employed, go with a SEP IRA. The maximum you can contribute is 15 percent of compensation or $30,000, whichever is less, for either. The difference lies in the paperwork. For a SEP IRA, it's child's play; for the Keogh, you need an advanced degree.

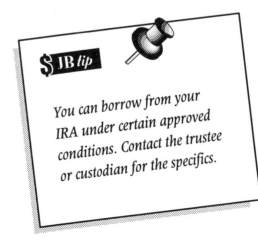

$JB tip

You can borrow from your IRA under certain approved conditions. Contact the trustee or custodian for the specifics.

You cannot withdraw any moneys without penalty prior to the age of fifty-nine and a half, with the exception of death, permanent disability or early retirement at fifty-five or later. The penalties, as stated before, include a declaration of whatever is withdrawn as ordinary income and an overall 10 percent penalty on that amount. This penalty is not tax deductible (as is the penalty for early termination of a certificate of deposit) and is collected by the financial institution you deal with.

Assuming that you will be employed, I strongly recommend that you begin an IRA account and participate in a 401(k) program through your employer. If you were to deposit $2,000 a year into an IRA account over the next forty-seven years, your hard investment, that is, actual dollars deposited, would be $94,000. Your accumulated total by the time you reach Life Phase 6 (sixty-five years old) would be $3,821,179.60. This assumes that you have earned a minimum income of $2,000 for each of the years in which you make the contribution and that the investments made with your funds will give you a 12 percent average return per annum. Some years you could have exceeded 12 percent, others, less than 12 percent—but overall, an average of 12 percent.

WHERE TO PARK YOUR FUTURE

There are several areas in which you can allocate your retirement contributions. You can put it into a bank or savings and loan and earn its passbook interest. It is highly recommended that you not take this as one of your options, since the only one who really wins is the bank or savings and loan, which lends it out at a higher rate in its normal daily operations.

You might consider placing it in a time deposit with the same financial institution. Such time deposits come in all sizes, shapes, and terms, and you should verify what interest they offer as well as what penalty they collect at early termination. A time deposit is a far better choice than a passbook. I would limit the duration of a time deposit to four years or less.

Don't forget the savings-and-loan scandals. The taxpayer ate billions of dollars in losses from financial institutions that were so mismanaged, greedy, corrupt—you name it—that the average law-abiding citizen was forced to bear the losses.

Many had their life savings lost or depleted. If you have been blessed with accumulating more than $100,000 in cash, *do not* put any dollars over that amount—not one dime—in an account with the same institution. The FDIC insurance only covers *up to $100,000.* If you have $187,322, and the savings and loan or bank is closed—too bad. You just lost $87,322!

Insurance coverage is per Social Security number. If you are a participant in a trust with a separate tax number, you have some protection. Still, this was a miserable situation for money in the high-flying eighties.

You might also place your money in mutual funds, which have different objectives. This would be my first choice. One example is the money market fund. Money market funds invest only in money-related issues such as U.S. Treasury obligations, certificates of deposit, commercial paper, and banker's acceptances. Money market funds often offer substantial interest rates consistent with U.S. Treasury obligations and liquidity. Also, the money market fund does not charge a commission, although an ongoing administrative fee is structured within it.

Other funds may charge a commission as high as $8^1/2$ percent. Such a fund is known as a load fund. If you choose a load fund, be sure to verify what its track record is, since if you make a contribution of less than $10,000 it may take several years before you are able to offset the cost of the commission.

A consistent contribution of $2,000 a year will yield you a handsome nest egg. Just remember that if you choose to place your dollars into a money market fund it is important to keep track of what is going on in the interest-rates market. If interest rates decline substantially, then the yield on your money market funds will also decline, thus reducing your overall return.

If you choose to invest in mutual funds, work with a mutual fund company that has a family of funds (for example, money market funds, growth funds, income funds, bond funds, and overseas funds). Mutual funds offer a large variety to choose from, and they allow you to switch from one to another without incurring substantial cost. And, there is a variety—more than 4,400 funds to choose from!

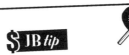

$ JB *tip*

*It doesn't matter if you don't get a tax
deduction for your contribution. The
advantages of tax-deferred compounding
outweigh any taxes you have to pay on
the earned income.*

Another area to consider for placement of retirement dollars is stocks
and/or bonds. If you are adept at structuring individual stocks yourself,
then you should use a discount broker. If you believe in the market but
are not particularly good at selecting stocks yourself, then you may want
to engage a stockbroker.

If you use a stockbroker, remember that you will be paying commissions and often a transaction fee every time you buy or sell. This is
because in order to qualify as an IRA, the stocks must be governed by an
independent administrator or trustee. This applies to all issues. But most
mutual funds, as well as banks and annuities, have their own trustee, so
the annual charge is minimal.

Regardless of how your IRA dollars are placed, the account will be
valuable to you in the long run. Remember that the amount compounds
and can grow substantially over time. If you earned 8 percent on a
$2,000-a-year contribution, over a thirty-year period your hard dollar
contribution would be $60,000 and its overall value would be approxi-
mately $245,000. That's not peanuts!

Every working person under seventy should begin an IRA *this year*,
even when you can't take a deduction on your taxes for it! And, in fact,
the earlier in the year you commence it, the better. The tax code allows

you to do all the paperwork and make your contribution up to the time of tax filing, which is normally April 15, for the preceding year.

If you are qualified to contribute to an IRA, do it. If you have the opportunity to participate in a SEP or Keogh plan, do that also. There are significant advantages in investing early in the year in these accounts. So, if at all possible, make your contribution at the beginning of the year, or consider making an installment contribution. This will increase the amount of your retirement fund significantly over time.

HOW MUCH NEST EGG DO YOU NEED?

Money pros say you need 70 to 80 percent of your *pre-retirement* income to maintain your present standard of living. Why the drop? They assume that kids are gone, commuting costs disappear, insurance costs are reduced, mortgage costs are nil, and your tax bracket will be lower.

However, note that inflation will most likely reduce the value of a dollar between now and when you retire, meaning that a $40,000 income ten or fifteen years from now will definitely not buy as much as a $40,000 income today. Inflation will eat away at your nest egg. Early on, it makes money sense to do some guesstimating. The following chart will help you determine what income you will need. It takes into consideration the number of years until you retire and various inflation rates.

INFLATION MULTIPLIER CHART

— ◆ — ◆ — ◆ — ◆ — ◆ — ◆ — ◆ — ◆ — ◆ — ◆ — ◆ — ◆ — ◆ — ◆ — ◆ — ◆ — ◆ — ◆ — ◆ —

Years in Future	Average Inflation Rate						
	2%	4%	6%	8%	10%	12%	14%
1	1.02	1.04	1.06	1.08	1.10	1.12	1.14
2	1.04	1.08	1.12	1.17	1.21	1.25	1.30
3	1.06	1.12	1.19	1.26	1.33	1.40	1.48
4	1.08	1.17	1.26	1.36	1.46	1.57	1.69
5	1.10	1.22	1.34	1.47	1.61	1.76	1.93
6	1.12	1.27	1.42	1.59	1.77	1.97	2.19
7	1.14	1.32	1.50	1.71	1.95	2.21	2.50
8	1.16	1.37	1.59	1.85	2.14	2.48	2.85
9	1.18	1.42	1.69	2.00	2.36	2.77	3.25
10	1.20	1.48	1.79	2.16	2.59	3.11	3.71
11	1.22	1.54	1.90	2.33	2.85	3.48	4.23
12	1.24	1.60	2.01	2.52	3.14	3.90	4.82
13	1.27	1.67	2.13	2.72	3.45	4.36	5.49
14	1.30	1.73	2.26	2.94	3.80	4.89	6.26
15	1.33	1.80	2.40	3.17	4.18	5.47	7.14
16	1.36	1.87	2.54	3.43	4.59	6.13	8.14
17	1.39	1.95	2.68	3.70	5.05	6.87	9.28
18	1.42	2.30	2.85	4.00	5.56	7.69	10.58
19	1.45	2.11	3.03	4.31	6.11	8.61	12.06
20	1.48	2.19	3.21	4.66	6.73	9.65	13.74
21	1.51	2.28	3.40	5.03	7.40	10.80	15.67
22	1.54	2.37	3.60	5.44	8.14	12.10	17.86
23	1.57	2.46	3.82	5.87	8.95	13.55	20.36
24	1.60	2.56	4.05	6.34	9.85	15.18	23.21
25	1.63	2.67	4.29	6.85	10.83	17.00	26.46
26	1.66	2.77	4.55	7.40	11.92	19.04	30.17
27	1.69	2.88	4.82	7.99	13.11	21.32	34.39
28	1.72	3.00	5.11	8.63	14.42	23.88	39.20
29	1.75	3.12	5.42	9.32	15.86	26.75	44.69
30	1.79	3.24	5.74	10.06	17.45	29.96	50.95

Source: *Smart Money Family Financial Planner*, Berkley Publishing

Here's how to use the chart. Assume you are planning to retire in fifteen years and you've guessed that the annual rate of inflation during those years will be 6 percent. Your annual income today is $40,000. What will you need fifteen years from now to match that amount at a 6 percent annual inflation rate? Take $40,000 and multiply it by the appropriate inflation multiplier from the chart: $40,000 x 2.40 = $96,000. Now multiply this amount by 75 percent (remember, your expenses should be lower) and you get $72,000. Surprised?

Now that you have an idea of how much annual income you'll need in retirement, you must multiply that amount by the number of years you expect to be retired. According to "official" mortality tables, men are now living to an average age of seventy-two, and women are living to age seventy-seven. Remember, this is average, and until new "official" mortality tables are created, these ages will seem low. If you are thirty, the odds are that you may not retire for at least thirty years. Let's say you then live another thirty years. If you multiply thirty times $72,000, you need a nest egg of $2,160,000—a giant one! (This figure does not include inflation that continues to raise your cost of living *after* retirement, but for simplicity we'll assume your savings keep up with inflation through your retirement years.) Unshock yourself—here's some good news.

- Moneys you put into your nest egg/retirement accounts will continue to grow in value after retirement starts.

- There will probably be *something* from Social Security.

- Moneys you save and invest now in any type of tax-favored retirement account have a tremendous plus: compounding.

◆ SUMMING UP ◆

You must keep an eye on retirement, no matter how old—or young—you are. Any change in the tax laws that affects where you can place investment dollars for retirement purposes must be identified. This is where a good financial planner and CPA come in handy.

Be sure your retirement planning is on track. Even though it will probably be many years before you retire, effective retirement planning begins today.

- Guesstimate what you will need for retirement.

- Start saving today.

- Begin funding an IRA today.

- If you are self-employed, begin an SEP or Keogh.

- Know what Social Security has credited to your account. Contact the Social Security Administration at 800-772-1213, and request a Personal Earnings and Benefits Estimate Statement (PEBES). It's a good idea to check every three years—you have thirty-nine months to correct a mistake, if you find one.

- Use your employer's 401(k) to the maximum amount allowed.

- Adjust your W-4 to reflect a reduction in taxable income for any IRAs, SEPs, Keoghs, 401(k) participation.

- Find out retirement benefits from your job, and if you are married, your spouse's job.

$ JB *tip*

If you are out of the workforce and married,
have your spouse fund an IRA for you.

Because you have a substantial number of years ahead of you, I would recommend that instead of starting your IRA in a bank or savings institution, you consider placing your funds with either a quality mutual fund or (if you are savvy enough to select your own stocks or have the good fortune to establish a relationship with a good stockbroker) a self-directed account that invests in stocks and other security issues.

Chapter 10

—◆—◆—◆—◆—◆—◆—◆—◆—◆—◆—◆—◆—◆—◆—◆—

Hiring the Experts

*A*s long ago as 19 B.C., the poet Virgil counseled, "Always believe the expert." Throughout Proverbs, which Solomon began writing about the tenth century B.C., Solomon advocated the counsel of others.

> Fools despise wisdom and discipline. (1:7)

> Plans fail for lack of counsel, but with many advisers they succeed. (15:22)

> Listen to advice and accept instruction, and in the end you will be wise. (19:20)

Jesus taught the wisdom of working together, and the apostle Paul, writing at about A.D. 58, said in Romans 12:16:

> Live in harmony with one another. Do not be proud, but be willing to associate with people of low position. Do not be conceited.

The money game can be complex. Even after you have set specific financial goals for yourself, you need a definite strategy. Haphazard investments won't do. In the money game particularly, the Bible's advice,

"Listen to advice and accept instruction" (Proverbs 19:20), is both essential and relevant.

It is relevant that Solomon advocated not just advice, but good advice, from reputable sources: "The tongue of the righteous is choice silver, but the heart of the wicked is of little value" (Proverbs 10:20).

There are many reliable written sources, such as the *Wall Street Journal, Forbes, Barron's, Business Week, Fortune,* and *Money* magazines, the *Kiplinger Tax Letter,* and *Value Line Survey.* There are even some good TV programs that deal intelligently with financial matters. But the truth is, you can swamp yourself with information, reading so many newspapers and magazines and survey guides that you have no time left for investing.

You will find it useful to develop a store of financial consultants to keep you abreast of tax and law changes, to interpret changing interest and T-bill rates, and to give the kind of advice experts have access to and an understanding of. The old axiom, "It's not what you know but who you know," can be more appropriately restated as, "Who you know can contribute to what you know."

These financial advisers should have several things in common.

1. They should have been working in their area of expertise for at least five years—let them make their "beginner's mistakes" at someone else's expense.

2. They should be willing to tell you if they will receive a commission on the product they are offering to sell you. Do not hesitate to ask about commissions and how much they are. If you choose to go ahead and place your money, you at least know who gets what.

3. They should be available, consistent, and reasonably experienced. When I say "available," I do not mean that they should be able to pounce on the phone the moment you call. That's almost too available. What you want is someone who will return your phone call and respond to

your needs in a fairly short period of time—usually the same day. Consistent, in this case, means not oscillating with every new idea that comes along. You want someone who can evaluate a particular situation and make a well-informed recommendation. Given the complexity of today's financial arena, an experienced financial planner should be able to refer you to other experts when the need arises.

4. They should be able to give you in writing (and you should ask for it) a clearly stated presentation of the nature and scope of the investment. You need to know:

   a. What a particular investment is all about
   b. What the financial projections are in both the best and the worst cases
   c. Who the principals are (who's in charge, who's in management)
   d. What the risks are

Why do you need this information? You need it to protect yourself. When you deal with several experts in multiple areas, you may get conflicting opinions and recommendations from time to time, and the advice you have received may turn out to be the absolute worst. Or a recommendation may be valid at the time it is given but turn out to be harmful in the long run. It is difficult and costly to verify that a recommendation was inappropriate or negligent. Any kind of litigation costs a substantial amount, and in the majority of cases, the only person who wins is the attorney. But if you have a clear description of the projects and its risks in hand from the outset you may be able to avoid such pitfalls.

IT'S OPPORTUNITY CALLING—OR IS IT?

There is one other area you should be concerned about before you actually settle on a group of financial experts.

The calls usually come around dinnertime—offers for gold coins, mutual funds, mortgage insurance, home equity loans, penny stocks, or credit counseling. Although you're probably immune to many of these telephone pitches, you may find yourself intrigued one evening. Should you or shouldn't you?

Never, Never, Never Respond to Pressure

Trouble signs are often easy to spot. Many "boiler room" operations employ fast-talking scam artists who know how to elicit *yes* answers from you until you've committed money for worthless or nonexistent products or services.

If you are uncomfortable with a caller, say so. Don't worry about being rude. A legitimate salesperson will recognize your discomfort and begin again or excuse himself or herself from the call. If you have trouble communicating your objections, hang up. A person who merely wants to make a quick sale will persist unless you act to end the encounter.

You should never be pressured to act quickly to take advantage of a one-time or limited-time offer. No sales offer or investment idea is so urgent that you don't have the time to investigate. Remember, if something sounds too good to be true, it probably is.

If you are interested in a product or service, request written information. A legitimate offer will be backed up with literature that more fully explains the product or service. Don't fall for the line that "to keep operating costs down" the offer is only being made by telephone.

You've heard it before, but it bears repeating: *Never give out your credit card number or authorize its use unless you know exactly how it is to be used.* If you do act and later suspect that you have made a mistake, you may be allowed a grace period during which you can change your mind. Check with your state department of consumer affairs.

Get Names and Numbers

Legitimate sales people encourage scrutiny of their goods and services. Ask for references of satisfied clients if you feel that such information would be useful. A caller who insists that to keep more profits for yourself you must not let the word get out is hoping to gain the confidentiality that will allow him to continue an illegitimate operation.

If you are interested in more information, ask for a caller's name and telephone number and an address for the firm he or she represents. You can check out most companies and individuals through several organizations designed to protect consumers:

- *The Better Business Bureau.* The nation's almost 200 local Better Business Bureaus collect reliability reports on providers of goods and services. Consumers file complaints with the bureau, which are processed and forwarded to the businesses in question, including charitable organizations. You have access to the reports and any complaints against a company.

- *The National Association of Securities Dealers.* The NASD operates a toll-free number, 800-289-9990, to disclose information about registered firms and individuals. From it you can find out whether a caller offering financial products is a registered broker. You will also learn whether the agent, or his or her firm, has ever been fined or undergone disciplinary action by the Securities and Exchange Commission, the NASD, or other self-regulatory organizations or state regulatory agencies. The outcome of arbitration decisions is also available.

- *The Securities and Exchange Commission (SEC).* A person who claims to be an investment adviser should be registered with the SEC. To verify an investment adviser's registration, call the SEC's public reference branch at 202-270-7450.

- *State Departments of Consumer Affairs.* More than forty states require investment advisers to register with state securities agencies. Obtain your state's department of consumer affairs number from the telephone book or call the

North American Securities Administrator's Association at
202-737-0900 to get the number. Some states staff consumer protection divisions that deal solely with telephone
solicitation and sales problems.

- *The Direct Marketing Association.* If you wish to stop
  receiving solicitation calls, you can write to: Telephone
  Preference Service, Direct Marketing Association, P.O. Box
  9014, Farmingdale, NY 11737-9014. The association will
  remove your name from the lists used by its member
  firms. If you order a product from another member firm,
  however, your name will be added to the list again.

Realize Many Are Legitimate Calls

Although telephone calls that interrupt your personal time may be
annoying, some worthwhile goods and services are offered over the
phone. Many brokerage firms use the telephone to contact prospects or
current clients. An investment professional can have valuable information
and services to offer.

If you are looking for reliable financial information, however, the telephone should be merely a starting point. The investments that are most
appropriate for your situation cannot be determined in a three-minute
telephone conversation. A financial consultant who has your best interests at heart will be willing to spend the time to meet with you personally.

If you fear that a one-on-one meeting with a financial consultant will
produce more pressure than you desire, ask whether you may first attend
a seminar about a given topic of interest to you. Many full-service brokerage firms offer lunch hour or evening seminars to present investment
products and services in greater detail.

When it comes to evaluating telephone offers, one of the best things
you can remember is that building wealth should be a long-term proposi-
tion. When it comes to financial gain, no get-rich-quick scheme can com-
pete with the time-proven strategies that should guide a lifetime of sound
saving and investing.

THE FINANCIAL PLANNER

A financial planner is a qualified professional who acts as a kind of contractor or general engineer and helps to devise a game plan and orchestrate the subcontractors who are the experts in specific fields.

A financial planner is like a general practitioner—a sort of "family doctor"—who gives an overall diagnosis, then refers you to the proper specialist. The planner's job is not necessarily to find the precise investment for you, but to give the best advice for your particular circumstances.

Planners will consult with other specialists, such as attorneys, accountants, and insurance brokers, in order to give you a comprehensive view of your present and future financial status. Planners can contribute advice that may help you define and/or realize some of your objectives.

Most financial planners have a variety of licenses. They sell a mass of products that are available on the market. These products could include the purchase and sale of mutual funds, stocks and bonds, insurance, limited partnerships, and almost any other product that looks like it might mesh with a client's objectives.

Most financial institutions—banks, insurance companies, stock brokerage, and accounting firms—offer some form of personal financial management. Often, however, their recommendations are geared only to the financially substantial individual. If you don't have a lot of money for investment purposes, seek some of the independent financial services available almost anywhere.

For sources, you may want to contact either the International Association for Financial Planning (IAFP Registry, Two Concourse Parkway, Suite 800, Atlanta, GA 30328; call 404-395-1605) or the Institute of Certified Financial Planners (760 E. Eastman, Suite 301, Denver, CO 80231; call 800-282-7526).

The IAFP is made up of accountants, bankers, real estate agents and brokers, securities representatives, money managers, financial consultants, attorneys, and insurance agents and brokers. The ICFP consists of more than 91,000 members; a directory is available that lists them. Look in your Yellow Pages under "Financial Planners."

The IAFP is comprised only of those who have completed the two-year course sponsored by the institute. Any individual holding a CFP degree is not necessarily right for you. The degree does, however, indicate a willingness and desire to know more about tax laws and products versus just selling something to get a commission.

In choosing a financial planner, chemistry is one of the things to look for. There is no sense dealing with someone, no matter how competent, who gives you an uneasy feeling. Your consultant should share your general financial goals and life values, respecting you as a woman and as a Christian. There should be some similarities in background and circumstances. And, since the client-professional union should be long-term, it would be unusual if there were any major age gap between the two of you.

Listen to recommendations from friends and acquaintances, and don't be afraid to ask specific questions. Here the advice is the same as that given earlier for any financial adviser: You should expect your planner to be available, willing to return phone calls on the same day and to spend time explaining information and recommendations to you; consistent, centered in a strategy and overview that will consider all new ideas and opportunities without becoming a slave to them; and experienced (in professional practice at least five years).

Establish at the beginning exactly how your financial planner will be compensated. A good planner should not be a salesperson, and he or she should not earn fees solely from commissions. A fixed-fee consultation plan will ensure that your planner is unbiased and available, able to give you clear professional evaluation of financial opinions.

YOUR CORPS OF SPECIALISTS

Once you have a professional financial planner, a group of financial contacts is your next goal. Investment counselors, Certified Public Accountants (CPAs), bankers, and tax attorneys can provide you with information that will help you anticipate economic trends.

For example, if you had been aware that interest rates in March and April of 1980 were the highest they would be that year and would drop dramatically in the next three to four months, that information could have changed your personal borrowing plans. Or, if you had known that throughout 1979 and the early 1980s we would experience some of the highest inflation and interest rates in years and that a recession would follow, you could have planned your purchasing and borrowing—and investing—to correspond with these trends.

The key, then, is to determine and use the best information sources available. Specialists did not know when interest rates peaked or that we were headed for a recession. They did know that a combination of events creates other events.

Insurance Agents

One of the first professionals you may encounter is the insurance agent. The insurance industry is going through a major revolution at the time of this writing and will continue to do so. Insurance itself comes in all sizes and shapes. The most common is casualty—your housing contents, your house, automobile, jewelry or art, medical and dental. There are also life and disability insurance. Many insurance agents have expanded into financial planning, selling mutual funds and limited partnerships.

$ JB tip

Deal with an agent who is able to offer you rates from several different companies.

Rates and products vary substantially from company to company. Because of the competition and change within the industry, review your policies at least every three years and/or if there is a major tax law revision. Before you sign on the dotted line, make sure you fully understand its contents and limitations. *Read the policy!* Keep in mind, your needs will change as your family grows or moves away.

Bankers

Bankers are essential to any financial strategy, and by now you should have established a working relationship with a banker. Review pages 53–56, which discussed the role of the banker and the questions you should be ready to ask your banker.

The CPAs

Most of us are obligated to pay taxes. Therefore, a member of your team should be a good Certified Public Accountant. There are plenty of CPAs in the United States. Unfortunately, many of them merely do bookkeeping tasks. You need someone who will plan and make recommendations that are appropriate for you no matter what your life phase is. There are accountants who specialize in certain areas such as the medical field, small businesses, or various forms of commercial real estate.

Find a CPA whose practice is mainly with people like you, in both their professions and their income. Be alert to information that tells you whether the CPA is merely doing bookkeeping or is rendering true tax counseling.

When you interview accountants, make sure you ask how they are compensated and what their track records are for previous clients. Ask if any of their clients are audited or get large refunds. If a high percentage are audited, does it mean the CPA is too aggressive, interpreting the tax laws very loosely, or does it mean that the majority of the clientele is part of a high audit area, such as doctors and dentists? If refunds are hefty, why? Withholding should be changed to reflect a decrease in tax obligation each year. A CPA should query you as to your anticipated income, determine what expenses could be tax deductible, and advise you of appropriate W-4 changes.

One final suggestion. Ask your accountant if she will stand by you in the case of an audit and/or appear in your behalf.

Remuneration for this member of your cast is usually billed on an hourly basis plus computer costs, if applicable.

Tax Attorneys

If you've had any large windfalls, or have made a significant amount of money, you should to consult a tax attorney. Tax attorneys combine a knowledge of law with the expertise of an accountant. They are expensive, are not right for most of us, but are certainly there if the need should ever arise.

Tax attorneys charge for their time by the hour. They will also charge for all phone calls, paperwork, and copying. Be organized when dealing with them—otherwise your bills will mushroom.

$ JB tip

Make sure that anyone who claims to be a tax attorney is just that—a minimum of 75 percent of his professional time should be in this area. Ask.

Real Estate Brokers

If you are considering a commercial real estate investment, deal with someone who has considerable experience in real estate, specifically in the commercial field. There are many areas in real estate and each has specialists. If you want to buy single-family houses, condominiums, or town houses, find an agent or broker who specializes in residential properties.

If you are considering purchasing small buildings that might be appropriate for professional offices, then deal with someone who specializes in commercial properties. If you have the financial resources and the nerve to invest in large shopping centers or even in developmental deals, deal with brokers who focus on those areas. Each of these investments will have different tax consequences as well as financing packages.

Continuing education is a requirement of a licensed agent or broker. Membership in the National Association of Realtors is desirable.

Property Managers

If you own or are a partner in complexes such as apartment buildings, it may make sense to hire a Certified Property Manager. Managing property is an art that demands years of experience and know-how. Firms that handle several thousand units are often very efficient because they spread their costs and have extensive computer resources. As a result, you can get ongoing income and expense statements that will allow you to keep up-to-date on your property, noting any irregularities as they arise.

Stockbrokers

If you are contemplating the purchase of stocks or bonds, you may engage a stockbroker. As in the case of insurance, the securities industry has gone through a substantial revolution over the last decade. The stockbroker's primary function is the selling of stocks, bonds, and mutual funds. Most have branched out into selling limited partnerships as well. Some have even entered the insurance area and are selling not only life insurance but also annuities.

LIVE AND LEARN

Life Phase 1 is probably the phase during which you will seek an education. I don't mean simply college or graduate work; I also mean an overall awareness of what is going on in your financial life. If you are attending college or thinking of returning, why not add to your schedule some basic accounting classes that deal in tax matters? This will familiarize you with some of the tax jargon you will be exposed to throughout your life. There are also other ways to become educated.

In my *Financial $avvy for Women* workshops given across the country, I recommend various free seminars that are sponsored by brokerage firms, even though the purpose of these seminars is often to pitch a specific product. It could be real estate or oil and gas; it could be stocks in general.

Brokerage firms hope to bring in new clients this way. If you do not wish to be contacted, politely refuse to give your address and phone number.

You will hear such terms as "depreciation," "accelerated depreciation," "recapture," "cost basis," "phantom income," "minimum tax bracket," "acquisition costs," "speculation," "high risk," "raw," "developmental," "commercial buildings," "triple net lease," "adjusted basis," "leverage," and "non-recourse loans." Relax—these terms may be intimidating at first, but with a little time and effort you will soon be familiar with them.

Community Colleges

In addition to seminars, most community colleges offer investment courses taught by qualified professionals covering such topics as financial planning, beginning investments, and the stock market. These classes will acquaint you with financial terms and practices, give you examples of various investment opportunities, and discuss such things as taxes and interest rates. Just remember when you have a lot of new data thrown at you, you may not be able to absorb it all. So don't be afraid to take the same class a second time. I know a few financial planners who spent two years in fifth grade!

Cash Flow

Your "education" in financial matters should also include a close look at how you spend your own money—something that has already been discussed in chapter 3 (see the cash flow chart on pages 35–36). Working out your cash flow will give you a good idea of where your dollars go. Most of us are spenders rather than savers or planners. Many of us seem to think that we are immortal. But as my Aunt Betty always said, "There are three sure things—death, taxes, and arthritis." Aunt Betty might add—"Good money management just might help you face all three."

Life Phase 2: 25–35

◆ — ◆ — ◆ — ◆ — ◆ — ◆ — ◆ — ◆ — ◆ — ◆ — ◆ — ◆ — ◆ — ◆ — ◆

I do wish that more women would become owners of the soil.

—Amelia Bloomer, 1855

Chapter 11

—•—•—•—•—•—•—•—•—•—•—•—•—•—

Decision Making

$\mathcal{A}$s Life Phase 2 begins, you have completed your education and you may also be considering adding to or building on the skills you already have. This is an exciting time in which you are truly on your own, personally and financially, and are probably turning your labor into money. You have become your own person. You make firm decisions in your personal life, as well as in your career. Women in this life phase do a significant amount of job-hopping in order to advance their careers. They often become involved with professional groups and networks.

If you have not already married, you are statistically most likely to do so in this phase. If you are married, this and the next phase are when you and your husband will begin your family. If you are married, it is highly probable that both you and your spouse work. That will allow you to accumulate savings and purchase a home, often a primary objective in this life phase. Not only are you aiming for a high comfort level in your career choice, you are also beginning to develop some solid financial skills. As a consequence, you develop a strong interest in tax savings.

During this period, housing and child-care costs, medical bills, and car payments may put enormous pressure on your household budget. These demands can create a type of financial paralysis—you know you need to plan for your kids' college education and your retirement, and yet you are stretched thin financially. Unfortunately, college and retirement planning usually end up at the bottom of the "to do" list.

CHART YOUR COURSE

In the first few months of each year you should sit down and map out your objectives and plan what you believe you can realistically accomplish by year-end. In addition, you should reevaluate your overall tax obligation, if you had one in the preceding year, and do some rough estimates of where you may be spending your money and what tax benefits might be derived from it.

It is easy for money to slide through your fingers during this period, and it is important to get a fix on your cash flow and to label areas where you spend money frivolously. Two continued temptations from the first phase are eating out and buying clothes. If one of your primary objectives during this particular phase is to purchase your own home, curbing excess spending will be crucial to achieving that goal.

Of course, you may receive a windfall or have the ability to borrow funds from relatives at attractive interest rates, enabling you to purchase a home without going through the belt tightening and cutbacks most people find necessary. Be aware of your present tax bracket, especially if your goal is home purchase—the rent you pay plus tax savings via mortgage payments and real estate taxes may make the impossible possible.

Now is the time to revisit chapter 6, "Taxes: Lightening the Burden," particularly the section about the W-4 and changing your withholding. When you buy a home, it is important to immediately project your overall tax obligation. Unless you pay all cash and have no mortgage, your federal and state obligations will be significantly reduced. By increasing your withholding allowances on your W-4, you will increase your monthly cash flow—cash flow that may be critical in meeting your new mortgage payments.

A WAY TO SAVE: DEFERRED COMPENSATION

Deferred compensation has already been discussed in terms of types of income, but more needs to be said here. You can spread out the reporting of income through the means of deferred compensation. The result is that you save on taxes.

For many persons, deferred compensation comes in the form of a

401(k) plan. (See chapter 9, "Retirement Planning Begins Today," for more on this subject.) Many companies have 401(k) programs, which allow an employee to invest a percentage of her income (only Social Security taxes are withheld) each pay period in a special investment/savings account. Today, between contributions by your employer and yourself, annual amounts can reach the lesser of $30,000 or 25 percent of your net salary after your deductible contribution is subtracted. When you withdraw moneys at a later date (you choose when), you are then responsible for federal and state taxes. Most plans will allow you to borrow if emergencies occur. The 401(k) program is the best deal in town!

LIQUIDITY

During this phase, as in all the others, you need to maintain the liquidity funds you established in Life Phase 1. As I noted earlier, three to six months of after-tax income is generally sufficient. This, of course, is over and above funds you will be investing. Once again, liquidity refers to the ability to terminate your investment position within seven days and receive the market value of your cash back. Items such as bank accounts, money market funds, tax-deferred annuities, and T-bills are all liquid.

Liquidity funds should be invested in items in which the principal is guaranteed and/or that have a very minor likelihood of changing in value. The fewer the strings attached, the better. If you have to terminate your position in an annuity, for example, there may be a penalty, although annuities are technically liquid, in that you can get your cash out in a relatively short time. As noted earlier, certificates of deposit and time deposits also have penalties if you terminate the contract before the maturity dates.

Stocks and mutual funds are liquid in the sense that they can be terminated with proceeds in your hands in a fairly short period of time (in seven days, as a rule), but there is no guarantee of the value of the principal. The stocks you own outright and the mutual funds that invest in them will oscillate in price, and you may have to liquidate at a loss. Bonds can also change in value, again depending on interest rates and the quality of the company.

Some IRA funds, 401(k) accounts, or other types of retirement accounts you participate in can be quickly liquidated and some cannot. Before you place funds in any investment, you must know what will happen if you need them in an emergency. If you can't get them within a seven-day period and you have no other available funds for emergencies, forget it!

INSURANCE: DISABILITY AND LIFE

The various types of insurance and your need for insurance were discussed in chapter 7. Revisit that chapter now. During this life phase you will definitely need disability insurance and you almost certainly will need life insurance as well.

BANKS

In this phase you will continue to build your credit, and as you do so you will not only get to know your banker better but you will learn about various programs and how they can benefit you. You will also recognize the value of having more than one banker. Why? Because money tightens and loosens and interest rates go up and down. The bank that offered "a great deal" yesterday may be offering far less today.

It makes sense for you to at least check the Sunday business section of the major newspaper in your city. Often it will compare various financial institutions on such items as home loans, automobile loans, and unsecured loans and what the bank is willing to pay in various types of savings programs. It is surprising how wide a variation there can be between one financial company and another.

INVESTING

In this phase you may want to invest in the stock market or in mutual funds. For further information on these investment options, read sources cited in the bibliography.

PURCHASE OF A HOME

This is the life phase in which purchasing a home usually becomes reasonable. The process of home buying is discussed in chapter 12.

KIDS AND MONEY

Life Phase 2 is the time when the majority of women begin their families. The financial side of raising children is discussed in chapter 13.

◆ MS. MISC. ◆

As you begin to build savings, you should make use of the available money market funds. You may be tempted to invest funds in the many tax shelters offered by various brokerage firms, as well as private syndicators. But unless you have a substantial income and the opportunity to build your net worth in the other recommended areas, I would advise you to stay clear of tax shelters at this time. Most individuals pursue tax shelters when their income reaches a federal and state combined tax bracket level exceeding 40 percent. This will probably not happen in your present life phase. It is in the next three phases that earnings and revenues are often at their highest.

◆ WINDFALL! ◆

The company you work for has announced banner earnings, and you are one of its best sales reps. The company is giving you a bonus of 25 percent of your yearly salary. Your earnings came in at $30,000, so your bonus will be $7,500. Your company also has a credit union from which you can borrow up to $3,000 unsecured. With your recent 10 percent pay increase, you are comfortable borrowing $2,500 to add to your $7,500.

In this particular life phase, there are two recommended investments for your $10,000. If you haven't already purchased a home, this might be your chance to do so. The person who makes $30,000 a year will be able to afford approximately $800 a month in mortgage payments.

You might want to consider placing your funds in the stock market.

Invest your dollars in the young emerging companies. You are looking for growth. Financial services, global communications, and biotechnology fields are viable candidates. Consider purchasing stock in a company approximately six months after it first hits the public market. By that time the price may have settled down, the speculators have made their quick profit or loss, and a firm assessment of the company can be made. For more information on investing in the stock market, read my book *Financial $avvy for Women* or *Stocks* by Austin Pryor.

BE WILLING TO WORK AT IT

Because money management has no fixed answers and no fixed circumstances, it will require a good deal of time, hard work, and energy. The Bible tells us that hard work is a virtue: "He who works his land will have abundant food, but he who chases fantasies lacks judgment." (Proverbs 12:11). It also alerts us to the value of patience in money and investments: "An inheritance quickly gained at the beginning will not be blessed at the end" (Proverbs 20:21).

If you attempt too much too quickly and expect that everything you do will work perfectly the first time, you may be in for some disappointments and surprises. It is necessary to keep working to reach your goal. As I have told client after client, class after class, you will certainly make mistakes, but by diversifying and always asking questions, you can learn to minimize your losses and maximize your capacity as an effective, informed investor.

NOW IT'S UP TO YOU

The information given in this book for this life phase will help you devise a coherent, consistent financial plan. But you are the one who must finalize it and implement it. "All hard work brings a profit, but mere talk leads only to poverty" (Proverbs 14:23). Your money sense will enable you to produce your own financial plan, which will then free you to focus on other things. "Dishonest money dwindles away, but he who gathers money little by little makes it grow" (Proverbs 13:11) should become one of your rules to live by.

"The wise woman builds her house, but with her own hands the foolish one tears hers down" (Proverbs 14:1). You can build your house through sound financial management. You can tear it down with procrastination and excuses. The rewards for having and using your own money sense are immense. In the end, they will give you the kind of freedom and security that is fast becoming every Christian woman's birthright.

Quiz

The company you work for is going public—selling its stock for the first time. As a bonus, you have been given 1,000 shares for your loyalty and hard work. You are tired of paying rent and have determined that if you sell your stock, you will receive $20,000, enough for a down payment. Should you buy a home?

(a) Yes—if your rent is more than the mortgage plus real estate taxes cost.

(b) No—you think that real estate prices will crash any day.

(c) No—you believe it's wrong to borrow money.

(d) No—wait for an inheritance that might come someday.

Answer: All answers are basically wrong. If you pay taxes, your mortgage can actually be more than your rental payments. Unless you have bundles of cash, some money must be borrowed initially to buy a home. You can increase your payments by at least one each year and be mortgage-free in eighteen years instead of the normal thirty years. Real estate has cycles of ups and downs, rarely crashes.

◆ PHASING UP ◆

During Life Phase 2, most women take on new responsibilities. Some marry; many couples become families. Budgets are strained as mortgages, medical bills, child-care costs, and car payments (sometimes for two cars) take their toll.

If you have not yet started a retirement fund or IRA, review chapter 8 on retirement planning. If you are employed outside the home, find out if your company has a 401(k) program. If it does, participate. Many companies have a matching incentive—this is like free money. If your spouse has one, ditto.

Your IRA should be started in a no-load mutual fund. If you don't have the lump sum at the beginning of each year, make regular monthly payments. When you pull down these funds thirty years from now, you will pat yourself on the back for being so brilliant.

If you have not yet purchased insurance, review chapter 7 on insurance programs. If you have been blessed with kids, you need disability and life insurance coverage.

If you have children and have not yet begun plans for financing their college education, begin now. Some mutual funds will allow an account to be opened with as little as $25 invested each month. The catch is that to participate you must deposit money on an automatic withdrawal program from your checking or saving account. Still, these mutual fund programs are a good idea. Chapter 13, "Kids and Money" will offer numerous ideas for financial planning for the expenses children bring.

In addition, your Phase Focus should be:

$ To invest for capital growth.

$ To start building an education fund for your kids when they are born (and maybe, one for you too).

$ To purchase life insurance to provide for your dependents.

$ To buy a home or a bigger home for an expanding family.

$ To closely manage your needs for credit.

$ To provide for childbearing and child care costs.

$ To name a guardian for your kids—make a will (details in chapter 15).

$ To add to your Liquidity Fund.

$ To save 10 percent or more of your income by tithing to yourself each month.

◆   RETIREMENT BONUS   ◆

If you had invested $2,000 every year from the age of eighteen in an IRA account earning 12 percent per year, you would by the end of this life phase have accumulated $109,499.40.

Chapter 12

— ◆ — ◆ — ◆ — ◆ — ◆ — ◆ — ◆ — ◆ — ◆ — ◆ — ◆ —

Purchase of a Home

You've decided it's time for the big investment; you want to buy a house. The first thing to decide is how much you can really afford to spend on housing on a monthly basis. In calculating that amount, you will need to consider what your current tax bracket is, how much you are paying in taxes in addition to your withholding, and the amount of rent you are currently paying. In order to determine your current tax bracket, refer to page 87.

Let's assume that you are single and making $30,000. You have no deductions, with the exception of a $2,000 contribution to an IRA account. Your taxable income will be reduced to $25,500 ($2,000 contribution, $2,500 personal exemption), leaving you with a federal tax obligation of $4,547. If you are required to pay state taxes, then your taxes will be greater.

TAXES BEFORE BUYING A HOME	
Gross Income	$30,000
IRA	-2,000
Personal Exemption	-2,500
Taxable Income	25,500
Federal Tax, 1994	4,547

Let's also assume you are currently paying rent of $500 a month, for a total of $6,000 a year. This, of course, is not tax deductible, although some states do allow a renter's credit. Let's say that you find a condominium or small house that has a current market value of approximately $85,000. Let's also assume that you have been able to save a 20 percent down payment, or $17,000, and that you obtain a $68,000 mortgage at 8 percent.

Real estate taxes will be $850 annually. In addition, mortgage payments are approximately $6,500 for a combined annual cost of $7,350. (During the first few years of any payment involving a loan, the percentage of principal being repaid is at a minimum, so for illustration's sake I will assume that less than $50 will go toward your principal the first year.) Dividing the $7,350 by 12 results in a monthly payment of approximately $613.

MONTHLY HOUSE PAYMENT CALCULATION
—◆—◆—◆—◆—◆—◆—◆—◆—◆—◆—◆—◆—◆—◆—◆—◆—

Cost of House	$85,000
Mortgage Payments	6,500
Real Estate Taxes	850
	$ 7,350
Monthly Payment Including Taxes ($ 7,350 ÷ 12)	$ 613

You may think there is no way you can afford to pay $613 per month. But there may be. You are already spending $500 per month for rent. The key here is to consider the various tax benefits you will obtain by purchasing a home. Under current tax laws your mortgage interest, up to one million dollars, as well as real estate taxes, is fully deductible. Often when individuals begin to itemize deductions, they will discover that numerous contributions, accounting fees, state and/or personal taxes, excess medical expenses, and miscellaneous professional obligations add up to a tidy sum. And by the time they total up all these areas they often have reached or exceeded $3,500.

Keep in mind that as a single taxpayer you must have deductions greater than $3,700 to pass your zero bracket amount ($6,200 for married filing jointly). The IRS has stated that taxpayers (single, married, or head of household) must have gross deductions in excess of a certain amount before they can begin to use the itemized tax forms. That "certain amount" marks your zero bracket.

Now let's assume you have done a detailed analysis and have found that medical payments are in excess of $7\,1/2$ percent of your adjusted gross income. Adding contributions, professional obligations, investment and accounting advice, and state personal tax withholdings, you have $3,000 in deductions. If you include that amount with your real estate taxes (approximately $850) and add that to your interest payments, you arrive at a gross deduction of approximately $10,250. You would then deduct the $3,700 disallowance (zero bracket amount for singles) and arrive at an excess-deduction total of $6,550.

EXCESS DEDUCTION CALCULATION
—◆—◆—◆—◆—◆—◆—◆—◆—◆—◆—◆—◆—◆—◆—◆—◆—

With Other Deductions	
Excess medical, states taxes,	
contributions, professional dues,	
accounting, etc.	$ 3,000
Interest	6,400
Real Estate Taxes	+ 850
	$10,250
Zero Bracket Adjustment	-3,700
Excess Deductions	$ 6,550

Taking your gross income of $30,000 and adjusting for the $2,000 contribution for your IRA, the $6,550 for your excess deductions, and $2,500 for your personal exemption, you will arrive at your taxable-income base of $18,950, or a federal tax obligation of $2,843. Before purchasing the residence, your federal tax obligation was $4,547.

TAXES AFTER BUYING A HOME

—◆—◆—◆—◆—◆—◆—◆—◆—◆—◆—◆—◆—◆—◆—◆—◆—

Gross Income	$30,000
IRA	-2,000
Personal	-2,500
Excess Deduction	-6,550
Taxable Income	$18,950
(Federal Tax = $2,843)	

With the purchase, federal taxes have been reduced to $2,843, for an overall savings of $1,704. Dividing that number by 12, your monthly federal tax withholding is reduced by a minimum of $142. When you add that amount to the rent that you had previously paid ($500), you have a total of $642.

You have calculated the cost of the residence plus taxes to be $613 a month. Now, take $613 and deduct it from $642. You will find the increase in your monthly cash flow is $29. Of course, this does not take into consideration any expenses you might incur for repairs or maintenance to the house, so you need to be sure your budget has surplus and your liquidity fund is adequate to cover unexpected expenses.

You may feel that you want to buy even if prices are not increasing, but, in fact, have actually declined. Again, you need to sharpen your pencil and get your calculator out. Go through the steps from the preceding pages and decide whether the math works out in your situation.

If the difference is one that you do not feel you can financially handle, then you should probably continue to rent. But if the difference turns out to be minor—and if the thrill, pride, and emotional satisfaction of owning a home could offset a flat real estate market—then consider buying.

As soon as you have crunched the numbers and determined that, yes, indeed, taxes will be reduced if you buy—here's the next step. If you have purchased the house, then you need to visit your payroll department immediately and complete a new W-4 form.

By adjusting your withholding at the time of purchase, you will increase your cash flow, because less will be taken out each pay period. Otherwise, you would get a large refund after taxes were filed—a refund that does not pay you interest. And a refund that you can use each month.

What if you were fortunate enough to purchase a home that then appreciated substantially in value? This increase in value is referred to as equity buildup, and is arrived at by calculating the appreciated value of your property less the balance of your mortgage.

In the previous example, you purchased a home that cost $85,000, and you made a down payment of $17,000. Suppose that its value increased to $125,000. Your current equity would value at $57,000—which could represent a substantial portion of your net worth.

HOME EQUITY CALCULATION

Original Purchase Price	$ 85,000
Down Payment	-17,000
Mortgage	$ 68,000
Increased Market Value	$125,000
Mortgage	-68,000
Equity	$ 57,000

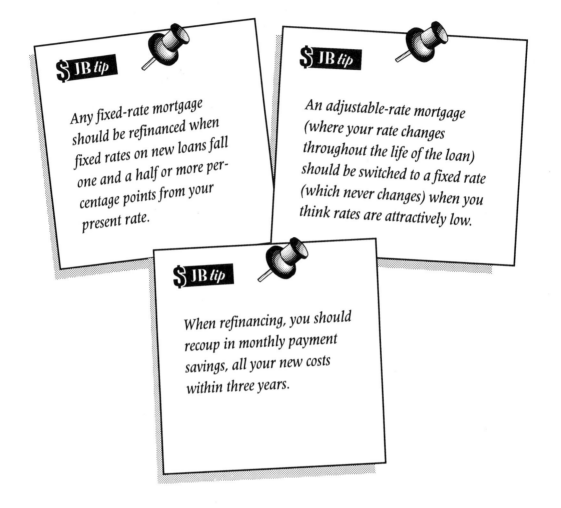

$ JB *tip*

Any fixed-rate mortgage should be refinanced when fixed rates on new loans fall one and a half or more percentage points from your present rate.

$ JB *tip*

An adjustable-rate mortgage (where your rate changes throughout the life of the loan) should be switched to a fixed rate (which never changes) when you think rates are attractively low.

$ JB *tip*

When refinancing, you should recoup in monthly payment savings, all your new costs within three years.

ABOUT MORTGAGE COSTS

In order to help you determine what a mortgage would cost monthly, I have included two tables. They both illustrate loans ranging from $20,000 to $100,000 at interest rates varying from 7 percent to 12 percent. The difference is that one is for a fifteen-year mortgage, the other for thirty years.

MONTHLY MORTGAGE PAYMENTS

15-year, fixed-rate loan (monthly principal and interest payments):

Loan Amount	Interest Rate										
	7%	7½%	8%	8½%	9%	9½%	10%	10½%	11%	11½%	12%
$ 20,000	179.77	185.40	191.20	196.95	203.00	209.00	214.93	221.08	227.32	233.64	240.04
25,000	224.70	231.75	239.00	246.18	253.75	261.25	268.66	276.35	284.15	292.05	300.05
30,000	269.64	278.10	286.80	295.42	304.50	313.50	322.39	331.62	340.98	350.46	360.06
35,000	314.59	324.45	334.60	344.66	355.25	365.75	376.12	386.89	397.81	408.87	420.06
40,000	359.53	370.80	382.40	393.90	406.00	418.00	429.85	442.16	454.64	467.28	480.07
45,000	404.47	417.15	430.20	443.13	456.75	470.25	483.58	497.43	511.47	525.69	540.08
50,000	449.41	463.50	478.00	492.37	507.50	522.50	537.31	552.70	568.30	584.10	600.09
55,000	494.36	509.85	525.80	541.61	558.25	574.75	591.04	607.97	625.13	642.51	660.10
60,000	539.30	556.21	573.60	590.84	609.00	627.00	644.77	663.24	681.96	700.92	720.11
65,000	584.24	602.56	621.40	640.08	659.75	679.25	698.50	718.51	738.79	759.33	780.11
70,000	629.18	648.91	669.20	689.32	710.50	731.50	752.23	773.78	795.62	817.74	840.12
75,000	674.12	695.26	717.00	738.56	761.25	783.75	805.96	829.05	852.45	876.15	900.13
80,000	719.06	741.61	764.80	787.79	812.00	836.00	859.69	884.32	909.28	934.56	960.14
100,000	898.83	927.01	956.00	984.74	1,015.00	1,045.00	1,074.61	1,105.40	1,136.60	1,168.19	1,200.17

30-year, fixed-rate loan (monthly principal and interest payments):

Loan Amount	7%	7½%	8%	8½%	9%	9½%	10%	10½%	11%	11½%	12%
$ 20,000	133.06	139.84	146.75	153.78	161.00	168.20	175.52	182.95	190.47	198.06	205.73
25,000	166.32	174.80	183.44	192.23	201.25	210.25	219.40	228.69	238.09	247.58	257.16
30,000	199.59	209.76	220.13	230.68	241.50	252.30	263.28	274.43	285.70	297.09	308.59
35,000	232.85	244.72	256.82	269.12	281.75	294.35	307.16	320.16	333.32	346.61	360.02
40,000	266.12	279.68	293.51	307.57	322.00	336.40	351.03	365.90	380.93	396.12	411.45
45,000	299.38	314.64	330.20	346.01	362.25	378.45	394.91	411.64	428.55	445.64	462.88
50,000	332.65	349.60	366.88	384.46	402.50	420.50	438.79	457.37	476.17	495.15	514.31
55,000	365.91	384.56	403.57	422.91	442.75	462.55	482.67	503.11	523.78	544.67	565.74
60,000	399.18	419.53	440.26	461.35	483.00	504.60	526.55	548.85	571.40	594.18	617.17
65,000	432.44	454.49	476.95	499.80	523.25	546.65	570.43	594.59	619.02	643.69	668.60
70,000	465.71	489.45	513.64	538.24	563.50	588.70	614.31	640.32	666.63	693.21	720.03
75,000	498.97	524.41	550.33	576.69	603.75	630.75	658.18	686.06	714.25	742.72	771.46
80,000	532.24	559.37	587.02	615.14	644.00	672.80	702.06	731.80	761.86	792.24	822.90
100,000	665.30	699.21	733.77	768.92	805.00	841.00	877.58	914.74	952.33	990.30	1,028.62

As you enter your later life phases, one of your goals should be to own your home outright. It is unbelievable how much money is paid out in interest. If you were to borrow $50,000 over thirty years at 8 percent, your monthly payment would be $366.88. Doesn't sound like much, but if you multiply $366.88 x 12 months x 30 years—Ta Dah—you have paid out $132,076.80!

$ JB *tip*

On a thirty-year loan, if you make one extra payment a year, you will reduce the time you pay your mortgage off by twelve years. Now, that's a Ta Dah!

$ JB *tip*

If you can afford the larger monthly payment, the fifteen-year mortgage makes money sense.

WHERE TO FIND MONEY

Home ownership is your only hope of having free housing when you retire—renters pay forever. Mortgages eventually are paid off.

So, how do you get the money for your first home? Unless you win the lottery or have an inheritance due any moment, you might try the old fashioned way: *Save for it.* That means no toys, entertainment, fancy vacations, dinners out. It means living in a cheap apartment. A second job, perhaps. It means that if this is your objective, being myopic makes sense.

Here are some other ideas to help you gather your nest egg:

1. *Move.* If you can't afford San Francisco or Connecticut, how about Denver or Minneapolis.

2. *Fixer-Uppers.* If you can stand the mess, find a wreck and resurrect it.

3. *Make an appointment with the Relative Bank.* Grandparents, parents, even cousins sometimes are willing to help out. (Hint: This is business, so propose signing a note, etc.)

4. *Lower your debt.* The less consumer debt you have, the more you can borrow for a mortgage.

5. *Commute.* The farther you are willing to drive, the less expensive the house.

6. *Borrow from Profit Sharing, 401(k).* Some plans allow you to borrow from your company's plan. This assumes, of course, that you have money in it.

7. *Withdraw from Profit Sharing, 401(k).* If your company allows this you might try it, but use caution; a penalty is involved. Ask, because it does add to your taxable income, and run the concept by your accountant.

8. *Get a VA or FHA loan.* These don't require the normal 20 percent down. FHA can require as little as 3 percent for property under $50,000, 5 percent on older property, and 10 percent on new homes. With the VA, often no money is required down. You need to be or have been connected with the armed forces to get these—but what a deal!

9. *Be prepared to buy private mortgage insurance.* With it, you can usually pay just 10 percent down.

10. *Sell your investments.* Isn't this one of the reasons you invested?

11. *Scratch the vacation.* Put the money aside that you would have spent.

12. *Buy a foreclosed house.* Some are duds, others great buys for minimal dollars. This is how my daughter bought her first home through HUD (Housing and Urban Development). Less than $2,000 down with closing costs and three years later, it has appreciated $30,000! Not bad.

13. *Lease with an option to buy.* To do this may require some money up front ($1,200 to $10,000) to hold the price for one to five years. If you don't buy, you may lose your option deposit. This is how I bought my present house.

14. *Make a deal with the seller.* If you find a house that has been on the market for a while (that's how I was able to convince the seller to do a lease-option), the seller is more flexible. Your rent for the first few years could be based as if you were paying a mortgage. Some, or—if you are a great negotiator—most of it, could be the down payment. Within three years (or so) you must get new financing.

15. *Buy in a new development.* Builders routinely make deals. They are carrying construction loans that are usually more expensive (higher interest) than a standard mortgage.

16. *Buy an older home.* In the same range of square-footage, older homes usually cost less than the new, improved version.

17. *Buy a condo or town house.* They usually cost less (but don't appreciate as much as a single family house).

18. *Do an equity-sharing deal.* This is a shared arrangement where someone (a relative, friend, or investor) puts up the down payment. When it's time to sell, any profits are split. Caution—put everything in writing, including under what circumstances a sale will occur.

19. *Buy a house with a friend or relative.* This could be one of those last-resort measures. What will you do if she wants to sell and get her money?

20. *Find a job with a company that has a piggy bank for employees who want to buy homes.* Many companies offer low interest rate loans to help with down payments and closing costs.

21. *Work a second shift.* This can be for a very short period of time as you save every dime you get paid.

22. *Assume an outstanding mortgage.* Many loans are assumable—meaning that you come in and pay the difference between the selling price and the outstanding loan. If real estate has been flat or has declined, you might get in with little money. Assumable loans are qualifying (meaning you pass the credit check) or non-qualifying (no credit check). Credit doesn't matter. What matters is whether you have the money for the down payment.

23. *Borrow from your credit card.* Don't do this.

24. *Pray.* You might want to start here. Whatever your goal is, take the time to center yourself and ask for direction.

You may come up with some ways I haven't thought of. The bottom line is: If you want a home, with work and creativity, it can happen.

WHEN DOES RENTING MAKE MONEY SENSE?
There are circumstances when you shouldn't buy. At least, not yet.

- If you live in a rent-controlled apartment, that's a steal (meaning low rent); it may make sense to stay put.

- If you are uncertain of your future—especially your employment—over the next year or two, it makes sense not to lock up any large sums of money.

- If you are newly divorced, you need time to determine what your living strategy is. A lot happens after a divorce—tying money up in a house immediately doesn't make sense. Put it in a money market fund while you weigh your options.

- If your job may have changes on the horizon and you anticipate that you could be moving within two years, you may lose money on the selling costs of a home you had just purchased.

- If you believe that properties will decline or are declining, you may want to wait a year before you buy. Not all houses appreciate in value. Some cities, regions, even states suffer poor economies at times. In the eighties, California property values skyrocketed. In the nineties, many Californians saw their property values plummet.

- If you have not funded your liquidity fund, you are more comfortable with the idea of renting than of buying at this point in your life, or you have not yet saved/invested the amount you've set as a personal minimum for a down payment, renting may be the best option temporarily. You may want to make specific goals at this time, rather than thinking, "Eventually I'll probably buy a house."

Ideally, as homeowners retire, they live mortgage/rent free. Housing expenses relate to maintenance and real estate taxes. *If you decide not to buy*, do a little math and estimate what your housing (fair market rent) would be upon retirement. Will you have the cash to cover your housing expenses until you die?

If you choose not to buy, in addition to your regular savings and investments, additional funds should be set aside to cover your housing needs when you don't have regular income from a job.

Chapter 13
- ◆ — ◆ — ◆ — ◆ — ◆ — ◆ — ◆ — ◆ — ◆ — ◆ — ◆ — ◆ — ◆ —
Kids and Money

*H*aving children adds a new dimension to your financial picture, as well as to your personal life. Their impact on your financial game plan cannot be ignored. Children are a responsibility, and providing for your family is both a joy and an obligation. "If anyone does not provide for his relatives, and especially for his immediate family, he has denied the faith and is worse than an unbeliever" (1 Timothy 5:8).

Providing for your family basically means planning ahead. "The prudent see danger and take refuge, but the simple keep going and suffer for it" (Proverbs 27:12).

PLAN AHEAD!

A prudent plan for managing your income must include moneys for unforeseen emergencies, savings for education (particularly for college), and ways of seeding dreams for your children. If children are new in your life, it's a good idea to examine a cash flow analysis of your income and anticipated expenses to see if you need to change your spending habits.

Though your greatest expenses are still in the future (underwriting the teenage and college years), the routine costs of infancy are a surprise for most new parents. Even normal hospital delivery and initial pediatrician costs can bankrupt you if you don't plan ahead.

CHILD CARE

Child care is another big expense. Under current tax law, two-income couples and single working parents can claim a tax credit for a portion of these child-care costs, which is subtracted from any federal income taxes owed. You should also check your employee benefit plan; some have provisions that augment child-care costs.

EMERGENCY FUNDS

Here the rule about liquidity funds applies in double force. Keep an emergency reserve fund of three to six months of ongoing living expenses in safe, liquid vehicles, such as money market funds or short-term insured certificates of deposit. And finally, those college expenses will come due all too soon. Some financial institutions can provide personalized analysis of what your child's education might cost and what you can do now to meet those future bills.

A COLLEGE EDUCATION—ON A TUITION TERM?

A college education will probably be the largest outlay of money you'll ever make in a four-year period. College costs, which are high today, are likely to continue rising at a rate of 7 percent a year, according to education experts.

That means that one year at a private school could cost more than $55,000 starting in the 2010 academic year—or about $220,000 for a four-year degree. Sobering numbers for any parent.

With a little planning, however, you may be able to bring down that total. As college costs have risen, both university officials and parents have found ways to make a college degree more affordable without compromising the quality of education.

Reducing the Costs

There a growing number of ways you can reduce your total educational bill. Among them, you and your child might consider:

- *Starting your child at a community college.* Your child can attend a local or state college for two years and then transfer to a big-name university for the final two years.

- *Finding ways for your child to finish college in less than four years.* Passing advanced placement exams and taking college courses in high school can start your child on the way toward a college degree before he or she even gets there. Mega-costly Stanford University has been a vocal advocate of completing college in three years.

- *Enrolling more than one child at the same college.* Many colleges give tuition breaks to families with more than one child in attendance.

- *Sending a child to your alma mater.* The children of alumni get tuition breaks at many schools.

- *Working for the school your child attends.* Children of faculty and even nonteaching employees at some colleges receive significant tuition cuts.

- *Choosing an in-state institution.* Establish residency in the state where your child is attending college to benefit from the usually lower resident tuition fees.

- *Investigating new work-study programs.* Many colleges alternate study with periods of career-related work to reduce the cost of the education.

- *Prepaying tuition.* Some states also have plans that allow you to prepay tuition costs at in-state colleges. Generally, you pay a sum of money based on current tuition and your child's expected enrollment date. The plan will guarantee that your child's tuition is covered when he or she is ready to attend, no matter what tuition costs at

that time. Even some private colleges are beginning to
institute similar programs.

- *Shifting responsibility to the student.* Have your child
  work before and during college to pay a large part of the
  costs from his or her own pocket. Many parents believe
  that students get more out of college if they have a
  financial investment in it.

Colleges, states, many brokerage firms, and even banks are offering
"guaranteed tuition" programs. The Michigan Education Trust is innova-
tive. The first of its kind, it permits parents of kids any age, even newborns,
to pay as little as $3,000 now for four years of tuition later at any of the
state's fifteen public colleges or twenty-nine community colleges. The
amount paid will depend on how close enrollment is. Other states have
copied the concept.

You do need to ask a few questions before you start writing checks.

- If you prepay, what happens if the school shuts down
  before your child enters?

- What happens if your job moves you from the state school
  you enrolled your child at—will he or she still be eligible
  for the cheaper resident rates?

- What happens if your child doesn't want to attend the
  college you selected?

- Could your child be "not accepted" when enrollment time
  comes?

Before you make such a long-term commitment, you must
explore all the angles of the pre-payment options.

Smart-Saving Strategies

As a parent you'll also want to employ smart college saving strategies. The key is to start early and save regularly. You should start by establishing a target amount and a time frame. Generally, the more time you have, the more you will be able to make long-term investments that might fluctuate in value but give your underlying capital the opportunity to grow.

No matter what degree of risk you are willing to accept, a variety of saving alternatives are available. Among conservative options, series EE savings bonds, which have always been exempt from state and local taxes, now are federally tax-free to parents—depending on total household income—if they were purchased after 1989 and are cashed in to meet educational expenses. EE bonds are a "no-brainer," but they work! All U.S. Savings Bonds are registered and printed with the Social Security numbers of their owners. Your children should have Social Security numbers by the age of two.

Zero coupon bonds are a popular college investment because they pay all interest, along with principal, at maturity. To meet college costs, you can buy bonds that will mature during your child's college years. There are two types of zero coupons, taxable and tax-exempt. Taxable zeros might be appropriate as gifts, depending on the tax situation of the recipient. Tax-exempt zeros will generally produce lower returns, but they may be a better choice for higher income parents. Baccalaureate bonds are special types of municipal zero coupon bonds issued by some states; their interest is exempt from federal and, in some cases, state and local taxes.

Most financial advisers believe that if you have the time, stocks and mutual funds should comprise a hefty amount of your college kitty. That's because stocks have outperformed bonds and other fixed-income investments, returning an average 10 percent a year since 1926. A well-balanced portfolio of individual stocks and no-load growth mutual funds can help you minimize risk while accumulating college funds. As your child reaches college age, you can gradually shift assets out of stocks and into cash instruments. If you give gifts of stocks or bonds to children under eighteen, you must register the securities in your name or in the name of another adult as custodian for your children. Use the child's Social Security number for the registration. Earnings and gains will legally belong to him or her and will be taxable as the child's income if the earnings are less than $1,200 or the child is over fourteen years of age.

In order to take advantage of your child's lower tax rate, you may also want to talk with your financial adviser about investing in your child's name through a custodial account. With custodial accounts, remember, your child legally gains control of the money at age eighteen or twenty-one, depending on state laws, and can do whatever he or she wishes with the money.

One other thought. Don't forget to invest in yourself—your own education. Unless you are a great entrepreneur, statistics show that the more educated you are, the more money you make. More to save, to invest—to write those big tuition checks with!

Sensible Borrowing Alternatives

Whether or not you've saved regularly during your child's pre-college years, you may still need to borrow to meet college costs. Even if you're not eligible for federally subsidized loans, a variety of attractive loan alternatives may be available.

Interest expense on home equity loans up to $100,000 generally is fully tax-deductible. Other types of consumer loans, including credit cards and personal loans, no longer have that tax advantage. Credit lines frequently offer an interest-only option so you can defer principal repayment until after your child graduates, when your overall expenses may be lower.

If you have a 401(k) plan where you work, you may be able to borrow against its assets. A 401(k) loan might carry a lower interest rate than another type of loan. According to federal guidelines, however, you must repay the loan within five years.

The federal government offers loans through commercial lenders that are not based on financial need, some for parents and some for students themselves. In addition, college and university loans may be more widely available as schools become more creative in devising financing options and payment plans. Check with school financial aid officers for information on these options.

THE MAGIC OF COMPOUNDING

The number of years from now that college starts	Sum accumulated at								
	4%	5%	6%	7%	8%	9%	10%	11%	12%
1	1.04	1.05	1.06	1.07	1.08	1.09	1.10	1.11	1.12
2	1.08	1.10	1.12	1.14	1.17	1.19	1.21	1.23	1.25
3	1.12	1.16	1.19	1.23	1.26	1.30	1.33	1.37	1.40
4	1.17	1.22	1.26	1.31	1.36	1.41	1.46	1.52	1.57
5	1.22	1.28	1.34	1.40	1.47	1.54	1.61	1.69	1.76
6	1.27	1.34	1.42	1.50	1.59	1.68	1.77	1.87	1.97
7	1.32	1.41	1.50	1.61	1.71	1.83	1.95	2.08	2.21
8	1.37	1.48	1.59	1.72	1.85	1.99	2.14	2.30	2.48
9	1.42	1.55	1.69	1.84	2.00	2.17	2.36	2.56	2.77
10	1.48	1.63	1.79	1.97	2.16	2.37	2.59	2.84	3.11
11	1.54	1.71	1.90	2.10	2.33	2.58	2.85	3.15	3.48
12	1.60	1.80	2.01	2.25	2.52	2.81	3.14	3.50	3.90
13	1.67	1.89	2.13	2.41	2.72	3.07	3.45	3.88	4.36
14	1.73	1.98	2.26	2.58	2.94	3.34	3.80	4.31	4.89
15	1.80	2.08	2.40	2.76	3.17	3.64	4.18	4.78	5.47
16	1.87	2.18	2.54	2.95	3.43	3.97	4.59	5.31	6.13
17	1.95	2.29	2.69	3.16	3.70	4.33	5.05	5.90	6.87
18	2.03	2.41	2.85	3.38	4.00	4.72	5.56	6.54	7.69
19	2.11	2.53	3.03	3.62	4.32	5.14	6.12	7.26	8.61
20	2.19	2.66	3.20	3.87	4.66	5.60	6.72	8.06	9.64

The table above tells you what any sum of money will rise to in any year in the future, if it compounds at a given rate. Look down the left-hand column for the number of years into the future you want. Read across to the rate of increase you expect. Where those lines intersect, you will find a compounding factor. Multiply that factor by the sum you started with to see what it will rise to in the years ahead. Use this table to estimate the price of college in the future or to estimate what your current college savings will be worth in a given year.

Meeting your child's college costs can be managed, but you need to start now. Talk with your financial adviser about sound planning, regular investing, and financing strategies. He or she can also help you review your college investment plan periodically to see that it remains in line with your changing personal needs and market conditions.

In any case, long-term planning for "kid contingencies" is essential.

Financial Gifts

Another way to provide for college expenses is to begin now with gifts of money, stocks, and bonds. In accordance with the annual gift tax exclusion permitted under federal law, you and/or your spouse may each make gifts to your children of up to $10,000 a year per child without incurring a gift tax. If you or your spouse wish to make larger gifts, the unified estate and gift tax credit should be discussed with your accountant or attorney.

Informal Trust and Custodial Accounts

Under the Uniform Gifts to Minor Act (UGMA), you may be the custodian of the funds or investments. You have the legal authority to hold and manage them on your children's behalf. If your children are under fourteen, any gains, dividends, or interest under $600 will be tax free. The next $600 requires your child to file a tax return. Any earnings over $1,200 are taxed at the parents' tax rate.

Both these types of accounts allow you to put money into a savings program for your children. With the informal trust account, you are considered the legal owner of the funds in the account, while the money in a custodial account legally belongs to your children.

With UGMA, you legally must transfer holdings to your eighteen-year-old. If you have a teen who has some problems, this could be a problem/tragedy. If you diligently save and invest for your child's education and he or she turns out to have zero regard for money, your dreams and plans may go out the window, if not down the drain.

If you have already set up holdings for a young problem teen(s), don't put any more money into them. As your child hits the teen years, watch closely. As your child's eighteenth year approaches, if you know it would be a disaster to turn over all the money, consider buying zero coupon bonds that mature in several years.

Tell your child that when the bonds mature, they will yield such-and-such an amount of money. Your child could sell the bonds before maturity, but will probably not think of it. Give him or her some of the money at eighteen, just very little of it.

Now that I've said that, let me recommend the better way. Some states have legislated a Uniform Transfers to Minors Act (California did in 1985). This allows you to pick any age between eighteen and twenty-one for the disbursement of funds. Check to see if your state has passed a UTMA. Any parent will tell you there's a big difference between eighteen and twenty-one when it comes to money sense with kids.

WILLS AND YOUR CHILDREN

A final area of planning mandated by children is that of making a will. This kind of protection is every bit as important as the accumulation of your estate. It is, after all, your net worth, and even if you are just starting out with a "negative" net worth, you have intangible assets, such as yourself, your children, and your personal belongings, that must be protected.

For starters, a will designates whom you want to take care of your children. A few years ago, a front-page article in the *New York Times* remarked on how many parents "neglect to name a guardian for their children" in event of the parents' death. Perhaps their own death is not real to them, but it does seem incredible that parents will give minor children every advantage they're able to, but leave their entire future to chance by not making a will or naming a guardian to look after the youngsters' welfare.

Chapter 15 gives more information on wills. Proverbs 14:24 says, "The wealth of the wise is their crown, but the folly of fools yields folly." You are no fool; make a will.

PASS YOUR MONEY SENSE ON

Money and kids go together. We have seen how children make money management even more important. But there is another aspect to responsible parenting: training kids to be savvy about money. As a woman, and now as a financially astute woman, you operate on the basis of valuable insights and concepts. By modeling your own values and demonstrating the fundamentals of financial responsibility, you can give your children an early understanding of both the importance and the techniques of financial stewardship.

These are the seeds you sow for the future:

> Train a child in the way he should go, and when he is old he will not turn from it. (Proverbs 22:6)

> My son, observe the commandment of your father, and do not forsake the teaching of your mother. (Proverbs 6:20 NASB)

TODAY'S CHALLENGE

A mother's challenge is to prepare her children to live in the world as it really is, to accept money as the basis of our economy's barter systems, and to learn at home that industry and responsibility bring rewards, while laziness and irresponsibility bring difficulties.

Teach Them Young

But just how do you go about teaching children about budgeting, saving, and thoughtful spending? In the early days, you begin by playing counting and number games. Letting children handle and count coins familiarizes them with money and helps them learn the value of the various coins and bills. Taking young children shopping also helps, but taking them is not enough—let them actually shop with you. You can let them make their own purchases, such as coloring books, stickers, or snack items. It is never too early to show children one toy that costs $1 and two others that cost 50¢ each. Let them decide if they want the higher priced, presumably better item, or two less costly toys.

What About Allowances?

The pros and cons of regular allowances are often debated, but I think the positive values far outweigh the negatives. An allowance gives school-age children practice in handling money. Without the discipline of an allowance, children will find it harder to make decisions such as, "Shall I spend this money on stickers or put some in my piggy bank?"

What Kind of Guide Are You?

Help your kids by devising a simple method to keep track of how much they spend each day, what they spend it on, and how much is left over at the end of the week. The budget found on page 192 was used by my niece Crissy when she was younger.

This is the first step in establishing a simple budget, and it's one way you can begin a lifelong habit of planned spending. Like adults, children have fixed and flexible expenses.

At the age of six, a child's allowance should consist of "walking around" money to be spent on whatever she wishes. By the time she is nine or ten, she should be able to compare her expenses to the size of her income (allowance, special jobs, baby-sitting) and develop some idea of budget categories: spending money, fixed expenses (lunch or school supplies), and savings. If she loses money, which happens fairly often, don't replace it except for what is needed to cover the necessities she normally pays for.

Let children observe how you plan family purchases, from bringing a shopping list to the grocery store to setting aside money regularly for such major expenses as vacations. Seeing how you make the family budget will help them relate more easily to their own budget.

CRISSY'S BUDGET

—◆—◆—◆—◆—◆—◆—◆—◆—◆—◆—◆—◆—◆—◆—◆—◆—

Month_____ Week _____

Money Received	Sat.	Sun.	Mon.	Tues.	Wed.	Thurs.	Fri.
Allowance	—	—	—	—	—	—	—
Odd Jobs	—	—	—	—	—	—	—
Gifts	—	—	—	—	—	—	—
Others _____	—	—	—	—	—	—	—
TOTAL	—	—	—	—	—	—	—

Money Spent	Sat.	Sun.	Mon.	Tues.	Wed.	Thurs.	Fri.
Candy	—	—	—	—	—	—	—
Toys/Games	—	—	—	—	—	—	—
Gave to Friends	—	—	—	—	—	—	—
Pets	—	—	—	—	—	—	—
Clothes	—	—	—	—	—	—	—
Church	—	—	—	—	—	—	—
Savings	—	—	—	—	—	—	—
Snacks	—	—	—	—	—	—	—
Movies	—	—	—	—	—	—	—
Other _____	—	—	—	—	—	—	—
TOTAL	—	—	—	—	—	—	—

Total Money Received $_____

Total Money Spent $_____

Over/Under $_____

SAVINGS AND CHECKING ACCOUNTS

If your son or daughter doesn't have a bank savings account by the age of thirteen, a visit to the bank is in order. Although policies vary, most financial institutions will accept accounts for children who can sign their name legibly, and many will waive the minimum deposit requirements for opening an account if the saver is under eighteen.

One word of caution here. Some banks and savings and loans have a minimum service charge on accounts. Try to avoid such a charge, as the fee could exceed the amount of interest earned on the account, and savings could become a disincentive.

You, or the new account representative, should explain the advantages of security in savings and extra earnings in the form of interest, as well as the forms and procedures for savings deposits and withdrawals.

Kids and Checking Accounts

A checking account for teenagers can also be useful, but this is a lot harder to implement. Most banks still require that checking account customers be at least eighteen years old. Some won't even consider joint accounts with the parents. Eventually, those policies will go the way of the dinosaur. Meanwhile, it's worth the effort to search for a bank that will accommodate teenagers. If your child is willing, the lessons inherent in a checking account are numerous.

Classes for Kids

Even the American Bankers Association (ABA) recognizes the value of economic and financial education for teenagers. It inaugurated a personal economics program back in the eighties, which now extends throughout the United States and reaches more than a million teens. The program goes into every high school in a county for one week a year, one hour a day, and holds classes on how to balance a checkbook, use consumer credit, and understand various bank services.

Kids Can Bank on It

However, it was not until the summer of 1987 that any practical application was made of this belief. Now there is The Young Americans Bank (YAB) in Denver, Colorado, established through the vision of Bill Daniels.

The Young Americans Bank is for anyone under the age of twenty-two. It offers savings accounts, checking accounts, CDs, personal loans, and business loans. Equally important, it is providing an education: how to negotiate a loan, sign a check, and manage a savings account.

In 1994, the bank had 16,465 savings accounts with an average balance of $357. The average age is nine. The average age of checking account holders is sixteen, with an average balance of $390. Kids report that their reasons for saving include buying a car, computer, Nintendo or Sega, and paying for college. Those with a checking account said they wrote checks for business expenses, shopping, mail orders—and pizza!

YAB routinely holds programs on starting a business and how money works in our society, and it has created Young AmeriTowne®—a "hands-on" lesson in free enterprise.

$ JB *tip*

The Young Americans Bank has depositors from every state. You can get information by calling 303-321-2265 or by writing YAB at 311 Steele Street, Denver, CO 80206.

Daniels thinks lack of training is the chief cause of poor money management in America today. He believes it leads to budget problems, heavy reliance on credit cards, and ignorance about the value of money market and stock market mutual funds. Every city should have a YAB!

TEENS AND BUDGETS

During high school, teenagers should be able to budget for a month at a time, or even for each quarter. A seasonal clothes budget or a special trip, in addition to the allowance, is a good way to teach this kind of longer-range budgeting.

Giving Teens Credit

Buying on credit is not about to disappear. So it's increasingly important for your kids to understand the rights and responsibilities that go along with it. My daughters have been on their own for years now. But while they were in their teens, I did two important things.

First, I put them on one of my MasterCard accounts, where each card user's name appeared individually and each was given a credit card. My job was to monitor them closely, and if they made any charges, to make sure that each paid her share of the bill. By having their names added to the account, they would establish their own credit file, which was my primary objective. Every time a payment was made, even if I had made it, they also got credit.

The secondary objective was to familiarize them with money management. When something was purchased, it had to be paid for—"Those who play, have got to pay." In our house, that particular MasterCard was known as the "kids' account," and the adults did not use it.

My daughters are close in age, but during their teen years, there was a broad gap in their sense of responsibility. Sheryl abused her privilege by charging beyond her stated limit, resulting in her card being taken away immediately. Of course, as a parent, I had to make good the funds that were charged and have her pay me back. If I did not, I would have jeopardized her sister, who had been meeting her obligations by paying her charges when each bill arrived.

The second thing I did was introduce each daughter to my banker when it was time to buy her first car. We went through the whole formal process of making a loan application. Of course, I had to guarantee the transactions, with my name being added to the documents after they had completed them. But as far as my daughters were concerned, the loans were in their name and they had the obligation to make the monthly payments. If they weren't paid the bank would take the cars back. My daughters didn't know that I had cosigned.

As payments were made, the bank reported the transaction on the appropriate credit report. Using a credit card and participating in the loan process for a car significantly increased my children's awareness of what credit and money were all about. When Shelley turned eighteen, she received an invitation to get her own Visa card, which meant she no longer used the kids' MasterCard. That was one of my goals for each of my girls—to be able at some point to begin their credit lives on the right foot.

As each daughter turned eighteen, the bank released me as guarantor on the remaining loan balances, if any. During the entire period, loan payments were made from their checking accounts, never mine. There were some rough spots—like the fact that their checkbooks never balanced in the beginning—but they learned. At one point things got so bad in one account, the only solution was to close the account and open a new one (guess which daughter!)—just to know exactly what the beginning balance was. But that was OK. It was part of the learning process.

◆   SUMMING UP   ◆

Teaching youngsters about money in their formative years can promote their intellectual development. It also helps adults rethink the basics of the value of money and the importance of making it grow. Children need to understand that we seldom receive anything for free. We work for what we receive. But if we work, we have a right to expect to benefit.

The Money Sense Parent's Creed reads:

A parent provides her child with a hands-on learning experi-

ence while maintaining an atmosphere of trust and communication that is critical to the learning process. The parent
teaches through experience, and her guiding principle is
clear: Learn by doing.

If children function as responsible, cooperative, giving family members,
and if they understand and accept the "game rules," they should participate in the benefits.

Gifts of knowledge, understanding, and self-discipline can have their
own rewards for you as a mother and parent. "Correct your son, and he
will give you comfort; he will also delight your soul" (Proverbs 29:17
NASB).

Life Phase 3: 35–40

So what if Christopher Columbus was credited with discovering America? Queen Isabella gave him the money.

—Judith Briles

Chapter 14

- ◆ — ◆ — ◆ — ◆ — ◆ — ◆ — ◆ — ◆ — ◆ — ◆ — ◆ — ◆ — ◆ —

Branching Out:
Starting Your Own Business

If you are between thirty-five and forty, you probably feel you have many years of experience behind you. You have undoubtedly made mistakes, but possibly you have been able to turn them to your advantage. You most likely are stable and know what you want, and you may be ready to branch out. Perhaps that's why a second or side business often evolves during this period. I have often heard women in this life phase, myself included, say they really feel that they have reached adulthood. Most likely, you will consult an attorney for the first time to make a will.

This particular phase is the shortest. Because it builds on the experiences of the two earlier phases, there are fewer problem areas. So take advantage of what you have already learned and enter confidently into this one.

DO YOUR OWN THING?

During this phase, the stability and experience you have gained may encourage you to think about starting your own venture. If this is the case, it is absolutely essential to begin to build up cash. When you have written up a business plan for a company and estimated the amount of capital needed to start, it is wise to double the estimate. Until you are actually at the helm of a business, you will probably not realize what the overall costs are. Often, as much as 40–50 percent can be hidden in items and expenses that you did not realize were essential to the ongoing operation of a small business.

> ## $ JB tip
>
> *The National Association for the Cottage Industry is a group that lobbies on public policy matters affecting home businesses. It publishes newsletters, provides insurance policies for both health and business insurance, and offers seminars. Membership is $45 a year. Write to Box 14850, Chicago, IL 60614.*

Whether you call it entrepreneurship or simply the desire to be your own boss, a growing number of women have decided to start their own business. Although naysayers point to the high failure rate of new businesses, there are millions of success stories. Why shouldn't yours be one of them? But before you begin, here are a few questions for you to ponder.

1. Are you willing to answer your own phone, open the mail (daily), and be available to respond to customers (here's the phone again) outside of 9:00 to 5:00? I have gotten calls at 5:30 in the morning and at 10:30 at night.

2. Do you complete tasks—or are there always unfinished items for "tomorrow"?

3. Do you have a minimum of six months' worth of moneys set aside to support you and your family while the business gets started?

4. Do you have a place that will be for work alone? The dining room table works for a couple of days and then chaos sets in. You need uninterrupted space.

5. Can you work alone? The hours can be long without people around you.

6. Will your idea make money?

7. Can you keep going when the chips are down?

If you answered yes (better yet, enthusiastically yes), good luck!

Small businesses employ more individuals than the Fortune 500 combined. Small businesses also fail. Eighty percent of the self-employed go out of business within five years of being started. Most of that 80 percent didn't have a written business plan.

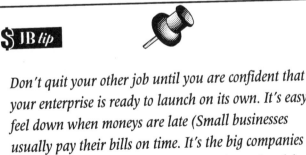

$ JB tip

Don't quit your other job until you are confident that your enterprise is ready to launch on its own. It's easy to feel down when moneys are late (Small businesses usually pay their bills on time. It's the big companies who hold back for 90 to 120 days. A ninety-day delay in payment could shut you down!) and the computer has crashed for the third time in one week.

Background Information and Experience

Before you contemplate starting your own business, it's advisable to have a few years' experience in your chosen field. It is not uncommon for women to tell me they would like to go into business and then admit that they haven't really identified which business, and they do not have the necessary experience to support their new venture. Owning your own company can be a wonderful experience, but there are always dues that must be paid in advance.

You will have to gain the experience that only the school of hard knocks brings. Behind every successful person there are failures—some spoken about, some unspoken.

Gaining experience ranges from negotiating lines of credit, hiring and firing, getting rid of too much supply (or inventory) when the demand no longer exists, having to postpone your monthly obligations because you must meet your payroll first, to even missing a payroll!

You also need to get some basic background information. Most community colleges offer classes and programs for the person who wants to begin a business or expand a hobby into a profitable enterprise. The instructors are often professionals who have themselves become entrepreneurs, or entrepreneurs who have become professors.

Often these instructors can refer you to accountants and attorneys who specialize in small businesses. After all, the needs of a very small business are quite different from those of IBM. When the senior management of IBM walks into a banker's office, it gets the bank's attention immediately. Without pre-existing banking relationships, if you walked into a banker's office to discuss your business venture, you might be met with a yawn.

Bookkeeping

It is also a good idea to get some experience in simple bookkeeping and/or accounting methods. I have observed many snafus over the years, where women have started small businesses now grown into interesting moneymakers, but have not thought to separate their business accounts from their family accounts.

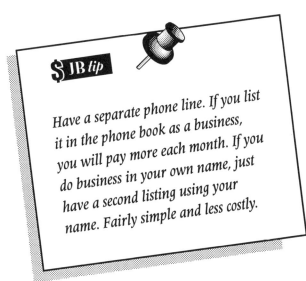

$ JB *tip*

Have a separate phone line. If you list it in the phone book as a business, you will pay more each month. If you do business in your own name, just have a second listing using your name. Fairly simple and less costly.

If you are going to start your own business, it is important to run it as a business. Segregate everything. Establish new checking and business accounts for your business, and operate under a separate name (or at least one that can be designated as a business name, as distinct from the one you use daily). Also, if you sustain any losses or expenses in the first two years, no matter the size, you more than likely have a legitimate tax deduction. If you intend to take these deductions as write-offs on your tax return, it is essential to have the appropriate records.

THE IRS SAYETH

The IRS recognizes that start-up companies, incorporated or not, incur expenses and losses before realizing a profit. Not every business is able to show profits immediately. I should caution you, though, that the IRS's patience won't last forever when you take these deductions. They have clearly defined rules about hobby-related businesses. If your business continues to show a loss or your expenses exceed your revenues after three years, you should consider closing the business down and moving in another direction. The IRS would like to see a business turn a profit for at least three out of five years.

Use your home office exclusively for business. Your desk should not sometimes be the dining room table. The IRS will disallow a home office deduction unless the space is exclusively for business. That doesn't mean your entire home must be an office, just the portion you use for work.

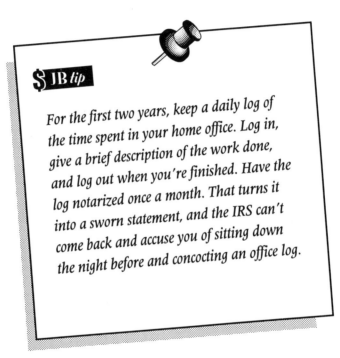

$ JB tip

For the first two years, keep a daily log of the time spent in your home office. Log in, give a brief description of the work done, and log out when you're finished. Have the log notarized once a month. That turns it into a sworn statement, and the IRS can't come back and accuse you of sitting down the night before and concocting an office log.

There are rules about taking losses on your tax return. You should consult your accountant, especially about how passive loss rules may affect you. Remember, you must demonstrate that you are operating in a businesslike manner and are attempting to make a profit. You cannot keep deducting business losses forever! If the IRS reclassifies your business as a hobby, you can deduct the expenses related to your hobby against the income you earn from your hobby, but you cannot offset additional losses against other income. If you believe you will make a profit in the fourth or fifth year, you can ask the IRS to delay a decision on whether you are, indeed, engaged in a potentially profit-making business.

INCORPORATING—OR NOT

One of the first financial decisions will be the legal form your business should take. You can set yourself up as a sole proprietor, a partnership, a Subchapter S corporation, or a regular business corporation, known as a C corporation.

There are some disadvantages in incorporating. One is that when you, as an individual and employee, contribute to Social Security, and the corporation contributes an equal amount on your behalf, the IRS can, if it wants to become sticky, question the amount paid to the owner/employee. If it is determined that the compensation is excessive, the IRS could reclassify some of the income as dividends. Keep in mind that dividends are not deductible for a corporation. Therefore, the corporation is taxed on the dividend and you will also be taxed on the same dividend that you declared originally as income.

Another disadvantage is that fringe-benefit programs, such as medical insurance the company pays for, must be nondiscriminatory. This means that the goodies you enjoy must be shared by all. Of course, if you are the only person in the corporation, this doesn't create a problem. State and local income taxes, as well as franchise and other taxes on corporations, require a regular filing of returns, reports, and other documents. If you dislike paperwork, make sure to hire someone competent to take care of those needs.

Normally the initial paperwork for incorporating is done through a qualified attorney. Several do-it-yourself books are available at your local bookstore. If you decide to do it yourself, NOLO Press in Berkeley, California, has published several excellent books.

As a rule, the decision of whether to incorporate or not is an accounting decision. Make sure to confer with your tax adviser or CPA. The IRS is looking increasingly closely at potential abuses in the corporation area, and it certainly makes sense to avoid any pitfalls. The IRS also continues to change the rules, another reason for conferring frequently with your CPA or tax adviser.

On Your Own—The Sole Proprietor

Most businesses start as sole proprietorships or partnerships. If you form a partnership, it will need its own tax ID number. If you want to start your business as a sole proprietor, your own Social Security number will suffice as long as you have no employees. If you do have employees, you'll need to obtain an employee identification number (EIN) in order to file your payroll tax returns. Get an EIN from the Internal Revenue Service by completing Form SS-4. You can even get the EIN issued over the phone by calling 816-926-5999.

As a sole proprietor, you don't have to file a separate tax return for your business. Just attach a Schedule C (Profit or Loss from Business) to your next personal income tax return. Examine your tax situation several times during the year. If you have money coming in, you may have to make quarterly estimated tax payments to the IRS to cover income and self-employment taxes. IRS booklet #505 provides information on the filing requirements.

If you have another job as an employee, FICA (Social Security Tax) is being taken out of your paycheck. In your business venture as a sole proprietor, you will still have to pay self-employment tax to the extent that your wages as an employee did not reach the maximum covered levels. Get some advice from your accountant here.

If you make a profit, set up a retirement account—IRA or Keogh. You can't deduct the IRA amount if you are covered by a corporate retirement plan in your other job. If you are employed in addition to your own business, you can set up a Keogh plan for your self-employment earnings even if you have coverage in a plan from your other job.

As a sole proprietor, you are personally liable for lawsuits against your business. Make sure you take out business liability insurance that will cover any problems. A million-dollar policy should not be considered unreasonable.

The Other Corporation—Subchapter S

Most people incorporate a business to limit the liability of the corporate shareholders. A Sub "S" corporation is limited as to the number and type of shareholders and classes of stock that may be offered. There can be no more than thirty-five shareholders, and no partnerships or corporations can be shareholders.

A Subchapter S corporation operates like a regular business corporation—except for one significant area. The corporation itself does not pay taxes on its income. Instead, the business earnings (and losses) flow directly through to the owner of the corporation. They are then taxed at the owner's individual tax rate. Rules for the deductibility of losses are complex and also depend on whether you are active in your business or are a passive investor. You definitely need a tax adviser here.

$ JB tip

If you are profitable, you can set up an IRA or you can set up a regular pension and/or profit sharing and 401(k) plan. Get accounting and legal advice before you commit to a plan.

WORKING OUT OF YOUR HOME

If you work out of your home, join the crowd. Many corporations are allowing—even encouraging—employees to work out of their homes. With commuting costs rising and family needs constant, companies are becoming more flexible, and with the widespread use of computers and fax machines, it is amazing what can be done without getting into a car.

Most businesses start out of homes today. Look what a garage did for Apple Computer! The IRS, being quite attuned to the cottage trades, has several requirements for deducting home office expenses.

One of the following must apply:

- You use the office to meet with customers or suppliers.

- The office is your principal place of business (and you do not have use of an office at your employee's place of business).

- The office in your home is a place that you use regularly and exclusively to conduct your employer's business, and it is for the employer's convenience.

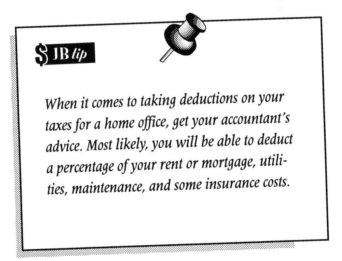

$ JB *tip*

When it comes to taking deductions on your taxes for a home office, get your accountant's advice. Most likely, you will be able to deduct a percentage of your rent or mortgage, utilities, maintenance, and some insurance costs.

In addition to the above, the Supreme Court issued a new ruling that further defined the circumstances under which expenses for home offices could be deducted in 1993. Here is the new test for deductibility of home office expenses; one of the following must be true:

- The home office must be the place where the most important function or service of the business is provided.

- The amount of work time spent in the home office must be greater that the amount of work time spent outside of it.

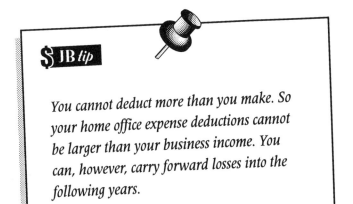

$ JB tip

You cannot deduct more than you make. So your home office expense deductions cannot be larger than your business income. You can, however, carry forward losses into the following years.

WHEN YOUR FAMILY WORKS FOR YOU

One of the advantages of owning your small business is that you can pay family members to work in your business. Because they are earning income, those family members can start their own tax-deductible IRA accounts (if they are not covered by a pension fund elsewhere), or they may be eligible to participate in your company's retirement plan.

Family members do pitch in to help when a small business is started. To formalize their help, you can pay them. Ordinary chores such as having the kids take out the trash do not qualify. But if your children help with the filing or make deliveries of product, then they can certainly earn a paycheck. Their money can easily be invested in a no-load mutual fund and used to start a college account. You get to deduct the wages as a business expense. Win-win.

If you pay a spouse on a regular basis, he can (if not covered elsewhere) take $2,000 of that income and open a deductible IRA account. In fact, even if your family employee is covered by a company pension plan at a full-time job, up to $2,000 a year in earnings from your company can still be put into a nondeductible IRA to grow and compound tax-deferred.

You can still claim children as dependents if they are under nineteen and are living at home (unless a divorce decree states otherwise), or if they are full-time students under twenty-four and you contribute at least half of their support. You won't lose your child as a dependent if he or she files a tax return. However, children who are claimed as your dependents cannot take their own personal exemption when they file their own returns. Only one of you can claim the exemption. If you are a sole proprietor, wages paid to a child under eighteen are exempt from Social Security taxes. If you are incorporated, Social Security taxes must be paid on a child's income, just as for any other employee.

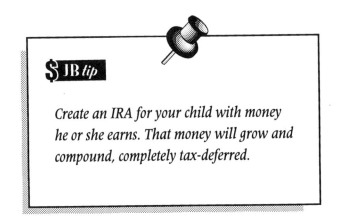

$ JB tip

Create an IRA for your child with money he or she earns. That money will grow and compound, completely tax-deferred.

WHERE TO GET MONEY FOR STARTING UP

Raising money for anything is hard. For a new business it's like banging your head against the proverbial brick wall. If you don't have enough of your own money, there is always a supplementary approach—OPM: Other People's Money.

Consider trading a percentage (for example, 25 percent) of your business income for start-up money from the Bank of Mom and Dad, a relative, or a friend. Both parties share in the profits—and the risks. And you don't have to start paying until money comes in. Make sure you put whatever you do in writing. And evaluate whether the relationship can withstand the pressure of the worst possible scenario.

If your venture is wildly successful, what happens if a "partner" wants out? Do your business estate/divorce plan when you start up, not down the road.

$) JB tip

Don't take out a home equity loan to fund your business. If it fails, the bank could foreclose and you would lose your home. Ugh!

PUTTING UNCLE SAM ON YOUR TEAM

The Small Business Administration has two booklets you should find useful: "How to Start a Home-Based Business" and "How to Raise Money for a Home-Based Business." Both are free. Contact the Office of Business Development and Marketing, 409 Third Street SW, Washington DC, 20024, or call 202-205-6665.

An excellent resource is *Free Money for Small Business and Entrepreneurs*, by Laurie Blum (Wiley & Sons). This is ideal for any business that benefits the public good.

The government sells all sorts of equipment, furniture, and supplies at bargain basement prices, if you know where to shop. Call the General Services Administration's headquarters, at 703-557-7785, to find out about government auctions in your area.

HUGE FINANCIAL RESPONSIBILITY

Years ago, my firm had a client who loved animals—all kinds of animals. When she first came to us for advice on financial planning, she had a significant amount of cash. She invested $10,000 in mutual funds. She wanted to allocate the remainder to the development of her business, which involved the training and care of unusual animals.

During this time she brought in a business partner, and the two of them bought an elephant. The objective was, of course, to take care of the elephant; but they also intended to rent him out for parties and parades. Everything seemed to go well, but then they had a falling out and the partner wanted to retrieve her money. The court stepped in and settled it. My client got custody of the elephant.

Now, if you have never raised an elephant, let me assure you its upkeep is not cheap. This particular elephant's room and board averaged $1,500 a month. When he was transported to his various engagements, the truck hauling his trailer only got about two miles to the gallon. But my client loved the elephant and wanted to do all she could to make sure that he was well fed and cared for.

She approached us about selling her mutual funds because she needed additional cash. I told her I had mixed emotions. I could certainly understand why she wanted to take care of the elephant and why she needed the funds, and I wanted to do everything that I could to help her. But my money sense side said that was a mistake, because I suspected that the money she would receive from selling her mutual funds would quickly disappear into elephant maintenance. She chose to ignore my advice, sell her mutual funds, and keep her elephant. Needless to say, she ultimately had to sell her elephant because she couldn't meet her bills.

My friend of elephants thought she was doing the right thing, and she was happy. At least, initially. What got lost was common sense and good judgment. She did not have the ongoing assets nor the location to care for the elephant.

It is not good business or money sense to become emotionally involved with your investments or your businesses. You are often so up to your ears in a day-to-day operation that you can't see what's happening. If you are going to start your own business, do it on a sound basis. If your purpose is to make a humanitarian contribution, make sure you recognize it as such. The amount of money you spend on it and/or your asset contribution will at least be deductible on your taxes. Your time will not be.

INVESTMENT CLUBS

If you believe in sharing information, an investment club may be a great way for you to enter the wide world of investing. Most clubs start with a group of friends, coworkers, or neighbors who have a common interest—investing in the stock market. Moneys are pooled, research and information discussed. Some clubs are very small; others have twenty to thirty members. When it comes to making an investment decision, you will not be alone.

$ JB *tip*

Investment clubs are terrific places to brainstorm with other members as to what products they are buying. If there are some with small children or grandchildren, what toys, TV shows, and movies are hot? Can stock be bought in them?

Most clubs have a monthly financial requirement, e.g., each member puts $100 in the kitty, with $25 added each month. The group decides, after a committee or individuals present companies for consideration, to buy so many shares of a stock or fund. Over a period of time, more shares can be purchased and sold. Investment choices are made by popular vote for all buys and sells.

The net result is that you will learn a lot about the stock market. Many clubs have local stockbrokers and financial planners speak at their meetings. If you have an interest in starting a club, contact the National Association of Investment Clubs at P.O. Box 220, Royal Oak, MI 48068, or call 313-543-0612 for an information packet.

$ JB tip

A collective group is a great place to find out who spends money on what . . . and who no longer buys what.

Nearly 25,000 people belong to investment clubs. Most are women. There are more than 8,000 clubs in America. When working with the National Association of Investment Clubs, dues are $30 per club, plus $10 per member per year. In return, NAI will send members the *Better Investing Magazine*. This is in addition to the partnership agreement, general information on how to form the club and how to set up accounting procedures.

Investment clubs may be a great way to put your toe in the stock-market water. They have some wonderful success stories. The great majority of members had little knowledge of the stock market when they started.

$ JB tip

Some of the most successful investors start very small. Beginning with $100 and a commitment of $25 per month can be a major building block to your financial house.

LIMITED PARTNERSHIPS

At various times in your life you may be tempted to participate in a limited partnership. Do not yield to such a temptation unless you are willing to risk the loss of all your invested capital.

BONDS

Bonds are an important form of investment, although they need to be approached carefully. For more information on bonds, read Austin Pryor's *Sound Mind Investing* (Moody, 1993), or *Money Markets and Bonds,* also by Austin Pryor (Moody, 1994).

WILLS

You will need to file a will during this life phase, if you have not done so already. Wills are discussed in detail in chapter 15. Estate planning (a broader subject) is discussed in chapter 19.

Quiz

You are sick of your job, your boss, the commute—everything. You decide that the only solution is to start your own business. The question is, what business should you start, and how should you go about it?

(a) You decide it doesn't matter, anything would be better than your present situation.

(b) Sign up for a course on entrepreneuring at your community college.

(c) Quit your job and put in a workman's compensation claim for stress.

(d) Combine resources with your best friend and go into business with her.

Answer: (b) Start building your business savvy. Until you know what and how, do not quit—unless you have a very fat bank account with at least three years of living expenses. Going into business with a close friend can often be disastrous. If you want to start a business with her, start with a solid business plan, including financials. Make sure you include a "buy-out" clause for both of you.

◆ PHASING UP ◆

During this life phase you should continue contributing to your IRA. Here, as in the two previous phases, your choices for investment placement are more than likely going to be stocks or mutual funds. You still have many years before what is considered the normal retirement age, and therefore your investment objectives will probably be growth oriented.

During this phase you should begin to build more and more liquidity. As in prior phases, your funds should be placed in instruments that not only are accessible but also offer you a reasonable and current market rate of return.

At this time your relationship with a bank—or several banks— should be excellent. You should definitely be on a first-name basis with your banker, and, if you have been presenting him or her with an annual statement of your income and expenses and net worth, he or she should be able to respond quickly when you need banking services.

Your Phase Focus should be:

$ Your will should be completed.

$ You should review your life insurance.

$ You should continue to put moneys into no-load mutual funds.

$ You may want to look for ways to start your own business.

$ If some of your investments turn sour, the world has not come to an end. Learn, accumulate, and invest with wisdom.

$ If you own your own home, a rental property may be your next piece of real estate.

$ Continue to tithe 10 percent to yourself.

◆   RETIREMENT BONUS   ◆

If you started your IRA at the age of eighteen and continued annual investments of $2,000, accumulating at the rate of 12 percent, by the time you reached the age of forty, you would have amassed $207,205.80

Chapter 15

— ◆ — ◆ — ◆ — ◆ — ◆ — ◆ — ◆ — ◆ — ◆ — ◆ — ◆ —

Making a Will:
Protecting Your Loved Ones

*T*he night before I wrote this chapter, one of my dear friends from California came for dinner and spent the night. A large, unframed oil painting of geraniums hangs in my kitchen. My friend loves it, and when we started talking about wills, she asked me if I died before she did, would I leave it to her? Knowing that I wouldn't be rushing to my attorney the next day to change my will—although it is a summer project—I immediately wrote a note to give the painting to Nicole if I died and taped the note on the back of the canvas for my family. I then told my husband that it should go to Nicole.

Until I get it done properly, my family was told that this is what I wanted done with the painting. If you were to die tomorrow, does your family know what you want done with your assets, your treasures?

Your daughters may love your jewelry. If you leave your jewelry to both of them, what happens if one moves a thousand miles from the other? Who decides who gets what, or how do they share?

Few people can reach perfect accord over what to do with mutually owned property. Anything that can't be divided should either be left to one person or sold and the proceeds split. In the case of heirloom jewelry or your art collection, the sentimental value may be higher than the real value. Find out which daughter wants which piece, and describe their choices in your will instead of leaving one or both the entire collection. When it comes to death and dying, few really plan for it or for those they leave behind. If no planning is done, those who are left behind may end up living with a monster.

I came across the column below several years ago, saved it, and now pass it on to you. It has been repeated numerous times in Ann Landers's syndicated column and is reprinted with her permission:

DEAR READERS: If you want to do something nice for your family, get your affairs in order.

I came across this gem in *The Survivor*, a splendid magazine for widowed people. I obtained permission from the author, Judge Sam Harrod III, of Eureka, Illinois, to reprint it.

IF YOU DON'T HAVE A WILL, YOUR STATE HAS ONE FOR YOU

The Statutory "Will" of John Doe.

I, John Doe, make this my "will," by failing to have a will of my own choice prepared by my attorney.

1. I give one-half of all my property, both personal and real estate, to my CHILDREN, and the remaining one-half to my WIFE.

2. I appoint my WIFE as Guardian of my CHILDREN, if she survives me, but as a safeguard, I require that:

   a. my WIFE make written account every year to Probate Court, explaining how and why she spent money necessary for the proper care of our CHILDREN;

   b. my WIFE file a performance BOND, with sureties, to be approved by Probate Court, to guarantee she will properly handle our children's money;

   c. when our CHILDREN become adults, my WIFE must file a complete, itemized, written account of everything she has done with our children's money;

    d. when our SON and DAUGHTER become age 18, they can do whatever they please with their share of my estate;

    e. no one, including my WIFE, shall have the right to question how our CHILDREN spend their shares;

3. If my WIFE does not survive me, or dies while any of our CHILDREN are minors, I do not nominate a Guardian of our CHILDREN, but hope relatives and friends may mutually agree on the one, and if they cannot agree, the Probate Court can appoint any Guardian it likes, including a stranger.

4. I do not appoint an Executor of my estate, and hope the Probate Court appoints someone I would approve.

5. If my WIFE remarries, the next husband:

    a. shall receive one-third of my WIFE'S property;

    b. need not spend any of his share on our CHILDREN, even if they need support, and

    c. can give his share to anyone he chooses, without giving a penny to our CHILDREN.

6. I do not care whether there are ways to lower my death taxes, and know as much as possible will go to the Government, instead of my WIFE and our CHILDREN. In witness whereof, I have completely failed to make a different will of my own choice with the advice of my attorney, because I really do not care to go to all that bother, and I adopt this, by default, as my "will."

(no signature required)

Sounds pretty bleak, doesn't it? Without writing one, everyone has a will. If you don't choose one on your own, you get the one your state picks for you. Would you choose the one from the Ann Landers column? I think not.

As you move through Life Phase 3 and your assets build up, you must begin to consider that you are mortal. Yet rarely do I see people under forty with a will that is properly put together, even though people ought to write a will as soon as they begin to acquire any assets or have children.

The average woman who works outside the home spends more than ten thousand days making money. It seems shortsighted not to spend one day making a determination of where your assets should go when you die. Unfortunately, more than 80 percent of those who will die today leave no will.

A friend was in her late thirties when her husband died of a heart attack. He was in his early forties, and they had three children. Because there was no will, the courts decreed she was to get one-third of his estate and the children two-thirds of it. And because the children were all minors, she would have to get approval from a judge in order to sell some of the assets of which the children were part owners, such as the second car. She actually had to prove to the judge that the selling of a car would not reduce the amount of the children's estate.

In addition, there was a significant amount of cash from life insurance proceeds, as well as a pension from his employer. The kids came out with more money than she did. Is this what you want for your spouse? Probably not. But most of us don't think about it until it is too late.

MAKE IT SO

If you don't have an attorney, or you are shopping around for one, by all means sit down and make a holographic will until you can get a formal document drawn up.

A holographic will is a will that is handwritten by you. In it, you recite who you are, your permanent address (and, if applicable, a secondary address), your place of birth, and your marital status. Your spouse should do the same. If there are any previous marriages, include that information and the names and addresses of your immediate family, which would include your sons, daughters, and parents.

If you have ever created a trust (see chapter 19, which deals with estate planning and probate), make sure you indicate the appropriate title for that. If you are entitled to any pensions, profit sharing, or other income, include that information. If you have insurance policies, include the numbers and beneficiaries—both primary and secondary—and whether you are covered under any group policies. Include a complete list of all your assets, as well as their current market value. If any of your assets are held under a name different from your present one, make sure that it is specified. If you have any safe deposit boxes, state where they are located.

You should indicate the name and address of an executor or executrix of your estate. You should name a guardian and give his or her address if you have children under eighteen. You should also designate a trustee, if that is appropriate, for the management of your assets until your beneficiaries reach the age in which the actual distribution will be granted. If you have any stocks, bonds, limited partnerships, retirement accounts, passbooks, time deposits, or any other marketable assets, make sure they are listed. Also indicate the location of your tax returns for the previous three years. Finally, you should spell out exactly what your plans are for your beneficiaries. Then you need to sign the document.

This document acts only as a temporary instrument. It is much preferred that you have an attorney who specializes in estate planning look it over and make whatever changes are necessary. If you have already gone over the location of your various assets and listed them, this should reduce your bill substantially. Remember, changes can be made as the circumstances warrant, and an addendum, or codicil, can be added to your new will.

$ JB tip

The only way to make small changes is to execute a formal codicil to the will, thus amending it. The codicil should be signed, dated, and witnessed according to your state's procedures.

If you have made any previous wills, state in your new one that it revokes any previous testaments. In addition, to be safe, destroy all copies of any old wills. If you have out-of-state assets, make sure you deal with them accordingly. Some states will demand that your heirs go through a separate probate in their state. It might be wise to liquidate your out-of-state assets and bring them into the state in which you currently reside and/or set up a separate will that covers the assets in the other state.

If you have any personal belongings of sentimental value, do yourself a favor and attach to the will a letter of intent that states exactly who gets which belongings. If the majority of your property is divided by percentage, the items covered in your letter of intent will be excluded from a distribution of the primary estate.

$ JB tip

Whenever there is a new tax law, ask your attorney if the new laws impact you.

You are probably wondering, *If I have done all this, why do I need an attorney?* For two reasons. First, the tax laws that deal with estates and trusts keep changing. Unless you are in the legal profession, it is highly unlikely that you are going to be up-to-date on the current laws. If your last will is dated prior to September 13, 1981, and you are married, call your attorney today to revise it. Why? Because any wills dated before September 13, 1981, pay more in estate taxes. Anything written after that date is covered under current law. The current law says that there will be no gift or estate taxes due on property left to your spouse. Second, inaccuracies in your wording could actually change your intent.

When should you update your will? One time to do so is when you move from one state to another. It is important to check whether the probate laws (laws pertaining to transferring the title on assets from the deceased to his heirs; see chapter 19) in your new state are comparable to those in the old one. If you have moved, play it safe and have a local attorney check your will.

Another time to update your will would be when the executor you have selected is no longer acceptable or has died; in this case you should name a new one. (It is often a good idea to choose an executor or executrix who is younger than you are.) In addition, if you have divorced or remarried, or if the number of children you have has increased or decreased, that should be noted in your will. Also, if you now have grandchildren and in-laws, you may want to include them.

If the value of your estate has risen or substantially declined, it may make sense to look over the distribution you previously stated. Or, if you have disposed of any real property listed in your previous wills, you should adjust the document accordingly. I recommend an overhaul of your will approximately every three years, given the way laws and personal objectives keep changing. If you have only a few changes to make in the will, it is not necessary to have the whole will rewritten. The changes can be handled with a codicil. Once again, a codicil is merely a statement added to the will and then initialed or signed separately.

NO EXCUSES PLEASE

People come up with plenty of excuses for not having a will. "I'm not dying this year." "I have nothing to leave anybody." "It's too morbid to think about death." "Tomorrow is another day." But none of these is really valid.

- You can/should have a will even if your financial affairs are a mess.

- When you do your will, only you and the attorney who writes it up will know the contents. Everyone else finds out when you die (unless you tell them before).

- You don't have to have any of your assets appraised. You just have to say which person you want to have the asset. Note that I said "which person" as in *singular*. Don't do sharing with your favored folks. It just doesn't work.

- No one has to know what you own—again, unless you tell them.

- If you change your mind about who you want to have what, change your will—the only time it becomes permanent is when you die.

Doing a will can be fun. Imagine how grateful your niece will be when she receives the treasure she has always told you she loves. This is your chance to have the last word—something many love to do and rarely get the chance to act upon.

As I wrote the initial drafts of this chapter, I knew that I was long overdue in doing another will. My excuse? Tomorrow was another day. When my friend Nicole said she would love one of my paintings, I ended up calling several close friends and asking if there was any item I had that they might like if I died. After the initial shock at my question, we would brainstorm about my various treasures. From my library to my pearls to the lead toy soldiers to an afghan I made. Each found a home. What homes do you want your memories and treasures to go to?

To recap, without a will, here's how the courts will deal with your former life:

- Depending on state law, not all of the property may go to your spouse.

- Your grown children may get some of the money that was meant for your spouse, leaving your spouse with too little to live on.

- A court will choose your minor children's guardian.

- Stepchildren will usually get nothing.

- Your friends will get nothing.

- Your family might battle with the courts.

- Your family will battle with each other.

- A fight might break out among your relatives over who gets the kids and who runs their inheritance (if there is one).

- A bigger fight might break out over the kids if there is no money to raise them.

- There probably won't be a trust to take care of your young children's money (if there is any).

- Part of the money that you meant for your spouse may go to your young kids. Your spouse, as guardian, can use the money only for their support. The court will have to approve certain expenditures and will require an annual accounting.

- Part of the family might be cut off from the family business.

- A business may have to be sold fast, because the estate might not be permitted to run it or because money is needed to pay estate taxes.

- You can't leave your favorite things to your favorite people.

- Your unfavorite people could end up with your favorite things—this is a bummer!

- The state will bend over backward to keep money safe for young children—then will hand it all over to them when they reach majority, usually age eighteen. If they're not ready for the responsibility, too bad.

- You can't leave a contribution to a church or charity.

- Your retarded or handicapped child may inherit money, disqualifying him or her from government aid.

- Everyone will be mad at you.

Some people have the view that if they are married, their spouse gets everything, so why bother with a will? But what happens if you both die in an accident? Who gets your property, your treasures, your kids? If you have child care for your kids when you are alive, why wouldn't you want to select the child care provider—now called a guardian—to look after them when you are not alive?

If you have no children and your spouse dies within five days of your death (fewer days in some states), everything passes to his relatives, leaving yours out. And vice versa. Is this what you want?

Single people may not care that everything goes to their parents. But it takes a will to include a friend, a roommate, a charity, or, in some states, even a sister.

Many people think that even if they don't have a will, their property will pass to the person who most ought to own it. Wake up. What's "right" under state law may be all wrong for your family and friends. Laws vary, but the following table gives you a general idea of what could happen if you die intestate. This means you left no will—at least, no one could find one.

Here is what's in store if that happens.

THE CONSEQUENCES OF DYING INTESTATE

If you are:	And die without a will, your property will go:
• Unmarried, no children, parents living	to your parents. Some states split it with your brothers and sisters.
• Unmarried, no children, parents dead	to your brothers and sisters; if you were an only child, to other next of kin.
• Unmarried, with children	to your children, but probably not to stepchildren. The court appoints a guardian for your minor children and heir funds.
• Unmarried, no relatives	to the state, not the federal government—forget about helping to reduce the national debt.
• Married, with children	depending on the state and size of the estate, all to the surviving spouse, or part to the the children. The spouse may get one-third to one half of your separately owned property, part or all of the community property, and all of the joint property you held together.

• Married, without children   depending on the state and size of the estate, all to the surviving spouse, or part to the spouse, part to your parents, and perhaps even part to your siblings. The spouse may get one-half of your separately owned property, part or all of the community property, and all of the joint property. Some states give everything to your spouse; others divide it among spouse, parents, and siblings.

I know that a lot of this sounds grim. Well, it is. But there are some bright spots. Some items will pass to those you want to have them if you own them jointly—such as in the nine community property states (Arizona, California, Idaho, Louisiana, Nevada, New Mexico, Texas, Washington, Wisconsin) and any property held as tenants in common that does not have a named beneficiary.

Here's what passes without the need for a will:

• All joint property automatically goes to the other owner.

• Property disposed by contract, such as a partnership with buy-sell provisions, goes to the person named.

• Any property with a named beneficiary, such as life insurance, Keoghs, IRAs, SEPs, employee pension, and profit-sharing plans goes to the beneficiary. U.S. Savings Bonds, tax-deferred annuities, and bank accounts that are in trust for others go to them.

• Property put into a revocable living trust goes to the beneficiaries of the trust.

- Lots of personal property—the china, books, knickknacks, even the stereo—is often divided by private agreement, without a will, assuming that no one in the family lodges a formal protest. In many states title to an automobile can be transferred without going through probate.

If you have assets with a named beneficiary, such as life insurance and IRAs, make sure you review them. Do you want the named beneficiary to continue to be your beneficiary?

WHY BOTHER . . . ?

You may have thought, *If I told my friends and relatives who gets what, why bother with the will stuff?* Here are a few good reasons:

- To name a guardian for your children and your children's inheritance.

- To give away property you didn't expect to own. This especially affects married couples. This usually happens with accidents. If your spouse dies and you die a few days, months, even a year later, your property and the kids now have the state deciding what's what.

- To dispose of any property you get after your death. You actually can get rich when you're dead. If you die in an accident, a court might bring in a big judgment payable to your estate. What do you want done with the money?

- To avoid a family uproar.

- To avoid all the problems of joint ownership and named beneficiaries. Single people should have wills.

- To dispose of your half of jointly owned property, if both you and the other owner die in the same accident.

- To make sure that your probate-avoiding tactics work. (See chapter 19.) If you set up a living trust, you need a so-called pour-over will. It guarantees that any property you forgot, or that comes to you after your death, will be added to your trust.

$ JB tip

When leaving money to charities, be precise with name and address. Otherwise, you may have several groups with similar names petitioning the court for "their" money.

DOING IT YOURSELF VS. PAYING A LAWYER

The do-it-yourself model of a will (the holographic will) should be used as a temporary solution when you can't get in to see the attorney until the end of the month. You should use a holographic will to cover most of the things you want to deal with until you can get an official, attorney-drawn one made up.

An attorney should charge from $150 to $300 for a fairly simple will. You can pay big dollars if the will is complex. Here is why consulting an attorney who specializes in wills makes money sense:

- To say exactly what you mean: Is it niece Mary or Aunt Mary who gets your jewels?

- To advise you on how to hold property.

- To reduce death taxes. If your estate is under $600,000,

you owe Uncle Sam nothing, but not all states match the federal $600,000 for exemptions.

- To advise you on any twists in the law. For example, if you leave Aunt Mary your home and there is a mortgage on it, your estate may be required to pay off the mortgage, thus leaving niece Mary out of getting the cash you thought would go her way. A lawyer can help you see that that doesn't happen.

- To ask you questions you might not think about. Do you want a beneficiary's share to go to her children or to her spouse if she were to die before your treasures got to her? Or would you want it not to pass to her family members, but instead go to a battered-women's shelter?

- To make your will challenge-proof—and believe me, challenges will arise. You need the right number of witnesses (varies state to state) who can testify that you signed the will and were of sound mind when you did it.

For the do-it-yourselfers, one of the best guides is Nolo Press's *Simple Will Book* by Denis Clifford. It is available in many bookstores, or you can contact Nolo Press at 950 Parker St., Berkeley, CA 94710.

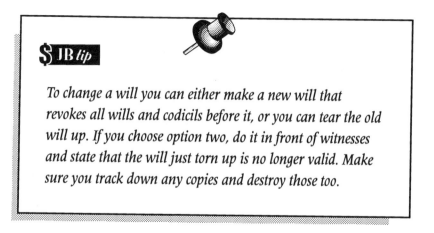

$JB tip

To change a will you can either make a new will that revokes all wills and codicils before it, or you can tear the old will up. If you choose option two, do it in front of witnesses and state that the will just torn up is no longer valid. Make sure you track down any copies and destroy those too.

Get it in writing. The only time "oral wills" will be valid is if you are in imminent danger of death, there isn't much property involved, and several witnesses have heard you.

Video wills aren't valid. But videotaping your reasons why you are giving whatever to whomever can cut the family feud down.

WHO SHOULD GET THE CHILDREN?

The first response is usually Grandma. Certainly grandparents want the best for their grandchildren. But if Grandma is seventy-five, this is not such a hot idea. First, she's raised her family—no parent in her right mind covets raising kids through the teen years again. Second, you are setting your kids up for losing their parents again in a fairly short period of time. Grandma could easily die naturally within the next five to ten years. Now, if Grandma is young, under fifty-five, that's another story.

Your better bet is a sibling, however. Or, if you have a "second family," an older married child, or even a close friend who shares your values and way of life, you might elect to designate him or her to care for your children.

If your kids are old enough to understand the question, ask them where they would want to live if something happened to you. The older your kids, the more critical it is that they be involved in the decision.

In addition to the "care" guardian, you need someone to handle the money side. Usually, the care guardian does both. But if she or he is not skilled at handling money, it may make money sense to get someone who has common sense in the money department.

If you are divorced, the kids usually go to the ex-spouse, if he wants them. Courts rarely step in if the other parent is fit (unfit could be an abandonment, no contact or financial support for at least two years, drug addiction, etc.).

Put your choice of guardian in your will. Spell it out clearly so that your kids are protected. The last thing they need is to be Ping-Pong balls.

HOW TO LEAVE MONEY FOR YOUNG CHILDREN

Name a Legal Guardian

One way to leave money for young children is to name a legal guardian for the children's funds. State law determines what can be spent on the children and what investments can be made. The guardian makes an annual accounting to the court. When the child comes of age—at eighteen or twenty-one, depending on your state—he or she gets the money.

Use the Uniform Gifts to Minors Act (UGMA)

You could also use the Uniform Gifts to Minors Act (UGMA). In most states, you have to make the gift during your lifetime, rather than by will. The funds are left to an adult who acts as custodian for the child. The law determines how the money can be spent and invested. A custodian usually has more flexibility in handling money than a guardian does, such as not having to go to court every time something is bought or sold. The funds go to the child when he or she comes of age, usually at eighteen.

Use the Uniform Transfers to Minors Acts (UTMA)

You could use the Uniform Transfers to Minors Act (UTMA), if your state has adopted it. The UTMA allows transfers by will as well as through gifts during your lifetime. The custodian can hold the assets until the child is eighteen or twenty-one (twenty-five in California). This is much better than the UGMA—a few years extra in maturity can do wonders in preserving a nest egg.

Set up a Trust

You can leave the money in trust. This is the best solution for sums over $20,000 or so. Your trustee—a relative, friend, attorney, or bank—manages the inheritance and pays it to the child according to your instructions. Money can be doled out as needed for the child's education and living expenses. The remainder is turned over to the child at the age you set—it could be twenty-five or thirty.

You can state that the child gets the money all at once or in installments. You might want to give the trustee the power to withhold payments if it seems to be in the child's best interest. (Young people have been known to join cults. Is that where you want money to go?) You might make the child co-trustee in his or her early twenties. Sharing in investment decisions without yet having to handle the money solo makes sense. It's a good learning tool.

Set up a single trust for all the children. If one child has big medical bills, they can be paid out of common funds without looting that child's basic inheritance. Or, if you have already financed two kids through college, you may want to designate a greater amount to your third child for college costs, then do a split. Typically, all the money stays in trust until the youngest child reaches an age you specify. Then the trust dissolves and everyone gets his or her appointed share.

NAMING AN EXECUTOR

Since 1987, estates that have assets of $600,000 or less are excluded from federal taxes. The tax consequence for the state you reside in at the time of your death could be another factor. Some states have no death taxes, others do.

Anything over $600,000 will be taxed at 37 percent, up to 55 percent on taxable transfers over $3 million. For those of you who leave in excess of $10 million, Uncle Sam has a special rate that can get you to 60 percent. A good lawyer is definitely needed to strategize and plan tax reduction.

All of this can be very complicated—which brings me to the choice of an estate administrator, or executor (executrix for females). The job of an executor is to see that your will is carried out.

There are two schools of thought on who should serve as the administrator, or executor, of an estate. A bank, attorney, or accountant will charge a fee for this service. If you appoint someone close to you, such as a family member, he/she has the right to charge a fee, but probably it will be waived. I have mixed thoughts on this. It's wonderful to get your assets distributed. But it's hard work, and I think the executrix should get something for her time.

If you have put your affairs in order, listed where all the appropriate documents are, and made an inventory of your assets, then a family member or a close friend would serve with relatively little trouble. But if your affairs are in disarray, it might make sense to bring in an outsider or professional. If things are a mess by the time your relatives achieve final disbursement of your estate, you may no longer be their favorite Aunt Martha.

Let's turn the tables and suppose that *you* are named as an executrix of a will. What does this job entail? Your basic charge is to gather together all the assets of the deceased, pay the appropriate taxes and debts of the estate, and distribute the remaining assets to the heirs. Well, you may be thinking, that doesn't sound too bad. Unfortunately, there is more to it than that. The following is a list of items you will need to cover:

- Locate the last will.

- If the decedent hasn't appointed an attorney, find one to act as counsel for the estate. Use an attorney who has done this in the past and preferably specializes in estates.

- File the will for probate.

- Obtain several copies of the certified death certificate. You will need this over and over again for proof for banks, insurance companies, Social Security, stock transfers, and so on. If possible, also know the whereabouts of birth and marriage certificates.

- File a claim with Social Security for the burial allowance of

$255. This is a one-time benefit for any widow or widower who has ever paid into Social Security.

- If the deceased has any life insurance, contact each of the companies for the appropriate forms, fill them out, and then submit them with the policy. This is often the largest amount of cash funds that you will receive during the probate process.

- If the deceased was a veteran, check into the possibility of veteran's benefits.

- If there are young heirs, file the appropriate forms with Social Security to get the available benefits for survivors.

- If the deceased was working, verify whether or not there are any pension benefits forthcoming.

- Make an inventory of all the decedent's assets, including contents of any safe deposit boxes.

- Close bank and brokerage accounts and open a checking account for the receipt of proceeds of the estate during the administration process.

- Make a list of all liabilities, as it is important to verify the validity of claims that have been or will be presented for payment.

- Maintain records of all income that is earned during the life of the estate.

- Invest any surplus funds in short-term Treasuries, money market funds, and money market checking accounts.

- Determine the names and addresses of all heirs, next of

kin, legatees, and devisees.

- If necessary, obtain court permission for allowance for support of the surviving family.

- Determine the value of all assets as of the date of the decedent's death. If the value of the assets has changed six months later, you will again determine their overall value. Estate taxes will be determined on the lower of these assessments.

- Pay all bills of the estate.

- Arrange for any appraisals of real estate or personal property. Collect any debts that are owed the decedent.

- Publish a legal notice on claims against the estate in a newspaper that is acceptable to the court.

- Set up appropriate bookkeeping records for the estate. Make sure there is an accurate record of all disbursements and receipts. If required, sell assets to raise funds for the payment of any debts and taxes.

- Notify all beneficiaries of their individual bequests.

- If the decedent owned a business, obtain audits and appraisals of the books and records to determine the value of the business interest.

- Provide an annual account. (This includes arranging for the preparation of federal and state death tax returns and income tax returns.)

- If the decedent owned any personal property that has tax obligations, pay those when they are due.

- Determine the appropriate time to make distributions to the beneficiaries.

- Obtain an estate-tax-closing letter from the IRS.

- Prepare a detailed accounting to the court that is acceptable and final.

- Obtain an order of distribution from the court.

- Arrange for transfer and reregistration of securities, if any, with respective transfer agents.

- Pay all bequests.

- Petition the court for the discharge of the executor.

Take a very deep breath. This is not an easy job. Still want to do it for free?

We have all heard horror stories about the widow who was notified shortly after the death of her spouse that an order had been placed for some specific item. Be aware, unfortunate as it is, that there are individuals who prey upon the sorrow and misfortune of others. They scan the death notices and then send out invoices for goods that were never ordered and certainly never received. Don't let yourself be caught. If you are the executrix, it will be your responsibility to oppose in court all incorrect or invalid claims against the estate.

Depending upon the complexity of the estate, there may be many more requirements. Needless to say, this is not something you want to take on as a lark. It's serious business and must be dealt with as such. When you are considering your estate, make sure that the person(s) you select to serve as the executor or executrix is able to do the job.

That person does not need to be an expert in estate law or a high roller in investments. What is needed is someone who is fair-minded, well-organized, honest, reliable, and sensitive to the concerns of the heirs.

CHANGING YOUR WILL

You should change your will when:

- you have children—either by birth, adoption, or marriage.

- your net worth takes a jump, or a dive.

- your child(ren) marries, separates, or divorces.

- one of your heirs dies.

- one of your children has an illness that may go on forever.

- there are any changes in the inheritance or property laws—federal or the state you live in.

If you have only one child, write a will, and then have another child, what happens? Without being specifically mentioned, the second child will get something. It could be the same—or different. It depends on what state you live in and what its laws are. Birth and adopted children are treated the same. Stepchildren aren't. Unless you specifically say your stepchildren are to have something, they won't.

$ JB *tip*

Execute only one will. For extras, make photocopies.

$ JB *tip*

Whenever you move to another state, have your will checked.

Assembling all these bits and pieces can be a tedious and time-consuming chore. But it will be time well spent, should the unforeseeable occur. Do yourself, as well as your heirs, a favor and make sure you have this base covered.

Providing for your family means planning ahead—for whatever. Proverbs 27:12 forewarns:

> The prudent see danger and take refuge, but the simple keep
> going and suffer for it.

Any woman who cares for her spouse, her children, her parents, her friends, her church, and her community will not postpone drawing up this critical document any longer. There is only one time that will work. *It is called now.*

Life Phase 4: 40–50

Youth is the time of getting, middle age of improving, and old age of spending

—Anne Bradstreet, *Meditations Divine & Moral*
(1964)

Chapter 16

—◆—◆—◆—◆—◆—◆—◆—◆—◆—◆—◆—◆—◆—

Consolidation

The fourth life phase, from forty to fifty, brings us into what is commonly known as midlife. Not only can these be your most productive years and a time when you are at the height of your glory, but they can also include major crises in both your personal and business lives. If you didn't do so during the previous phase, this may be the time when you decide that you want to be your own boss, and that is often a very difficult choice for individuals who are already successful working for someone else.

In this phase, you may take a close look at your friends and work environment. If you have been married and out of the workforce for any length of time, this phase is often one of reentry, particularly if you have children who are in their teens. Changing roles can add stress to marriages, and women sometimes feel overwhelmed by the "superwoman" role they find themselves in. This can force on them a choice between the role of wife and/or mother and that of career person.

Although the midlife period is often considered an adventure, there will be times, especially concerning your finances, when you feel that everything is out of control compared to previous life phases. That may be entirely true, but as you reassess your personal situation, you should find that it will eventually settle down and your financial situation will begin to advance again. In my opinion, this is a time to be creative and take some calculated chances.

THROW ME A LINE!

Many will not agree with me that it makes money sense to have an open credit line available to you. But if you have a business—large or small—it is quite common to have some type of line of credit from your bank. It could be for a thousand dollars, or it could be for tens of thousands of dollars. Your needs will vary.

Perhaps you have to make deposits on equipment, but you are delayed in receivables. Meanwhile, payroll expenses and the rent bills march on. It's ironic how a small business will work so hard to get the big order and then the big order turns out to be a gigantic drag in paying its bill. Many big companies don't pay within thirty days. Ninety to one-hundred-and-twenty days is quite common.

How do you stay alive until the check arrives? If you don't have cash reserves and lots of other receivables coming in, you do what others do: Borrow short-term funds to meet your immediate needs. When the big check does arrive, you pay back the loan immediately. Otherwise, you may have a mini-Titanic in the making.

There will be rough times and other times when it appears that you can do no wrong. But if a financial opportunity arises, and you cannot come up with the cash necessary to take advantage of it, a line of credit could suffice. Always have it in readiness before any need arises. Rarely is there a charge to you until you actually draw on it.

Most banks offer lines of credit that are dependent upon your ability to repay. Some even offer you checkbooks that allow you to write a check to yourself or to whatever entity you desire, with the bank backing your check when it arrives as though it were a loan to you.

As a rule, these unsecured lines of credit are tied into the prime interest rate.

DON'T COUNT ON IT!

You must learn what you have accumulated from private programs and your IRA accounts. Also, since the government will probably increase the age at which you may begin to collect Social Security, as well as reduce the amount of benefits paid to recipients, it makes sense to find out exactly what you are entitled to from that program—and when. Social Security was never intended to be a retiree's sole support. It does offer supplementary income that is beneficial to a retired person.

Check again with the Social Security Administration as to the status of your earnings and whether they have been reported accurately. Mistakes do happen. Someone may put the wrong digit down on your Social Security number in error (and sometimes not in error), and you may not be accumulating the credits you should have.

Any local Social Security office can be contacted for a Form OAR-7004, an official administration form that requests a statement of your earnings. This form is also known as PEBES—Personal Earning and Benefits Estimate Statement. All you need do is give your name and address, your Social Security number, and your date of birth. For more information on this subject, refer to chapter 9.

The Social Security Administration will respond to you in writing with a complete record of your earnings since you began contributing to the fund. If there has been any error, make sure to contact the office directly. If you have changed jobs every two or three years, it is particularly important to make sure your earnings have been properly recorded. There may have been times when your Social Security contribution wasn't paid even though it was deducted from the paycheck: Your former employer took money from you. If this has occurred, contact your attorney for advice.

Another name for your Social Security number is TIN (Taxpayer's Identification Number). Both terms will probably be used on an interchangeable basis.

A TAXING BUSINESS

If you have a successful business and are anticipating selling or expanding it, it is important for you to look clearly at the tax ramifications. If you sell a company and make a substantial profit, more than likely you will incur a tax on the gain. If you are just now beginning to acquire an estate, you may contemplate making some gifts. Prior to selling your company, you may want to make transfers to family members. When the company is finally sold, the recipients will incur their respective taxes on the portion that they hold.

If you have already successfully transferred a portion of the assets to others below the rates that would incur gift taxes at that time, you will save yourself money. Transfers of $10,000 per person on an annual basis can be made without gift taxes. The gift tax is imposed on all transfers of money or property by an individual in excess of this exclusion. Any taxes that are imposed must be paid by the donor (the individual making the gift), not the recipient. Over the years, I have seen several people claim gift funds as taxable income on their tax returns. This, of course, is an absolutely unnecessary burden—certainly a windfall for Uncle Sam!

Any donor giving more than $10,000 is required to file the appropriate information on a gift-tax return. If you are contemplating making a gift in excess of the annual exclusion of $10,000, it would make sense to contact your tax adviser regarding the necessary forms. IRS Publication 904 illustrates how to determine the tax in a particular gift situation. Before you make a substantial gift, you also should determine how much the tax is and retain the necessary cash at the time you make the gift, so that you can pay the gift tax when due.

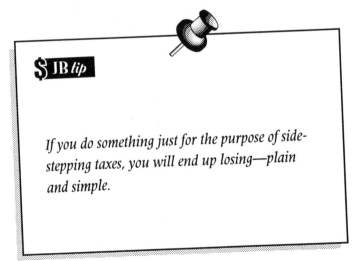

$ JB tip

If you do something just for the purpose of sidestepping taxes, you will end up losing—plain and simple.

CASH IN YOUR CHIPS

Aggressive accumulations in the various money market instruments should be of some benefit. In addition, some of the bond markets may be attractive.

AVOID THE TAX BITE

This life phase is usually the most productive in earned revenues. As a rule, tax obligations are at their greatest. That doesn't mean you should throw funds indiscriminately into various ventures simply to avoid paying taxes. What it means is that you should take a careful look at your spending and place accumulated assets into tax-sheltered, tax-deferred, or tax-exempt environments.

The short-term market is attractive in this phase. If you are purchasing bonds seek maturity dates of fifteen years or less. Municipal bonds are tax-exempt. The interest paid to the holder of such a bond is nontaxable if you live in the municipality of issue. If you invest in a bond fund that allows for a reinvestment of interest into additional bonds, the overall value of your holding can grow substantially. If you purchase any of the bonds at a discount, then you have the opportunity not only for tax-exempt income, but also for capital gain.

LESS IS MORE

This is the time when your assets are growing and your net worth is becoming more and more substantial. It is also the time to make an appointment with an estate-planning attorney to consider the feasibility of various trusts and their applicability to your own situation. Often individuals consider purchasing larger homes during this particular phase, possibly because their children are growing noisier and take up more space in the house. It's often a mistake to do that. Crowding in the old home doesn't last long, and you may later wish that you had kept your small house.

SOME GROWTH, MORE YIELD

Stocks that allow for some growth opportunity as well as a reasonable dividend should be considered during this phase, and especially as you enter the next phase. Stocks such as IBM are considered classic blue chips. But don't marry your stocks. Problems happen, and blue chips sometimes become red chips—worthless. This means you don't get to snooze. You must keep your ears and eyes open for opportunities.

NEW DIRECTIONS

Participation in your retirement accounts will begin to change as you approach the end of this life phase. You should be moving toward more preservation of capital and less aggressive growth. IRA dollars can be transferred now into (1) mutual funds that offer either bonds or income funds; (2) stocks such as utilities that offer fairly high returns via their dividend payouts; (3) banks; (4) money market funds; or (5) Treasuries. All are more appropriate places for retirement dollars than other options mentioned in earlier phases.

A few years ago, I spoke with a major bank representative who stated that the bank had five programs for IRA, SEP, and Keogh participants, ranging from a regular passbook account to a ten-year certificate of deposit. After talking with the bank officer, I decided to participate in a four-year certificate of deposit that had an interest rate of 8 percent, greater than the rate current six-month T-bills were offering. All in all, I was earning a reasonable rate of return and had not tied funds up for an extraordinarily long period of time.

This would enable me to evaluate the ongoing economy as well as re-evaluate other vehicles in which retirement funds could be placed upon maturity.

◆ MS. MISC. ◆

If you have been able to accumulate a respectable sum of money ($10,000 and up), you might consider placing some of it in U.S. Treasury obligations. Treasury obligations, as a rule, pay interest rates a few percentage points below the prime rate. They are guaranteed by the U.S. government, you can liquidate them within a very short period of time, and the interest is nontaxable on any state returns.

In this phase you should begin to reduce some of your personal living expenses—unless, of course, you have children in college. Now is also the time to begin aggressively building up cash, taking a close look at what your overall tax consequences will be. This is the phase when significant funds are paid in taxes to the local, state, and federal governments. Anyone who still pays in excess of 31 percent of her gross income in taxes at this stage should be looking at various legal methods that would reduce her liability.

◆ WINDFALL! ◆

A major windfall source during this phase is community assets or life-insurance proceeds from the death of a parent or spouse. Over and over again I have seen women receive substantial proceeds from life-insurance coverage and then allow it to "disappear." Friends and family members often come forward and give advice about how to invest. People who speak the loudest are often the most inexperienced and may even be relaying their financial fantasies.

This is not necessarily the time to procrastinate, but rather to take a close look at the various options available to you. Because of your age, it doesn't make sense to tie your funds up for a lengthy period of time. Nor does it make sense to get involved in any type of deal or new business opportunity that won't yield benefits quickly and that may entail large risks. If entrepreneuring still attracts you, act as a consultant, but don't tie up any funds you may need in the future.

You should be looking at investment and placement areas that guarantee your principal and some basic return. You also want liquidity. If you desire monthly income, there are investment instruments available that can provide it. You can put your funds in municipal bonds or bond trusts that yield monthly income. Government-guaranteed mortgages, known as Ginnie Maes (GNMAS, or Government National Mortgage Association), pay out a monthly income and give you a high rate of return, as well as a great degree of safety. Don't count on growth.

Quiz

You have just realized that you are getting older—a fact that your kids have accused you of for years. With your new wisdom, it dawns on you that you have not put funds away for your retirement. You thought Social Security was all that you needed. But that was when phone calls were a dime. What should you do?

(a) Start making phone calls—they are bound to increase in price soon.

(b) Contact your personnel or human resource department to find out what programs are available that will enable you to defer part of your income.

(c) Maximize your contribution to a company-deferred compensation program, start an IRA, and begin to increase investment in mutual funds.

Answer: (b) and (c) Start today—determine what's available and allocate moneys now. Every day you wait, you are one more day behind. Don't worry about the phone— it's one of the best bargains around.

♦ PHASING UP ♦

This is the phase where you begin to realize you won't stay young forever. The kids may start to leave home, and your marriage may experience a transition. This is the mid life, and crises do happen.

If you experience a divorce, this may be the first time you really had to crunch the numbers, even living on less. If you have remained single or are married, this will be the phase where you will probably produce the greatest amount of income.

This is also the wake-up call phase, because you finally realize you are marching toward what has been called the "over-the-hill" age. You acknowledge you have got to begin serious planning for retirement. Save. Learn. Invest.

Your Phase Focus will be:

$ Continue to diversify your investments.

$ If you have kids, add to their college funds. The plug will be pulled soon, if not already.

$ Explore your retirement needs.

$ If necessary, play financial catch-up.

$ Know your tax bracket. It may make money sense to shift moneys and investments to tax-deferred and tax-sheltered options.

$ If you haven't bought a home yet, buy one. With tax benefits and a slight nudge from inflation, buyers are ahead of renters. Renters pay until they die; buyers pay the mortgage off.

$ If you haven't written a will—do it. If you have made one, review it.

$ Tithe 10 percent to yourself.

◆ RETIREMENT BONUS ◆

If you had been putting $2,000 a year into your IRA account yielding the rate of 12 percent from the age of eighteen, by the time you reached fifty you would have amassed $682,858.80.

Chapter 17
Salary Negotiation

*J*s pay inequity a problem created since World War II? No. Judy Garland was paid $500 a week for her role as Dorothy in the 1939 classic, *The Wizard of Oz*. Her co-stars, Ray Bolger (the Scarecrow) and Jack Haley (the Tin Man) got $3000 per week. In other words, Judy Garland was paid 16 2/3 percent of what her male co-stars were paid! At least she made more than Toto, the pooch. He got $125 per week.

A Woman's Workplace Worth

It is well documented that women don't get paid as much as men do—even if they have the same skills and credentials and do the same job. One way—a key way—to reduce the gap (currently 71 cents on the dollar) is to know how to negotiate for equitable pay. It also pays big to know the facts. Too often, women don't get paid what they are worth because they don't know how to negotiate well.

First, ask around. Others may know the high and the low that you are interested in. Second, most companies, industries, and occupations have national associations. For example, I am a speaker, and I belong to the National Association of Speakers. I also work a great deal in the health-care field. Therefore, I belong to the National Association of Women Healthcare Professionals. I'm an honorary member of the Association of Women Surgeons and have been a member of several other associations.

If you live in a big city, you may find a branch or local chapter of a group of special interest to you. Besides looking in the Yellow Pages, you might try to call the 800 information operator (800-555-1212) to see if there is a national listing. Don't forget your public library. With reference books and computers, it is amazing the information you can pull together.

The National Association of Professional Trade Associations publishes a booklet annually which identifies main offices, people in charge, phone numbers and addresses, membership objective, when annual meetings are held, etc. Check with your local library to see if they have one. This one booklet can give you a substantial amount of information. Call your library and say you are looking for salary ranges for whatever occupation you have an interest in.

Once you identify what the top of the range is for someone with your qualifications and experience, ask for more than that in a salary discussion. In that way, you have room to move down. According to Nicole Schapiro, author of *Negotiating for Your Life* (Henry Holt & Co.), don't talk money unless you know what the range is for the position you are seeking. Schapiro also advises not to discuss dollars *until the position is offered*.

She also advises *what not to say*. Don't say, "Joe Smith gets this $___. I'm a woman, and I should get $___. Never do a salary negotiation with a legal threat behind it.

Before you go into a salary negotiation, put together a list of things that you would want in an ideal compensation package. Some organizations with low budgets have some goodies—perks—they can offer. These can range from life insurance, healthcare insurance, membership in specific clubs, extra time off, more sick days, or, preferably, personal days to be used at your discretion, extra vacation, flex time, job-sharing, a modem and computer hook-up at home that enable you not to come in five days a week, etc.

The downsizing of the nineties has had a major impact, especially on women. Be aware if there has been downsizing, and don't be afraid to ask if the company is at its "right size." Walk in the company's shoes. Be prepared to tell them how your work and your input will make a difference. You identify the value you bring with your employment. Most managers and employers will state that you will be up for review in a certain period of time. Ask to receive a job description and a copy of the evaluation form so you'll know ahead of time what criteria you will be judged by.

Jobs Aren't Permanent

Jobs are not permanent in the nineties. They keep shifting; there is more flexibility; and the part-time arena will expand. America's largest private employer is a temporary employment agency, Manpower, Inc. In 1993, the Milwaukee-based company employed approximately 600,000 people in the United States. That's more than the combined workforces of McDonald's and General Motors. Seventy-five percent of Manpower's employees are female, who are primarily placed in clerical and secretarial positions. (Why didn't they call it Womanpower?)

As companies downsize, they need some support help on a short-term basis. Repeatedly, they turn to the temporary help agencies. It is not unusual to pay temporary help more than permanent help on a per-hour basis. The rationale is that it's only for a short term—a few days, a few weeks. Of course, temporary employees do not receive benefits.

Creativity May Be Necessary

When negotiating for money, whether it's a new job or an increase in your present position, be prepared before you begin your discussion. If you have not thought through how the manager may respond to your requests, you may be tempted to cave in as soon as he says no. Many times, companies have budgets to pay for specific duties and tasks. If you're being interviewed or reviewed for situations that encompass only one or two functions, the reaction may be that there is no money.

You may do a terrific job, but you are at the top of your pay level. Don't be afraid to bring in your other skills, your other traits. Describe how those skills and traits can translate into other responsibilities; responsibilities that may have budgeted dollars attached to them.

A common fear many women have is that this is the only job. In reality, it isn't. There are others; it may take some probing to find them. Employers will pay you what they think you are worth. Your responsibility is to be able to prove, as in a show-and-tell with documentation and ledgers, exactly what you are worth, and why.

Applying technology requires a working brain—rarely physical strength. Which is good news for women. Skills for the new jobs being invented daily can be learned in apprenticeship programs, on-the-job, even through the local community college.

To equalize pay inequities, women must:

1. Determine if there is a disparity in pay for equal work that requires the same education and skills.

2. Approach management—the decision makers—and request an adjustment. Don't waste time grumbling about minor issues—present facts and data that support work done, value received and impact on a project or the company's profits.

3. The art of negotiation requires facts and no emotion. If your request falls on deaf ears, know what your next step will be. It could include networking with other divisions (which is wise to do anyway) and determining if there are positions that you can transfer to. It also includes leaving.

Business believes that women will work for less money than men will. History has proven that assumption to be correct. Pay inequities should be addressed early on.

Negotiation is a Problem to be Solved

Viewing negotiation as a matter of cooperating and resolving a problem versus creating a conflict is one of the first steps in creating a negotiating mentality. Negotiation plays a key role in your workplace and personal life. The most important step in any negotiation process is to be prepared. In any negotiation, 80 percent is planning and only 20 percent is action.

Being prepared means knowing what you want, and also knowing what the other side wants. You must have a clear picture of what your goal is in any bargaining process. Without it, the outcome could be significantly different from what you desire.

Savvy negotiators hope for the best but plan for the worst. It is important to have some type of ground rules. By developing common rules before beginning, you simplify the process and help to focus on the end results.

Sometimes, an impasse is created. It becomes evident that your desires may not be fully satisfied. If that's the case, one of the strongest strategies that you can have is to be able to walk away.

Keep It Clear—Know What You Want

The essence of any good negotiation is clear communication. Understanding that everyone has different communication styles and predetermining what each style is before a negotiation begins can put you ahead of the game. Negotiation is done on many levels, from simple bartering to problem solving and conflict resolution. It is a give-and-take, back-and-forth process of solving problems, large and small, that arise every day while you try to obtain or accomplish something.

Goals must be set. Knowing what you want or need to come away with is a strong card in your negotiation hand. If it is a material goal, name it and quantify it. If it is something intangible, describe it sufficiently to give it some substance. People are often more willing to give you what you want if they know exactly what you want instead of being confronted with general dissatisfaction.

Set your aspirations high because you'll never do better than what you aspire to. If you don't reach the highest level of your aspirations, you may be disappointed. But, in retrospect, you probably went further than you would have if you had set more modest goals, which is what most women do. Women rarely ask for enough when it comes to money. But don't look exclusively at money as you evaluate your present situation and future possibilities. How much fulfillment does your present career give you? How much do you like the company you work for? A move may be financially expedient but personally costly.

$ JB tip

Claim authority over your own life. It is a critical step in preparing to negotiate for your life—and that authority is a non-negotiable.

Don't confuse "authority" with "control." The desire to have total control over your life is unrealistic since you may depend upon others also. You cannot control the behavior of other people—in your own families or in the world—and you can't control the course of nature.

However, you can have authority over your life. You choose to be the final decision maker on important issues that concern your mind, your body, and your work.

What's Not Negotiable

You can't change some things. You can't change your age, but you can do a number of things to minimize its influence, such as practicing preventive health measures, exercising, diet, and regular checkups.

When you have a handicap, you have a handicap. You can't negotiate for better eyesight, unparalysis, or unslurred speech, etc. You can, though, negotiate for better circumstances that allow you to perform effectively both at home and at work. At some point, disease can become a part of life. If cancer hits, it's non-negotiable. It is the same with Alzheimer's, diabetes, AIDS, and other diseases. You can, though, determine what type and course of treatments you will participate in.

The Do's and Don'ts

- *Don't* go in cold. You can't wing it. *Do* bring in some facts that you prepared in advance.

- *Don't* pitch to the wrong person, anyone who can't do anything for you. *Do* see the decision maker.

- *Don't* force your style on someone by giving reams of paper to a bottom-liner, for example, or, one piece of paper to someone who only acts on reams of information.

- *Do* be aware of your employer's personality and work style; try to match it.

- *Don't* become overly emotional. *Do* stay calm and focused on your goal.

- *Don't* assume anything. *Do* know what you *do* know, and what you *don't* know.

- *Don't* argue or attack. *Do* be willing to make concessions without forfeiting your goal.

If you are feeling besieged with personal, professional workplace disappointments, feel needy, or just scared, entering into a negotiation in these times is probably not in your best interests. Hold off for a few days. As you practice negotiating, you'll learn to get what you need. At the same time, you'll build skills and exchange ideas when working with others—critical tools for survival and advancement in today's workplace.

Life Phase 5: 50–65

For age is opportunity no less than youth itself.

—Longfellow

Chapter 18

—◆—◆—◆—◆—◆—◆—◆—◆—◆—◆—◆—◆—◆—◆—

Contentment and Simplicity

*R*arely do midlife crises extend into Life Phase 5. In fact, this is generally a period of contentment. Investments begin to produce rewards you can measure; your children, if you had them, have probably reached adulthood and become independent; and you can loosen up and begin to have some fun. You have become proficient in the art of living and might enjoy the role of philosopher or teacher.

This is not a time to enter into a high- or extreme-risk involvement, however. The investments you undertake should be fairly clear-cut and intermediate in term. In this life phase you can bring to bear the experience you have achieved in the preceding life phases as you have lived and worked through various economic cycles—some of them good, some fair, and some absolutely dismal.

This phase, or the preceding one, puts you in the sandwich generation. Not only are you raising your children, you may find yourself the caretaker of your parents. Do yourself, and them, a favor and find out where their money is.

If you haven't consulted an estate-planning attorney by now, you should (more about this in chapter 19). In addition, you should take a closer look at the dollars you have accumulated and at the profit potential of investments you are already participating in. These will be your primary sources of future income and should allow you to reap some reward for your long years of work—but it's not always as easy as it sounds.

YOUR HOME

Home ownership and the selling of a home after you reach fifty-five bring into play a number of tax ramifications. If you haven't already taken your once-in-a-lifetime $125,000 exemption, consider doing so now.

ANNUITIES AND ESTATE PLANNING

This is a stage in your life when you will be approached about participating in annuities. It is also the stage at which you must review your will (or write one) and do serious estate planning. See Wilson J. Humber's *Saving the Best for Last* or Austin Pryor's *IRA's and Annuities* (both Moody, 1994).

◆ MS. MISC. ◆

As you cross over the halfway mark (fifty-five plus), it doesn't make sense to make long-term commitments for the latter part of this life phase. You should instead be taking profits and aggressively accumulating them in funds that will produce income as you enter the next phase.

If you decide to participate in an annuity, consider the commitment needed to get its full benefits. It is true that the placement of funds in an annuity allows you to change your mind and get your moneys back in seven days, thus satisfying your need for overall liquidity. But there are strings attached, and you will have to pay penalties on the interest you have accumulated if you withdraw too soon. Treasury obligations, tax-exempt bonds, corporate bonds, and high-yielding time deposits are all reasonable alternatives for your liquid funds at this time.

Finally, if you have not taken a close look at your insurance needs, as well as the possibility of using a trust, this is the time to do so. Assuming you have few dependents now, your need for life insurance may be substantially reduced, even eliminated. If you are married and die unexpectedly, your assets could go to your spouse without incurring any taxes. Of course, the question is: If your spouse dies, where will his accumulated assets go, and what tax consequences will they carry with them prior to the next set of heirs receiving them?

If you are unwilling to pass the responsibility and power of handling your money to someone else, either for your own benefit or that of your heirs, then trusts may not be your cup of tea. I would recommend that you enter this phase with some flexibility, so that you can make decisions and later change your mind if a decision proves inappropriate for you emotionally and/or physically.

If you have previously engaged an attorney to put together a trust, make sure you have it reassessed and/or revised each time a new tax act passes.

◆ WINDFALL! ◆

A $10,000 windfall during this phase can affect people in a number of ways. If you haven't done anything at all for your retirement and you recognize that it is not that far off, you may grasp the money and almost squeeze it to death. If this is your feeling, you should put it into preferred stocks, utility stocks, high-yield savings accounts, an annuity, or discount bonds. Rarely should it go into a speculative endeavor.

On the other hand, if you have been saving through the various life phases and a $10,000 windfall comes your way, you may look at it almost as a reward—something you can spend in order to have a good time. I have known many women who have taken a dream cruise or trip abroad, feeling that they would never have had the freedom to spend the money if Great-uncle Waldo hadn't left them the $10,000.

Another way of dealing with such a windfall is to place it, as you did in the previous life phases, in different investments, such as the stock market or an art collection, or even to lend it to the kids for a first home. A word of caution here: I have always felt that if you choose to lend funds to family members, it is best to consider them a gift. But you should get a promissory note as you normally would with any loan you make. If the money can't be paid back at the appropriate time, your mental note that it was a gift will reduce the anxiety and anger you may feel. Otherwise, you may end up terminating a relationship.

KEEP GROWING!

I think one of the worst things anyone can do in this particular phase is to stop working completely. Even though you may be able to take early retirement, don't just stay at home. Divert yourself into other channels—either by helping others or by reeducating yourself and focusing your energies on one of the hobbies you kept on the back burner during other life phases.

This is also a time to be checking in with various organizations, clubs, or even community colleges where classes on pre-retirement and retirement planning are offered.

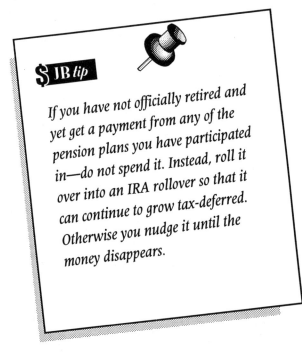

$ JB *tip*

If you have not officially retired and yet get a payment from any of the pension plans you have participated in—do not spend it. Instead, roll it over into an IRA rollover so that it can continue to grow tax-deferred. Otherwise you nudge it until the money disappears.

Quiz

You are getting phone calls nightly from a life insurance salesman. He has convinced you that at a minimum, you should review your insurance policies. He also has told you that you probably need to get new insurance. What do you do?

(a) Don't answer the door when he comes out for the appointment you set up.

(b) Keep the appointment and agree to buy new insurance, canceling your old policies.

(c) Get an evaluation from at least two other brokers before you cancel or buy anything.

Answer: (c) is the only reasonable answer. It's a good personal strategy to assess your coverage. In fact, you may not need any life insurance now — no dependents, kids gone, minimal debt, and your estate is under $600,000. There will, therefore, be no federal estate taxes.

◆   PHASING UP   ◆

By the time you have reached this life phase, you have probably received all four types of income. As you'll recall, *taxable income* includes the amount you received on your W-2 during your working years and the majority of any interest income that you receive from savings, bonds, and/or dividends.

You were introduced to *tax-deferred income* when you initiated your IRA or participated in a 401(k) program. Annuities also bring you a form of tax deferral. Remember that tax deferral is merely a means of deferring your tax obligations until a later date.

Tax-sheltered income is normally received from investments that have a form of depreciation attached. They actually produce cash flow, but because of the depreciation loss, the IRS allows that cash to come to you without a tax obligation attached. Capital gains are another type of tax-sheltered income. You never pay 100 percent of any gain to taxes, only a portion.

The final type of income is *tax exempt*. This is the income that is received from municipal bonds, for which you do not have to declare any federal tax.

There are other forms of partially exempt bonds, such as Treasury obligations. Treasury bills, bonds, and notes are taxable on your federal return but tax exempt on your state return. Tax-sheltered and tax-exempt incomes are the best kind. These are what you should be working for.

You will find this to be an era of simplicity. The control and placement of your funds is the cornerstone of your personal money management success. It has little to do with the overall dollars you have accumulated over a lifetime in a bank or savings institution. By this phase, you should be able to control your money as if it were a puppet and you the master puppeteer pulling the various strings.

During this phase, you concentrate on building your wealth and retirement accounts. It is also the time when you really do start thinking about tomorrow today.

Proverbs 14:1 resurfaces here. "The wise woman builds her house, but with her own hands the foolish one tears hers down." With the wisdom

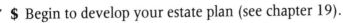

you have gained through the years, your house has a firm foundation for the rest of your life.

Your Phase Focus is:

$ Begin to develop your estate plan (see chapter 19).

$ Begin to explore retirement goals.

$ Evaluate and update retirement plans.

$ If needed, continue to pay college costs for your kids.

$ Review your health, life, and disability insurance.

$ Evaluate your investments and start moving more toward income-producing investments versus aggressive-growth investments.

$ Know your tax bracket so that you can compare returns on regular bonds and municipal bonds.

$ Never buy a limited partnership.

$ Continue to save at least 10 percent of your income.

◆ RETIREMENT BONUS ◆

If you had put $2,000 per year from the age of eighteen into an IRA earning 12 percent, your accumulated value at the end of this phase would be $3,821,179.60. What a great way to enter the sixth phase.

Chapter 19

Estate Planning

*Y*ou will die someday. If it were tomorrow, would your financial house be in order, or are you like 75 percent of America—tomorrow is another day?

The most common strategy for estate planning is to have a will. Refer back to chapter 15 for details, along with the dos and don'ts of putting together a will and selecting an executor. If three years have passed since you completed your will, dig it out and review it. Do you still want your ex-husband's sister to have your prized paperweight collection? If not, make an appointment with your attorney for a revision.

PAIN IN THE JOINTS

As you move through this phase, resist the temptation to place assets and properties into joint ownership with your children. Joint ownership is often the cause of horrendous problems. It is certainly convenient and does offer a means for transferring property when one of the owners dies, but there are strings attached.

Let's say you have your thirty-five-year-old daughter jointly listed on your money market checking account. You did that to ensure her access to the account if you become ill or are unable to go to the bank, and so that if you die she would have all the assets in that account.

Sounds good, but there could be problems. If your daughter is in a higher tax bracket than you, she must pay the income tax on her share of the interest earned through the year on that account. In addition, if your daughter's death precedes yours, the entire account could be taxed as part of her estate. Surprised? Most are when they get caught in this situation. A better alternative would be to give your daughter a power of attorney—written authorization for her to act on your behalf in all your financial affairs—and then, in your will, leave your assets to her.

DO YOU KNOW WHERE YOUR PARENTS' MONEYS ARE?

Most of us don't, and it becomes a real tug-of-war to get the details. Your parents probably come from the generation of not talking about what was made or invested. Yet in this life phase, you will most likely get involved with the management of your parents' money. And, most likely, if one parent is alive, it will be your mother.

Usually, you begin to learn the details when there is an illness or death. Don't wait for either. Begin a conversation now. Don't be surprised if they don't want to discuss it—after all, most of us don't like to talk about death and dying. If your parent mentions the medical and financial problems of her friends, you have a perfect opening. Ask if she is confident her financial affairs are in order. Ask what you can do to make sure that you will do everything she wants done if she died or couldn't make decisions for herself.

Here are the topics that are essential for you to probe:

1. Does she have any investments? When was the last time they were evaluated? It's quite common for older parents to buy and put certificates in a safe deposit box and forget about them. Update her holdings for safety, quality of the companies, and to determine if the investments match her income needs.

2. Does she have a current will? Remind her that having one will guarantee that her wishes are followed down to who takes care of her cat.

3. Does she have any life insurance policies? If your mother lives off her investments, pensions, and Social Security, and is not supporting anyone, why does she need life insurance?

   The only reason to have it is if her estate will exceed $600,000 and there is no cash or liquid investments to pay the tax required on estates over $600,000. Otherwise, she's wasting her money. Stop the premiums and cash in the cash value unless she's on her death bed.

4. Ask her where she wants to live if she becomes incapacitated. If she prefers a nursing home, start researching what is available. If she prefers home health, locate a visiting nurse unit so you know all the rules and requirements before the need arises. If she prefers to live with you or your siblings—are you set up, or are they, for Mom to move in?

5. Where does she keep her documents? You need to know what banks, accountants, attorneys, stockbrokers, financial planners, and insurance agents she has worked with. The paper trail is critical. Where does she keep records of her investments, her pensions, her birth certificate, and her Social Security information? Let her know you aren't interested in how much she has—you want to know where to find things so you can help out if there is an unexpected illness or an accident.

   Several books are available that would help organize her (and your) life. One is by Donald Upp called *One of These Days, We'll have to Get Organized*. You can get a copy by writing JADLU Press, Box 554, Jenison, MI 49429. Enclose a check for $21.95. This book covers everything from who to call if the water pipes break to funeral arrangements.

$ JB *tip*

Start on this now. My father is eighty-three. It is like pulling teeth to get information out of him. I should have probed ten years ago.

ZEROING IN

I need to mention one other Treasury security: zero coupon bonds. This bond has no current coupon, or interest payment. You buy it at a fraction of its mature value ($1,000). Interest is usually compounded semiannually within the bond. You might spend $456 to buy a ten-year zero in January 1995, yielding 8 percent. In 2005, you will get $1,000.

Zeros work well in saving for retirement. If you will have a mortgage when retirement approaches, buy zeros that will mature when you retire. You pay off the mortgage and increase your monthly cash flow at the same time.

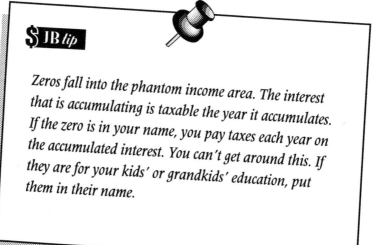

$ JB *tip*

Zeros fall into the phantom income area. The interest that is accumulating is taxable the year it accumulates. If the zero is in your name, you pay taxes each year on the accumulated interest. You can't get around this. If they are for your kids' or grandkids' education, put them in their name.

$) JB tip

When you own zeros, do not plan to sell them—hold them until they mature. Because interest rates, in general, move around, the underlying value of these bonds can change in value too. Buy them and stay put.

NOTHING IS FREE

When an attorney prepares your will, you will sign it in the presence of witnesses. You receive a copy and your attorney keeps a copy in his or her vaults. That's the one service an attorney offers free. Granted, your will won't take up much space, but there's a reason behind the freebie.

Your attorney bills you for the legal expenses of drawing up your will. When you die, your heirs will need an attorney to take your will through the court process of probate—changing the names on all your assets as directed by your will (discussed in chapter 15). Who best to do it but the person who drew it up? Ah, a method behind his/her madness!

The legal fees for handling an estate through probate can be many times the fees charged for writing the will. In many states, probate fees are based on a percentage of the gross value of the estate. If you have a young attorney, he or she will hope to outlive you and earn the probate fees. An older attorney will have shelves of wills in the vault, just waiting to be probated by a younger partner.

Alas, there's never a free lunch. Your attorney may have a breakfast on what he made preparing your will. When you die, he will be able to take a vacation on what he makes taking your estate through probate!

PROBATE

Probate has nothing to do with taxes. It is the legal process of changing the title on assets you own into the names of your heirs when you die. The probate court resolves disputes, pays off creditors, inventories your estate, and distributes your assets. If there's no will, it distributes your assets according to state law. Now this can be scary.

This process presents a double whammy:

1. It is expensive—legal fees can be as much as 10 percent of the total value of your gross estate. In states where the gross valuation of assets is the basis for determining legal fees, the court does not deduct the amount of any loans—including mortgages—from the asset side. Ouch!

2. It can take a long time (it shouldn't, but it often does). It is not uncommon for estates to take more than two years to process. If you own property in states other than your residence, the process is repeated in each state where you own real estate.

Probate is part of the Lawyer's Full Employment Act!

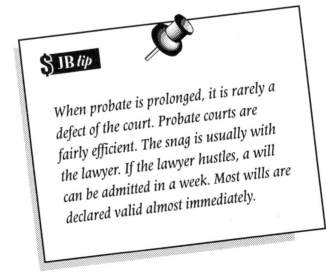

$ JB tip

When probate is prolonged, it is rarely a defect of the court. Probate courts are fairly efficient. The snag is usually with the lawyer. If the lawyer hustles, a will can be admitted in a week. Most wills are declared valid almost immediately.

THE LIVING TRUST (AKA INTER VIVOS TRUST)

A trust is a legal entity that can own, buy, and sell assets. When you personally transfer items to a trust, you no longer own them. The trust does. Have you lost control? Nope. Name yourself trustee and you are in charge. A living trust is like a will, in that in most cases it is revocable, meaning that you can change it as often as you want.

The primary purpose of trusts is to control the distribution and use of the assets, as well as to minimize taxes. There are several kinds of trusts. One is a revocable trust, which merely means that you can change the basic provisions of the trust, or totally void it. An irrevocable trust is a trust that cannot be changed.

A trust can be established at any time. If in your will you state that you want to establish a trust, then it will be titled a "testamentary trust." A testamentary trust provides that a specific percentage of your overall estate will be set aside and managed for a particular individual.

The person who manages the trust is called a trustee. This may be either an individual or an institution such as a bank. Some banks do an excellent job of managing trusts, others do not. Some individuals do an excellent job of managing trusts, others do not. Before you decide who is to be the trustee of your assets, make sure that you check out that person or institution thoroughly. Some of the biggest banks in the country have the worst track records.

There are two schools of thought on whether to have an individual or an institution, such as a bank, act as trustee. It is clear that a banking institution will have more experience and be aware of the necessary paperwork that has to be filed. It is (one hopes) competent and, if there is any mismanagement or fraud, has the necessary bonding to make restitution. Individuals, as a rule, do not have that.

But, there is still the nagging fear that once you let an institution take over the management and responsibility, it is out of your control. How can you handle that?

By making the bank or trust company serve as a "co-trustee" with a relative or a valued personal adviser of the grantor (you). A stipulation can be placed in a trust agreement stating that the individual trustee—for example, your spouse or your primary beneficiary has the right to remove the corporate trustee and name another in its place. Another method of dealing with that is setting up an *inter vivos* revocable trust. This will provide the opportunity to evaluate the trustee's competency during the grantor's lifetime.

Advantages of a Living Trust

Here's what a trust can do in a nutshell:

1. It allows for continuity of your personal finances and business.

2. It maintains your privacy after you die. Wills are public documents; trusts aren't. That is why very wealthy people are rarely reported to have zillions of dollars at their deaths. The great majority of their assets are buried in trusts—for their, their family's, and their attorney's eyes only.

3. All assets in the trust bypass probate.

The cost of creating a living trust can range from $500 to $2,500, depending on your needs and the attorney's fees.

The living trust is not the answer to all estate planning issues, but it certainly does create flexibility in managing estate issues. The living trust, by itself, *does not* save federal or state death taxes. But it *does* save all the costs of probating your will; at the same time it gives your estate a high degree of privacy, both in death and during your lifetime, should you become incapacitated and require a conservator to look after your financial affairs.

Transferring Your Assets to Your Trust

When you create a living trust, you have work to do. It is important to immediately retitle all your assets in the name of the trust as soon as possible. If you don't, and you die, everything treks through the probate court—exactly what you wanted to avoid!

Your attorney should provide the necessary papers to transfer title of your house. If you have a mortgage, your lender has to approve the transfer (lenders do this all the time, so it shouldn't be a problem). Some states require a new deed when real estate is put into a trust.

If you own any stocks, bonds, mutual funds, CDs, annuities, or any other financial assets that have your name on them—change them. Get certified copies of the first and last pages of your trust documents and the page that grants the trustee's (usually you) power.

Your renamed account will look like this:

> Elizabeth Ann Jones revocable living trust dated 1-29-95,
> Elizabeth Ann Jones, trustee.

From now on, you will add "trustee" after you sign your name on your checks for such things as stocks and CDs. Unless you have a Rolls Royce, keep your car in your name as it was, along with your household checking account.

For any items not in your living trust, you need a *pour-over will* that will distribute the leftovers after your death. The pour-over will handles the assets not placed in the trust—they will go through a regular probate. But, if you retitled everything promptly, this should be a minimal cost—all your valuable assets have been transferred already.

You don't need a new taxpayer ID number—your Social Security number is sufficient—and your living trust does not have to file a separate tax return. Everything is included in your regular tax return.

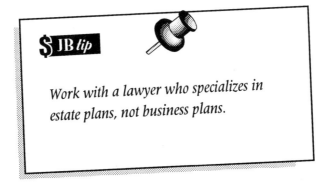

$ JB tip

Work with a lawyer who specializes in estate plans, not business plans.

$ JB tip

Most people know about wills and that's what they ask for when doing estate planning. Lawyers are quite familiar with the advantages of a living trust—but if you ask for a will, that's what you get. Ask about a living trust estate plan.

Leaving Money in Trust

A *testamentary trust* is set up by your will. Instead of leaving money directly to the beneficiary, you leave it in trust, to be managed by a trustee. Funds can be paid out for various purposes. At some point, the trust dissolves and the money is distributed. You get to decide when.

A trust can hold money until a child grows up. But don't try to control from the grave. By the time he or she is thirty, the child should be able to get the money and swim—or sink.

A trust can save estate taxes. If your net worth is over $600,000, talk to a lawyer about how to cut federal taxes. Often, you can do it without using a trust. The state may levy taxes on net worths less than $600,000; not all match the $600,000 federal exclusion.

A trust can manage money left to a spouse. A trustee runs the money. Your spouse receives the income and, if needed, payment out of principal. When your spouse dies, the remaining money goes to whoever is named. A family member, bank, or investment adviser is usually the trustee.

The spouse should be able to change trustees if the relationship isn't working. Again give the option—many surviving spouses do a better job than the friendly bank. Don't lock all your money in trust. Your spouse may have ignored managing money when you were alive, but could thrive when you're gone. Allow some flexibility.

A trust can provide for retarded or disabled children. State and federal programs cover basic medical and residential care, but only if the child has almost no money. This presents parents with a Catch 22: Money left to the disabled child will be consumed by the institution, guaranteed. If there's no money, the child will get only bare-bones support. A parental nightmare.

Middle-income parents may feel that they have little choice. They leave their modest assets to their healthy children and let the handicapped one get government aid. If this is the case, you should specifically disinherit the handicapped child (and tell your relatives to do likewise). You hope and pray that your healthy children will provide the extra comforts that their institutionalized sibling needs.

Do your entire family a huge favor and call a pow-wow. Be blunt about the situation and get their commitment that they will be there for their sibling. Promises made at times like these usually glue for life. Don't assume—tell them what you expect. If they can't commit, you know who to leave your money to.

If you have money, set up a trust. The disabled child (having little or no money) can usually qualify for government aid. The trust supplies extra maintenance and support, not dependent on siblings' generosity. For advice on how to do this, call your state or local Association for Retarded Citizens. Ask for the names of lawyers experienced in your state's public-assistance laws. For the booklet *How to Provide for Their Future*, send $8 to the Association for Retarded Citizens, P.O. Box 1047, Arlington, TX 76004.

A trust can assure that the children of a prior marriage will inherit. If you leave all your money to your new spouse, he can do anything with it, including cutting your children out. A trust prevents this. If you want, you can give your spouse an income for life while guaranteeing that your children will ultimately inherit when he dies.

DURABLE POWER OF ATTORNEY

You need a backup, someone who can act in your behalf if you are away, sick, in an accident—or if you can't function. Someone who is trusted—your spouse, friend, adult child, parent—is given your power of attorney. Age doesn't matter—both young and old should have a backup. This is a "doomsday" protection.

A durable power of attorney should be re-executed every four or five years. This shows that your intent still holds. If you want to cancel it, tell the person holding it that he or she is out and ask for your document back. If there are duplicate copies of the power of attorney, write to any institutions holding your money and tell them not to honor the person as your agent and let them know who the replacement is. If you are reluctant to trust anyone now, write a *springing* power of attorney. It only becomes active if you are incapacitated. Your springing power of attorney will define what that means. It will read something like this:

> I shall be deemed disabled when two physicians licensed to practice medicine in my state sign a paper stating that I am disabled and unable to handle my financial affairs. If this happens, then Susan Adams will handle my affairs.

You can use the same type of language to determine when the disability has passed.

LIVING WILLS

What did Richard Nixon and Jacqueline Kennedy Onassis have in common? The desire to die with dignity. Both had signed living wills prohibiting artificial life support.

Anyone who has been with a dying or comatose friend or relative hooked up to a zillion machines—sometimes painfully—understands the issue of the right to die. Many never authorize anyone to pull the plug and are kept alive because of state law or custom.

Living wills cover only terminal patients. You give the power to the doctor by specifying in advance which treatments you want and don't want should you become fatally ill.

Even if you have a living will, your daughter can say, "I don't care what Mom thought she wanted, continue to treat her." And the doctor probably will.

The best way to have your wishes carried out is to appoint someone to do it. You can do this in your living will. Even better, prepare a health care durable power of attorney. Most states have no problem recognizing this document.

Under a health care durable power of attorney, nonterminal cases—such as comas—are covered. You appoint a trusted relative or friend who knows your wishes to tell the doctor how far to go in trying to keep you alive.

A health care power of attorney should be drawn up by a lawyer so that it conforms to your state's laws and court precedents. Lawyers advise that you name two stand-ins to act for you, in case one isn't around when critical decisions have to be made. Your spouse, a relative, a close friend, and (possibly) your doctor are the most appropriate choices. To avoid inaction or delay, either one should be able to act alone.

Finally, shout it from the mountaintops. Let everyone know about your decision—children, spouse, doctor, friends. It isn't enough to sign a living will. You have to go out of your way to be sure it is honored. That is what I have done. I have told everyone who is close to me that I want nothing done to keep me alive just for the sake of breathing. I have told my husband, my kids, my friends, my doctors—and now you: Pull the plug!

As you have read this chapter, you may have thought, *Well, this doesn't sound too overwhelming.* If so, I have succeeded in my task—one of my missions in writing *Money Sense* was to demystify the money maze. Wills and trusts are loaded with potholes. Please, please get legal advice and use an estate planning attorney to guide you.

Life Phase 6: 65 and Over

Mrs. Nancy McKeen, of West Stoneham, Maine, has the honor of having killed the largest bear ever captured in that region. The bear was chasing her sheep, when she attacked him with a club, and, after a hard-fought battle, succeeded in laying him out. Mrs. McKeen is eighty-three years of age, in good health, and says she is ready for another bear.

—Alice Stone Blackwell, ed.,
The Woman's Column,
March 14, 1896

Chapter 20

—◆—◆—◆—◆—◆—◆—◆—◆—◆—◆—◆—◆—◆—◆—

Consumer Again

*B*ecause of the experience you have developed through each of the previous life phases, you are now in a position to be considered a master. Your depth of experience and common sense will guide you in the decisions you will make during this final phase. If you haven't already retired, you may be seriously considering it. You will hopefully live out your remaining years comfortably, without worry, stress, or strain from money-related issues (or bears). This is a time to stay away from debt and to keep abreast of any tax changes. In this final life phase, liquidity should be the key to what are often referred to as the golden years.

You are past the age of growth and capital appreciation and are now entering an era in which you will again become a consumer. As interest, dividends, or other gains come to fruition during this period, you will more than likely spend these moneys on ongoing living expenses. You could, of course, have other supplemental income such as Social Security, private pensions, and all the dollars you have been setting aside in your own retirement programs. By the time you reach the age of seventy and a half, you are required to begin withdrawing funds from your IRA, SEP, or Keogh accounts. These funds have accumulated over the years if you have been faithful and consistent in placing dollars there, and they should help enable you to enjoy this life phase.

If you haven't taken any classes on the needs of the retirement community, you should enroll in one. You might find a pastime that is enjoyable and sociable and provides you with extra funds. I know many women who spend this phase rediscovering family, friends, and fun. In the past they were too busy working to really let their hair down. They can now enjoy what they have been able to accumulate, spend their money, and make gifts to family.

THE TAX MAN COMETH

At this point, taxes should be fairly simple and not take up much time. Income will come from retirement accounts (some taxable, some nontaxable), interest and dividends, and possibly even from an avocation or offshoot of your previous career.

As a rule, your nontaxable income will be in areas such as municipal bonds and Social Security. You may owe taxes on up to half of your Social Security benefits if income from all your sources—pension, dividends, interest, municipal bond interest—exceeds $25,000 if you are single or $32,000 if you are married. This is subject to change by Congress. Other forms of income are partially taxable, such as a pension or profit-sharing account in which you contributed dollars that were taxed in previous years when you were employed with a particular company.

Income from time deposits, passbook accounts, and money market funds are taxable. If you are receiving funds on a monthly, quarterly, or annual basis from an annuity, a portion of those will be taxable. You will recall from Life Phase 5 that taxes on annuities are a function of your predicted life expectancy and the amount of money you funded the annuity with.

If you have stocks—in particular, utility stocks—a portion of the dividend you receive may be nontaxable. The company you own stock in will inform you at the end of each year which portion of the dividend, if any, will be excluded from taxes. Also, you may wish to have the company reinvest your dividends in additional stock, thereby making them nontaxable until such time as the stocks are sold.

Bonds, as a rule, are fully taxable. Exceptions, of course, are municipal bonds, if you are a resident in the state of their origin. If you own a municipal bond that originates in another state, you should declare the interest you receive as income on your state tax return.

You may also have income from rental property. Because of the IRS's allowances for depreciation, a portion of the rents may be tax sheltered. If you are receiving income from retirement accounts—IRAs, SEPs or a Keogh, 401(k), 403(b)—it is fully taxable, none of it being sheltered as you withdraw it.

If you sell your residence during this phase, not all the proceeds will be taxable. Remember that you have the opportunity to use the once-in-a-lifetime $125,000 exclusion for individuals over fifty-five years of age. Even if you bought a house several years ago for $25,000 and now sell it for $125,000, you will have no capital gains to declare.

I think it is a good idea to make a Taxable Income Chart with columns labeled *Taxable, Nontaxable,* and *Partially Taxable*:

RETIREMENT INCOME TAXATION CHART
—•—•—•—•—•—•—•—•—•—•—•—•—•—•—•—

Income Source	Taxable	Nontaxable	Partially Taxable
Social Security			◆
Corporate Bonds	◆		
Municipal Bonds			◆
Treasuries			◆
Annuities			◆
Dividends	◆		
Interest	◆		
IRAs, SEPs, Keoghs	◆		
Pension Plans	◆		
401(k), 403(b)	◆		
Inheritance		◆	
$ Gifts		◆	
Employment	◆		
Rental Property			◆
_____			
_____			
_____			
_____			
TOTAL	$ _____	$ _____	$ _____

Treasuries are tax free in your state, taxable for federal purposes; tax-deferred annuities will not be taxed on your original principal; depending on expenses, rental income and depreciation and income from rental property can fit in all three categories. If you are still earning money from a job, Social Security has limits on how much you can make before you have to give a percentage back—check with them, it changes each year.

After listing your incomes under the appropriate columns, and totaling the columns, you will have an idea of your gross taxable income. You can then proceed to adjust for your personal deductions. For example, if you are over sixty-five, you get not only an exemption for yourself, but also one for being sixty-five. If you have any other areas that give you some tax benefits, such as a mortgage payment, real estate taxes, or contributions, make sure you include those in your calculations.

It is important to do this because you no longer have regular withholding, unless you are still employed and receive a W-2 form at the end of the year. The government now wants you to submit tax-liability estimates on a quarterly basis. This means you will be sending in federal tax money every three months instead of having it withheld, as would happen with a normal paycheck. If you continue to work and receive wages in addition to receiving funds from other sources, you will calculate the amount withheld from your paycheck as well as the amount you need to pay quarterly. It is not a lot of fun to do all these calculations, but it is essential.

WITHHOLDING ON DEFERRED INCOME

Under present law, payers must withhold tax from some designated distributions. Designated distributions are defined as the taxable portion of payments made from or under:

- a pension, profit-sharing, stock bonus, or annuity plan.

- a deferred compensation plan in which payments are not considered wages.

- an IRA, SEP, Keogh, 401(k), or 403(b) plan.

- a commercial annuity contract.

- a partial surrender of an annuity contract.

The nature of the distribution determines the withholding rate:

Periodic payments (usually annuity payments) are treated like wages received from an employer.

Nonperiodic payments: These usually are subject to some withholding.

A recipient may, however, choose not to have tax withheld. The payer must advise the payee of that right.

During this phase, your income will come from a variety of sources. Money market funds, short-term certificates of deposit, annuities, income stocks (particularly utilities), Treasury obligations, municipal bonds, and short-term bonds are all valuable in this particular phase.

A word of caution here. You may find yourself holding as many as thirty individual issues of stocks and bonds. These are difficult for you to keep track of, and when you die they can become a headache for the executor of your estate and your heirs. Make life a little easier for yourself and your family. Slim your portfolio down to fewer investments so that you can track the dividends and interest due you and keep updated on each of the companies with greater efficiency and freedom.

SHARING YOUR WEALTH

If you have any real estate that is not returning a cash flow, you might consider selling it. If you have a substantial gain in some of your asset areas and are considering selling them, determine what the tax on your gains will be. If you plan on leaving assets to heirs, it may make sense to make a gift prior to sale. For example, you have a parcel of land originally costing $50,000. It has appreciated another $50,000, giving it an overall value of $100,000.

Depending upon your overall estate situation, you may elect to give a portion to five beneficiaries and then encourage the sale of the land parcel. The result is that you are not responsible for the capital gain because your beneficiaries now own it. Each has received, tax free, $10,000 as a gift. When they sell, they pay the tax on the gain. Remember also that when you make a gift, it is a gift and does not have any strings attached.

WHICH TAX IS WHAT?

Federal Estate Taxes

Several taxes may surface in the handling of your estate. The first is the Federal Estate Tax. This tax is levied on the current market value of any assets owed by an individual at her death. In making this calculation, the funds that have been spent on the estate administration, burial and final illness, debts, bequests to a spouse, and any charitable contributions are deducted. If the final amount is less than $600,000, then no Federal Estate Tax is due. In an estate of $625,000, you will pay 37 percent on the $25,000 over the exempt amount of $600,000. Uncle Sam gets $9,050.

State Taxes

State estate taxes are imposed by some states but not all. These will be based on the maximum federal credit that is allowed for the state death taxes.

Inheritance Taxes

Inheritance taxes are imposed by some states, but not all, on bequests made by a decedent in her will. Taxes will vary.

Federal Gift Tax

This is a tax on property that is transferred during an individual's lifetime. It is usually paid by the donor, or the person who is making the gift.

State Gift Tax

Here again, depending upon the state, the tax amount will vary.

TECHNIQUES TO REDUCE YOUR TAXABLE ESTATE

Give Your Money Away

You can give money to your church. Amen.

You can give money to charity. Make sure you give the exact name and location of your charity choices.

You can give your money away while you are alive. You can give $10,000 per year to everyone on your street. If you are married, you and your husband can give $20,000—and will everyone love you! Your gift can be in stocks, bonds, mutual funds—you name it. If it has grown in value since your purchase of it, you bypass taxes (no sale, no tax).

Marry

If you are single, you can marry! There are no estate taxes with a spouse. Tax does, however, come into play when the second spouse dies. If you have assets in excess of $600,000, see your estate planning attorney now and create a Bypass Trust. When done properly, you can end up leaving double the $600,000 amount to heirs, at the death of the second spouse, tax free.

Give Away Your Life Insurance Policy

You can give away your life insurance policy. This pulls it out of your estate. The new owner must pay the premiums. There is some delicate handling of who should be trustee, beneficiary, etc. so that it doesn't come back to your estate—it's attorney time again! Insurance companies are used to having their policies given away. Ask for an *assignment form*. If you still work and have insurance through your company, you can also give your group policy away.

Disclaim an Inheritance

If you are comfortable and don't need money, you can disclaim an inheritance from someone who will leave you money, and let it pass to the next heir—possibly your kids. This keeps the money out of your estate.

Create a Trust

You can create a trust. Through the use of trusts, part of the tax bite can be reduced. Trusts are discussed in greater detail in chapter 19, "Estate Planning."

All of the above assumes you have money to comfortably live on. *Do not give away money merely to avoid taxes.*

Prior tax laws stated that if any gifts were made three years prior to your death, they would be pulled back into the estate for tax purposes. Today's law eliminates this possibility and ensures that gifts made up to the day before your death will not be included in your estate.

If you are married, it may not make sense to own everything in joint name. With the current tax law, if one of you dies, there is no limit on bequests and gifts that would go to the surviving spouse. Everything you decide to leave to your mate is considered tax-free.

ESTATE UNDERTOWS

Funds Held Only Jointly

Let's say that you have $30,000 in a joint savings account at your local bank. You also have jointly owned stocks and bonds as well as other assets. If one of you were to die, jointly owned assets would be frozen pending probate. If you have had the unfortunate experience of going through probate, you know that it can take months, even years to fully settle the estate.

Unless the surviving spouse has personal assets to pay for ongoing living expenses, he or she may be in a fix. It could take several weeks or even months before the money is finally paid out to the beneficiaries. You would probably have been better off to put the $30,000 in three different accounts, $10,000 of it jointly held, $10,000 of it in your spouse's name, and $10,000 in your own name. That way, while the probate paperwork was being done, the surviving spouse would have immediate access to funds to take care of his or her living expenses.

An Outdated Statement of Marital Deduction

Under present law, a person can leave a spouse unlimited assets without tax liability. But if you have a will that is dated prior to 1981 that specifically states that the marital deduction of $250,000 is in effect in the transfer of assets, your estate could be taxed from one spouse to another when assets exceed $250,000.

To prevent that from occurring, include in your will the provision that if there is a marital deduction or transfer from one spouse to another, it should meet current law at the time of death.

Delay in Freezing the Estate

Sam's mother died and he served as executor. His brother-in-law was a CPA with one of the largest accounting firms in America. The stockbroker was a member of a highly prestigious firm, which had been swallowed up by an even larger, highly prestigious firm. The attorney was one of those high-priced attorneys who charges for every thirty seconds.

Sam wasn't totally tuned into the situation, being a stubborn scientist busy with his work and not a worldly financial type. Because of his lack of financial know-how, Sam assumed his brother-in-law and broker would have known of any legal constraints that could encumber or "lock up" the account when his mother died. Wrong assumption.

What was required but never took place was a serious discussion with and among all individuals regarding the modest, but significant $100,000 nest egg. The purpose of the nest egg was to fund the mother's lifestyle as a semi-paralyzed invalid, had she remained alive. It became evident that the nest egg was no longer needed because she was rapidly dying from cancer. Preserving money for the heirs and paying outstanding debts and taxes should have become the main objective, but no one seemed to see this, not even the professionals.

All kinds of goofy ideas were presented—many were acted on. Money was lost in investments that no one should have put money in. The estate was well under $100,000 when Sam's mother died. The broker became nervous about some of the trades and finally told the firm of the woman's death. At that time, the account was frozen—which it should have been when the mother died.

If the estate had been frozen at the appropriate time, approximately

$20,000 would have been saved. Investments that had been made on the "death bed" were inappropriate—all made either to make a quick buck or to avoid taxes. The irony was—the estate was so small, that there were no taxes due in the first place!

SOCIAL SECURITY AND YOU

You can start collecting Social Security as early as sixty-two. The amount you will receive will be a percentage of the full amount at sixty-five. (Retirement age is being gradually increased to sixty-seven.) You have several choices, particularly if you are married, so make sure you have the Social Security representative explain each one. If you defer receiving Social Security past sixty-five, make sure you sign up for Medicare.

You can contact one of the thirteen hundred Social Security offices nationwide—your phone book will give you the local number under "U.S. Government." If you don't want to go in person, you can make a phone appointment. Call 800-772-1213 to set one up, Monday through Friday, 7:00 A.M. to 7:00 P.M. Best times to call are early (7:00–9:00 A.M.) or late (5:00–7:00 P.M.) and on Wednesday through Friday.

Before approving any benefit, the government wants your Social Security number, certified original birth certificate, and the birth certificate of anyone else applying for benefits (could be spouse, even kids)—no photocopies—and proof of how much you made last year. That's it. If you don't have some of the above, the office will suggest substitutes. You can apply three months prior to receiving your first check. Checks can be mailed to your home or wired to your checking or savings account. Wires are usually received by the third of each month. Mail is mail—if you have great service, you'll get it within a week of the first day of the month. If you have wimpy service, have your moneys wired—I think it's the best way.

When Should You Start Collecting?

It depends. If you are over sixty-two and need money, the answer is now. If your health is poor, do it now. If no one in your family ever lives past seventy-five, do it now. Otherwise, hold off until you are sixty-five or older.

Why older? Benefits will actually ratchet up each year until you are seventy—after that, there is no real benefit in waiting. In January of each year, all Social Security recipients get a raise based on inflation.

It makes money sense to sit down with a calculator, paper, and pencil and work out your options. Earnings, age, marital status, and your spouse's age and earnings are all factors to the bottom line.

Social Security Limits

When you earn too much, your Social Security check is reduced. In 1994, "too much" was just under $8,000 if you were under sixty-five; for over sixty-five to sixty-nine, just under $13,000. This figure changes with the January inflation adjustment. If you earn over the limit and are under sixty-five, you are dinged one dollar for every two dollars you make. If you are over sixty-five, you are dinged one dollar for every three dollars you make. If you are over seventy, you can earn an unlimited amount without jeopardizing your benefits.

Social Security says that if you are under seventy and expect to exceed the limit, you must report it to them. They will adjust your check accordingly. Report your earning on Form SSA-777 (Social Security will supply it) and a copy of your tax return. If you earn more than you expected, you have to return the extra money Social Security paid out. If you don't, you will be penalized 20 percent on the amount overpaid.

What If You Go Back to Work?

You can stop your benefits, and when you start up again, Social Security will refigure your payments. You can also pay back everything you were paid. If this happens, you are treated as if you never retired. Then, when you do retire again, your amount is recalculated including the new FICA taxes that were paid in.

Taxes on Benefits

If you are single and have income from all sources (pensions, IRAs, annuities, royalties, interest, dividends, even municipal bond interest) of

$25,000 or more, you will owe taxes on half of what you receive in Social Security. If you are married, your magic starting point is $32,000.

Expect this to change. With the growing awareness of the problems within the whole system, Social Security will probably end up being fully taxed, at least the portion that is outside of what you originally contributed.

INVESTMENTS AND YOU

Don't stop investing—you could easily live another twenty-plus years. It's time for some shifting. In the past phases, you have concentrated on growth. With this phase, income becomes your primary focus.

Money market funds, CDs, and Treasuries are definitely part of this phase. So are bonds and, in particular, bonds that are short term—maturity within ten years. Don't place all your money in one type of income investment. Putting it all in CDs, or money market funds, or Treasuries, or other government bonds is myopic. Inflation isn't disappearing; you still need some growth potential.

For more detailed information on investing, read Austin Pryor's *Sound Mind Investing* (Moody, 1993) or other books listed in the bibliography.

Mutual Funds

Mutual funds are still a good choice. Keep at least 25 percent of your assets in funds that have some growth capability, with a little income. Ideally, select funds that yield some income and have had a track record of growth.

Utilities

Utility stocks are common ground for many in the last phase. Select utilities that have a PUC (Public Utility Commission) that has been receptive to rate increases in the past. Choose stocks that have had a constant record of earnings and dividends. The stocks you invest in should not have had dividends interrupted or reduced. Ever.

Another good method of investing in this phase is municipal bonds.

Alert-Partnership Warning

Brokers and financial planners may recommend that you put some of your money into a limited partnership that is designed to create income. Over the past decade, mega-millions of dollars have been lost by retirees via limited partnerships in gas and oil, public storage units, and the like.

The projections sound terrific—income every month, even increasing. *Do not touch anything that ties your money up without a GUARANTEED exit date.* In Life Phase 6, no money should be locked in. Access to liquidity is where you belong . . . meaning you can sell it or cash it in. In other words, *do not* buy an "income" limited partnership.

Sensible Investing

In investing for retirement, don't invest as if you were going to die next week. The great odds are that you won't.

- Keep some of your capital for growth (those stocks and mutual funds that pay income coupled with upside potential).

- Don't put all your money in "super safe" areas—such as government bonds. Spread your money around.

- Don't invest just to avoid taxes.

- Don't put your money—especially lump sum payouts—in high risk ventures (this includes your niece's new sock shop). If it fails, where are you going to get another lump sum?

Quiz

Your favorite niece has asked you to give her $30,000 to seed her cookie business. She has always been a good cook and you love her energy level—she always has plenty of projects going at once. You should:

(a) Write the check—as long as you get free cookies for life.

(b) Tell her you'll consider investing after you see her business plan.

(c) Tell her you will loan the money if she will sign a note with a scheduled payback period.

(d) Only consider loaning, investing, or giving her the money if you have funds in excess of what you need to meet your obligations.

Answer: Start with (d) if you have extra funds—over and above regular living needs and emergency funds—then look at (b) and (c). The first choice, (a), only works if you have tons of money that you can risk. You can buy cookies anywhere.

◆   PHASING UP   ◆

The best thing you can do at this phase in your life is to know what your money is doing. If you haven't taken a hands-on approach before, you must do so now. No one is going to be as loyal to your money as you are.

If you are married, statistically, 75 percent of you will be widowed in this phase. Going from wife to widow is painful; going from wife to widow to full-time money manager without an internship can be paralyzing.

Ideally your financial house should be in order. If you have been active in investment decisions, don't stop now.

You may not be able to control your aging process, but you can certainly control your hard earned money.

As I close this final phase, Proverbs 24:27 surfaces, "Finish your outdoor work and get your fields ready; after that, build your house." Your outdoor work has been your previous life phases. Now is the time to enjoy the home you have built.

Throughout this phase, you need to focus on:

$ Knowing where all your documents and important papers are—tell a trusted relative or friend.

$ Knowing where your retirement moneys are coming from.

$ Starting to withdraw funds no later than seventy-and-a-half from your various retirement accounts.

$ Staying tuned into policies that could impact your Social Security.

$ Reviewing your will, trust, and estate desires. Make sure everything reflects your wishes today, not ten years ago.

$ Evaluating your investments, shifting more toward income

and less toward growth as you get older.

$ Making gifts if possible. Take advantage of $10,000 tax-free gifts to as many people as you wish.

◆   **RETIREMENT BONUS**   ◆

If you started your IRA during Life Phase 1 and continued annual investments of $2,000, accumulating at the rate of 12 percent, sometime during Life Phase 6, you would have amassed more than $4 million! By the age of seventy and a half you must begin making withdrawals. When changes are finally made in Social Security payments, you won't care. As a millionaire, you can take care of yourself.

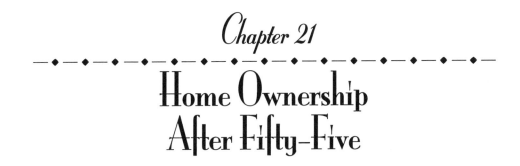

Chapter 21

Home Ownership After Fifty-Five

"*F*olly delights a man who lacks judgment, but a man [or woman] of understanding keeps a straight course," says Proverbs 15:21. By understanding the nuances of home ownership in this phase, you will maintain a straight course.

MOVING FROM A LARGER TO A SMALLER RESIDENCE

You may have realized a substantial increase in the equity of your home. If so, you may want to consider selling your residence and taking advantage of the once-in-a-lifetime $125,000 gain allowed for those over fifty-five who have lived in a house three years immediately prior to selling it. Your changing circumstances will make it possible to move to a smaller, less expensive home. In addition, with the cash that you receive from the sale, you may be able to purchase a house with a minimal mortgage or pay all cash. As you approach retirement, this aim should become a strategic part of your overall planning.

SHOULD YOU MOVE?

If you are happy with your home, maintaining it is not a problem, your mortgage (if there is one) fits your cash flow, and you really don't care if its value goes up or down—don't move! Stay put.

But if you are relying on the current market value to help support your retirement, put the FOR SALE sign out—now. You can't afford to risk losing money from your home if the market value declines.

UNCLE SAM IS YOUR PARTNER:
THE TAX IMPLICATIONS OF SELLING YOUR HOME

Every homeowner over fifty-five is sitting on a potential pot of gold. The government allows up to $125,000 in profits tax free from your home, if you sell it. This generosity of Uncle Sam only happens once in your lifetime and you (or your spouse) must be fifty-five to partake.

Let's say you bought your first home thirty years ago for $29,000 and sold it for $55,000. Then you bought a new home for $65,000 and sold it for $135,000. Finally, you bought the home you are in now for $145,000. You have just sold it for $220,000. What's your profit?

Here's how to figure it. (Note that my example does not have sales cost included, which will, of course, reduce your overall profits. Also, any fix-up costs within ninety days of your sale—not the closing date, but when the buyer and you sign the contract agreeing to price and terms—will reduce your taxable profit.)

EXAMPLE OF CALCULATION OF PROFIT
FROM LIFETIME HOME SALES

—◆—◆—◆—◆—◆—◆—◆—◆—◆—◆—◆—◆—◆—◆—◆—

Home	Buy-Sell	Profit
1	$29,000 — $55,000	$26,000
2	$65,000 — $135,000	$70,000
3	$145,000 — $220,000	$75,000
Total Profit		$171,000

How To Maximize Your Exclusion

1. This exclusion happens once in your lifetime. If you have never taken it, and you marry someone who has, you are out of luck.

The call? If a late marriage (or a remarriage) is in your game plan, you have a profit in your home, and your groom has already taken his $125,000 exclusion— sell your home before you say "I do." Otherwise, Uncle Sam says, "You don't."

2. If the house you are selling has a small profit, do not take the exclusion—you can't use any "leftover" amounts down the road. Pay the taxes owed.

The call? The exception is if you are selling to move to an apartment and it's NOT in your game plan to own again—take the exclusion.

3. If you are approaching "seniorism," are planning on marrying, and you both own homes with profits, considering selling both homes before the ceremony and getting a new one. That way you both get to take the $125,000 gold—times 2!

The call? You can do this on a joint tax return, as long as you have proof the sales were completed before your wedding. $250,000 tax free is a terrific dowry!

4. If you take the exclusion of $125,000, but you still have a profit that's taxable (as in the example of selling three houses and get-ting a $171,000 combined profit) you can defer gains over the $125,000 by buying a new house that costs at least as much as you sold the old one for minus your exclusion.

EFFECT OF THE EXCLUSION ON
THREE-HOUSE SALE PROFIT

—◆—◆—◆—◆—◆—◆—◆—◆—◆—◆—◆—◆—◆—◆—◆—◆—◆—

Combined profits of 3 houses	$171,000
55 Exclusion	– 125,000
Minimum cost of next house to defer remaining profit	$46,000

You now have a decision—to pay taxes on the gain or to buy another home. The maximum taxes on the $46,000 would be in the $16,000 area today. (Of course, with any new tax law, that's subject to change.)

The call? 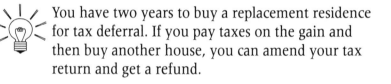 You have two years to buy a replacement residence for tax deferral. If you pay taxes on the gain and then buy another house, you can amend your tax return and get a refund.

5. If you take the exclusion and then change your mind, you have three years to amend your tax return from the time you took the exclusion.

WHAT IF YOU DON'T WANT TO MOVE?

Many can't imagine selling and leaving their home—memories, memories, memories. Memories are great, but what if you need money?

How about getting a housemate or renting out a room or rooms? This has pros and cons. Depending on the size of your home, another person could be too encroaching on your territory, or the company could be grand. Because of zoning regulations, you need to check out what's OK and what's not.

If you take this course, you need to consider such items as insurance (what if your tenant trips over your hose and breaks a wrist) and what you will do to get rid of someone who turns out to be undesirable. If your community has rent control, you may end up stuck with tiny rental payments from your boarder. Yuk to that.

$ JB tip

If you consider renting space: Get advice from your attorney or accountant, have a written lease, and check out if there is a landlord's type of association in your community. Others' experiences will be helpful.

Sell your home to your kids and lease it back for the rest of your life. Now, before you jump on this one, ask yourself a few questions: Are your kids there for you? Are they independent—emotionally and financially? If your kids are married, are their marriages strong? Is their income stable? Do they have steady jobs? *If you cannot answer enthusiastically yes to every question—do not even consider this option. No, nyet, not.*

A sale-lease back can be complicated. It demands that all concerned have terrific communication skills, are unselfish and equitable, and do not have one iota of greed or get-evenness in them. Here's how it works:

- You sell your home at a fair market value.

- Your kid(s) pony up the down payment—normally 10 to 20 percent.

- You are the bank—you carry the mortgage for the balance.

- The kids pay the monthly mortgage to you.

- You pay rent to them each month, which, ideally, should be smaller than the mortgage payment, at least in the beginning.

- The kids pay insurance, real estate taxes, and maintenance costs—this is a rental on paper and should be treated as such. They, in turn, get all the deductions that rental properties create, including depreciation.

- You pay utility costs.

$ JB tip

If this is at all attractive, all the details must be worked out with the help of your attorney. The last thing you want is for your son and his wife to split up and have the wife demand her share—now. Remember, this is a deal for your life; they are secondary players.

Local programs can assist low-income homeowners. Many cities offer special low interest home-region loans that don't have to be paid until you sell. Real estate taxes could be deferred until sale in some states.

$ JB *tip*

Check out your local senior-citizen center for programs available. Many mark the "senior" age at fifty-five.

You can give your home away. Many educational institutions, charities, and churches have programs that enable you to get a tax deduction and continue to live in your house for the rest of your life. You pay real estate taxes, maintenance, utilities, and insurance. When you die, the house goes to the group you gave it to. Before you even consider this possibility, be certain that you will not need the equity in your house.

$ JB *tip*

This doesn't work well if you are fifty and expect to live another thirty-plus years or if you are in a low tax bracket.

You can get a reverse mortgage—read on . . .

REVERSE MORTGAGES

These animals are fairly new, having come into existence in the eighties. The Federal Housing Administration (FHA) makes them available to any institution that offers FHA loans. I do not believe this is a viable option if you are under sixty-five.

Reverse mortgages allow to you to tap into the cash (the equity) in your home without having to move. They are good for as long as you live in your home. Here's how they work:

1. A lender agrees to make you a loan against the value of your house. The loan agreement rarely sets a maximum amount. In turn, you get a check each month.

2. The size of your check depends on your age, the age of your spouse, and how much equity you have in your house. If you are seventy years old, your home equity is $100,000, and the loan interest rate is 10 percent, an FHA lender might give you $276 a month for life. If you took out the loan at age eighty-five, the dollar amount would increase. You would get $604 a month for life. Private lenders generally offer larger amounts.

3. Checks continue as long as you live in the house. The total amount you can borrow is dictated by how long you stay there and receive monthly checks.

4. You pay no cash up front. All closing and insurance costs are included in the loan.

5. You pay no interest currently on the money you're borrowing. The interest compounds, to be paid off when the loan is settled. This loan can become quite large.

6. When you die or leave your house, it will be sold and the proceeds used to repay the loan, plus interest. Some lenders may take a percentage of the home's appreciation. Don't be surprised to learn that most of the money goes to the lender. If you want to save some of the proceeds for yourself or your heirs, look for a lender who offers an equity reserve. With a reserve, you always retain a fixed portion of the equity—say, 10 or 20 percent. You pay for this reserve by taking lower monthly checks.

7. If the loan exceeds what your house is worth when you sell the house or you die, the lender eats the loss (but check this out before signing up).

Regular monthly checks are the usual way of receiving money. Your lender may offer up to three other options: a fixed number of checks, a lump sum, or a line of credit that you can draw on whenever you want. With the line of credit, you can borrow as much or as little as you need. If you have never had problems with credit spending, this could work well.

Each check seems like income, but it is not. It's a loan—a loan against the equity in your home. If you are on Social Security, it won't raise your taxes or affect your Social Security.

The Pros:

- You can stay in your home as long as you are able.

- Checks can be used for anything.

The Cons:

- The loan is expensive—up front fees are buried in finance and interest charges that are added to whatever you withdraw.

- If you had the mortgage a long time and you decided to

"quit" the house there may be nothing left in equity. Will you need money for another home or to get into a retirement or nursing home?

$ JB tip

Protect yourself from going to zero—take a mortgage with an equity reserve.

- If you are under sixty-five, the checks are not hefty unless you have lots of equity—hundreds of thousands.

- Understand the terms of the contract. Can the lender force you out if it feels the house is declining in value? Make sure you can be away for a few months without having it interpreted that you no longer live in the house. If that's the interpretation that's made, the house can be sold.

- Being able to tap into money and stay put may be the wrong thing to do. You might be better off selling and moving to a condo, apartment, or senior citizens' home.

The following private companies will write reverse mortgages as long as you stay in your home. They usually pay larger monthly checks than you'd get from an FHA lender, especially on higher-priced homes.

1. The Individual Reverse Mortgage Account, Mount Laurel, NJ (800-233-4762; in New Jersey, 800-233-4767). It lends in California, Connecticut, Delaware, Maryland, New Jersey, Ohio, Pennsylvania, and Virginia.

2. The Home Income Security Plan (in Louisville 800-942-6550; in California, 800-431-8100), lending mostly in the metropolitan areas of California, Illinois, Kentucky, Maryland, North Carolina, Virginia, and Florida. It also offers a home-equity line of credit.

3. The Providential Home Income Plan in San Francisco (800-441-4428), offering loans and home-equity lines of credit in California, Florida, Illinois, Minnesota, and Wisconsin.

A number of state and local housing agencies also make reverse mortgages, usually to low-income homeowners and for limited purposes, such as paying property taxes or keeping the house in good repair. Some nonprofit agencies offer programs for specified terms, such as ten years. Two firms are working on true lifetime loans that would act like annuities.

For free information on where to find all these reverse mortgage programs, send a self-addressed, stamped, business-size envelope to the National Center for Home Equity Conversion, 1210 East College Dr., Suite 300, Marshall, MN 56258. For an excellent free booklet explaining reverse mortgages send for *Home-Made Money, a Consumer Guide to Home Equity Conversion*, from the American Association of Retired Persons, 1909 K St. N.W., Washington, DC, 20049.

SHOULD YOU PAY OFF THE MORTGAGE?

It depends. If you have lots of money—yes. A house free and clear stabilizes your living costs, reduces outgo, and usually makes you feel secure.

If you don't have lots of money, don't put all your savings into the house for it to be mortgage free. Many may disagree with me, but I think it's nuts to liquidate your liquidity. You will be house rich and cash poor.

If you paid off your mortgage and find Social Security and your pension just won't cover your income needs, you can:

• get a new mortgage or apply for a home-equity credit line—this could be tough if you are on limited income.

- sell your house and use the cash to buy something smaller and then add money to build up your reserves.

- explore a reverse mortgage.

$ JB tip

Get some advice here. Look at the tax consequences, if any, before you leap.

$ JB tip

Any time you have the possibility of lots of cash, those pesky investment sales folks appear. <u>Do not</u> put any of your money in anything that ties it up with nil possibility of liquidity. You are into low risk from now on.

Glossary

The Language of Money

*N*ow for those definitions. As you study money management, your understanding of these terms will deepen, but in the beginning what you most need is a thumbnail sketch that will enable you to recognize key terms.

Annuities

An *annuity* is both a "sum of money payable yearly or at other intervals" to an individual or a group and the "contract or agreement providing for" such payments. Some retirement accounts are held in the form of annuities. Insurance companies issue annuity contracts.

Appreciation

The *appreciation* of an asset is an increase of its monetary value. Fine paintings, sculpture, and real estate may appreciate in value (but do not always do so). The worth of a single unit of currency (a dollar, for example) may increase (come to exercise greater buying power), but does not always do so.

Bonds

Bonds are certificates issued by corporations and governmental bodies (local, state, and national) that receive interest and come due at a specific time. When you buy a bond, you are in essence lending money to the public or private entity that issued it. Treasury bills and notes are a type of bond and are exempt from state income tax. Municipal bonds are not taxable on your federal tax return.

Cash Flow

Your *cash flow* is your spending—where your money goes. If you are having cash flow problems, that means that you do not have cash on hand to meet your daily obligations and bills.

Certificates of Deposit

A *certificate of deposit* is an interest-bearing receipt issued by a bank that comes due at a specific time. It can be purchased individually or as part of a money market fund.

Commercial Paper

The term *commercial paper* refers to short-term money instruments with varying maturity dates issued by corporations as a way of raising money. Commercial paper carries no collateral and is paid off by the "good faith" of the borrowing company.

Compound Interest

Compound interest is interest paid on the basis of both the principal and previous interest credited to the account. Compound interest provides much greater gain to the lender or savings deposit holder than does simple interest.

Cost of Living

The *cost of living* is what it costs to live in a specific place at a specific time. The government computes the cost of living in this country by adding up the prices of a fixed group of expenses at a particular time (the Consumer Price Index, or CPI). You can compute your own cost of living by tallying up a representative number of your own expenses at a specific point in time.

Depreciation

Depreciation is an accounting decrease in the monetary value of an asset. Manufacturers are able to register this loss in the value of their equipment over time by declaring a depreciation when they compute their taxes. Rental real estate is subject to both depreciation (a house could bring less when it is sold than was required to purchase it) and appreciation (a house may be sold for a higher price than initially required to buy it).

Owners of real estate that is rented out to other parties can declare depreciation on the investment on their income taxes because of the wear and tear of the property over time. When they sell the property at a later date, they must "recapture" (declare as income) the dollars declared as depreciation on past income tax forms.

A unit of currency may depreciate. When that happens it takes a greater number of units to purchase the same amount of goods than were needed to purchase them when the currency had greater buying power.

Individual Retirement Accounts (IRAs)

An *IRA* is an account set up specifically to provide money for retirement. Regulations specify the amount of money you can set aside each year for this purpose and the amount of the deposit you can deduct from your taxable income. After you retire, you must pay taxes on the deposits and the interest they earned, but usually at a lower rate than would be the case if the income were taxed during your "working" career.

Interest

Interest is a fee paid by a borrower for the use of someone else's money. When you buy a bond, Treasury note, or certificate of deposit, or you deposit money in a passbook savings account, the corporation or governmental agency you "lent" the money to will pay you a fee for the use of your money. That fee is called *interest*.

Liquidate

When you *liquidate* (sell)an asset you turn it into cash.

Liquidity

Liquidity is the relative ability of an asset to be turned into ready cash. Your checking and savings accounts and certain types of securities (stocks, bonds, short-term certificates of deposit, and short-term Treasury bills, for example) have high degrees of liquidity, but Grandma's favorite rocking chair might not.

Money Market Fund

A *money market fund* is a mutual fund composed of money instruments (Treasury bills, Treasury notes, certificates of deposit, commercial paper, investment grade corporate and municipal bonds).

Mutual Funds

A *mutual fund* is an investment security set up to buy a wide range of securities and money instruments issued by corporations or by governmental bodies. When you buy into a mutual fund, you are in effect purchasing shares of the fund. Because the cash of numerous individuals and funds (for example, pension funds) is used by the mutual fund to purchase securities, the risk inherent in purchasing the securities is spread over a large pool and thus somewhat reduced. Mutual funds offer a good way for a small investor to begin to participate in the stock market.

Net Worth

Your *net worth* is the dollar value of your assets (such as property, financial investments, retirement accounts, checking and savings accounts) and moneys due you less your debts (what you owe others) and liabilities (financial obligations you must be prepared to meet).

Real Property/Real Estate

Real property, or *real estate,* consists of buildings and land.

Simple Interest

Simple interest is interest paid only on the basis of the principal (the money lent to an individual or corporation or deposited into a savings account).

Stock Certificates

Stock certificates are certificates stating the ownership of a portion (a share) of a corporation or company. When you buy stock you are buying a portion of a company and may receive dividends (funds representing your share of the money made by the company). Shares are bought and sold on *stock exchanges* and in the over-the-counter markets.

Treasury Obligations

A *Treasury bill* is a short-term government security maturing from one month to one year from the time of purchase. Treasury bills are for a minimum of $10,000.

A *Treasury note* is a government security maturing from one to five (sometimes more) years from the time of purchase. (Treasury notes are sold for a minimum of $5,000. All can be purchased individually or as part of a money market fund. When you buy a Treasury note you are in essence lending money to the government.)

A *Treasury bond* is a government security maturing from ten to thirty years. Treasury bonds are sold for a minimum of $5,000 when first issued.

Afterword

—◆—◆—◆—◆—◆—◆—◆—◆—◆—◆—◆—◆—◆—◆—

Work brings profit; talk brings poverty!

Proverbs 14:23 (TLB)

The key to your financial success lies only with you. Laws change, the economic environment changes. You must have the tenacity and experience to flow with these changes and turn them to your advantage.

Your hope for a successful financial future depends upon your ability to educate yourself in life, set goals, be resilient when you make mistakes, and use mistakes as part of your ongoing education. In the end, you take what you have learned and turn it into a more lucrative reward.

Simple? No, but then, when is anything worthwhile simple? Do what makes common sense because that's what makes *money sense*. Don't be greedy. Have patience. Keep learning. I believe in your ability to put it together. Now, it's your turn.

Bibliography

Berg, Adriane. *Financial Planning for Couples*. New York: Newmarket, 1993.

Briles, Judith. *The Dollars and Sense of Divorce*. New York: Ballantine, 1991.

_____. *Financial $avvy for Women*. New York: Master Media, 1992.

Burkett, Larry. *The Coming Economic Earthquake*, revised and expanded edition. Chicago: Moody, 1994.

_____. *Debt Free Living*. Chicago: Moody, 1989.

Card, Emily. *Ms. Money Book*. E. P. Dutton, 1990.

Cymrot, Alan. *Street Smart Real Estate Investing*. Dow Jones, 1988.

Dolan, Ken and Darla. *Straight Talk on Money*. New York: Simon & Schuster, 1993.

Donahue, William E. *The Complete Money Market Guide*. New York: Bantam, 1982.

Felton-Collins, Victoria. *Couples & Money*. New York: Bantam, 1990.

Humber, Wilson J. *Buying Insurance*. Chicago: Moody, 1994.

_____. *Saving the Best for Last*. Chicago: Moody, 1994.

Pryor, Austin. *Sound Mind Investing*. Chicago: Moody, 1993. (For a more focused look at individual topics, look at the Sound Mind Investing Strategies booklets by Moody, taken from this book. Booklets include *IRAs and Annuities, Money Markets and Bonds, Mutual Funds, and Stocks*.)

Quinn, Jane Bryant. *Making the Most of Your Money.* New York: Simon & Schuster, 1991.

Savage, Terry. *New Money Strategies for the '90s.* New York: Harper Business, 1993.

Schapiro, Nicole. *Negotiating for Your Life.* New York: Henry Holt & Co., 1993.

Schwab, Charles. *How to Be Your Own Stockbroker.* New York: Macmillan, 1984.

Tobias, Andrew. *The Only Other Investment Guide You'll Ever Need.* New York: Simon & Schuster, 1987.

Other Resources:

Read *Money, Time, Newsweek,* the *Wall Street Journal,* the Sunday *New York* or *Los Angeles Times,* and your local paper. Watch Wall Street Week on PBS.

Index

Moody Press, a ministry of the Moody Bible Institute,
is designed for education, evangelization, and edification.
If we may assist you in knowing more about Christ
and the Christian life, please write us without obligation:
Moody Press, c/o MLM, Chicago, Illinois 60610